American

The search for Ke

ROGER JINKINSON

Best Wishes

www.tales-from-a-greek-island.com
rjinkin@mac.com

ISBN 978-1-84327-995-2

Cover design Electric Book

The Racing House Press
20 Cambridge Drive
London SE12 8AJ, UK

Printed and bound by Lightning Source

DEDICATION

For my children. And my grandchildren.

Roger Jinkinson was born in Salisbury England, but lived for many years in London. An unusual career path found him meandering from school caretaker to deputy vice chancellor of a large university, then, at the age of fifty he gave it all up to go fishing. Now he spends half his time in Diafani, a remote village on the Greek island of Karpathos. He writes, takes photographs, dives to spear fish and keeps bees. The rest of the time he helps bring up his grand daughter in London. Roger's first book, *Tales from a Greek Island*, explores the life and history of his adopted village. It was well reviewed in the Anglo Greek press and well received by the villagers. There are two more books in the pipeline; *More Tales from a Greek Island*, and a novel, *Under Redwood*.

What they said about *Tales from a Greek Island*

His narrative approach and identification with the village and its values ring true. He is not writing about himself (as many expats do). The pages are full of idiosyncratic characters, of hunters and gatherers, fishermen, farmers, bee-keepers, musicians, poets, lovers, heroes...There is plenty of atmosphere and suspense and humour. And Jinkinson is engagingly informative about his natural surroundings. But what resonates most strongly, in the end, is his sense of wonder at the resilience of the human spirit.

Jonathan Carr - Athens News

Jinkinson knows how to tell a story. Each tale is just a few pages - none longer than 10 - but each is complete with a point, moral or message. That sounds a bit trite, but the stories are not; there's death and laughter in the lines... and Jinkinson's poetry in how he weaves a tale ... There is much conveyed in his plain, well-timed phrases: much about ritual, much about pain, much about the simple pleasures of local, peasant life. That sentiment is clear in every story, whether one is new to the country or also long enchanted with it.

Laura McDowell - Kathimerini English Edition

Contents

Acknowledgements

Three years ago I set out to write a story. Now the story is a book. It is time to let go.

Many people helped me. Some asked not to be mentioned. They have their reasons. My thanks to those who allowed me to interview them; some of their names appear as chapter headings. I am in awe of the power, perspicacity and intellect of the women - several in their seventies and eighties – who agreed to meet me. I am also grateful to Kevin's friends and family members who trusted me and passed on anecdotes, recollections and papers.

Special thanks are due to Anthony J. Papalas, author of a wonderful book, *Rebels and Radicals: Icaria 1600-2000*, whose knowledge of Icaria and post-war Greece helped me out of holes I was digging for myself and whose wisdom enlightened my search.

I met neither Anthony nor Vin Morgan, managing director, The Granger Papers Project, founded by Vin's great aunt and uncle. However, through the internet the project's resources enabled Vin and me to re-live eighty-year-old events from different perspectives.

Thanks also to Clive Coy a collector of memorabilia on Roy Chapman Andrews who kindly shared his collection. He will not agree with all I have written but he is clearly a gentleman and will not hold that against me.

Marc Dubin shared his files on Kevin Andrews and guided me through the mountain ranges he and Kevin shared.

The people of Diafani and Olymbos have magnificent memories and gave me more anecdotes than I could use. They knew Kevin Andrews well. They still sing his songs.

Finally my thanks to Roderick Robinson, my editor, who knocked this book into shape.

There will be mistakes. They are unintended.

A list of people mentioned in the text

Andonis
Shepherd, resin gatherer, Yerania mountains. KA became his *koumbaros* and was incorporated into his family.

Andreas
Gardener at American School in Athens, friend of KA.

Andrews, Alexis
Son of KA and Nancy Cummings.

Andrews, George
Son of RCA and Yvette Borup; KA's brother or half-brother. Married to Mary Nancy (surname unknown).

Andrews, Ioanna
Daughter of KA and Nancy Cummings.

Andrews, Roy Chapman (RCA)
Adventurer, explorer. Husband of Yvette Borup and possibly KA's father. Divorced from Yvette, he married Wilhelmina Anderson Christmas (Billie).

Anglin, Sir Francis
Head of customs, China, in twenties; friend of Chapmans.

Auden, W. H.
English poet; advised KA on at tempt to check well-being of Louis MacNeice's son.

Bernhardt, Sarah
French actress, self-publicist

Binder, Judith
Archaeologist, expert on classical Athens, friend of KA and Nancy Cummings.

Borup, Yvette
Photographer, explorer, great beauty. KA's mother.

Borup, George
Explorer; took part in Admiral Peary's 1908-9 expedition to North Pole. Drowned in boating accident with friend Winship Case, April 12 1912. KA's uncle, Yvette Borup's brother. Died before KA was born.

Cabot, Robbie
Author, close friend of KA.

Cammaerts, Francis
SOE officer in occupied France; friend of Xan Fielding; educationalist.

Campbell, Roy
South African poet; supported Franco but opposed Hitler; friend of Dylan Thomas.

Case, Winship
Close friend of George Borup; died with him in boating accident.

Caskey, J. L.
One time OSS member, later CIA operative. Head of American School of Classical Studies, Athens 1951.

Chapple, John
American publisher in Athens; unable to find time or money to publish new edition of *The Flight of Ikaros.*

Chess, Lura
Heiress, employer, friend of Yvette Borup, mother of Brian Howard.

Christmas, Wilhemina Anderson (Billie)
Second wife of RCA; rich

Christopoulou, Letta Duye
Close companion and friend of KA during last two years of his life.

Clift, Charmian; Johnston, George
Australian journalists and writers; lived on Hydra at same time as KA and Nancy Cummings.

Cook, Geraldine
Editor of final (Penguin) edition of *The Flight of Ikaros.*

Coudenhove-Kallergis, Anita
Metalworker, sculptress, jewelry worker, friend of KA

Coy, Clive
Palaeontologist, collector of RCA memorabilia

Cutting, Constance and Heyward
Friends of Yvette Borup; visited the Andrews in Peking.

Cummings, Nancy
Daughter of EE Cummings, married Willard Roosevelt, two children, Elizabeth and Simon. Divorced Willard Roosevelt, married KA, two children: Ioanna, Alexis.

Dreyfus, Alfred
French artillery officer wrongly accused of treason because of Jewish background

Dubin, Marc
Author, Hellenophile, friend of KA in later years.

Dugdale, John
British journalist, diplomat, politician, minister in Atlee government; friend of Yvette Borup in Peking.

Durrell, Lawrence
Novelist, poet, travel writer.

Earhart, Amelia
First woman to fly Atlantic solo; disappeared circumnavigating globe solo in 1937.

Emmet, Grenville
Wife of US representative to Netherlands in thirties; Yvette's cousin

Fermor, Sir Patrick (Paddy) Leigh

British author, scholar, soldier; played prominent role with SOE in Crete during WW2.

Fielding, Magouche
Widow of Armenian-born artist Arshile Gorky; married, divorced Xan Fielding. Mother-in-law of Martin Amis.

Fielding, Xan
Served with PLF in Crete and, later, with SOE in France. British writer, translated *Planet of the Apes* and *The Bridge over the River Kwai*. Married Magouche Fielding.

Finlay, John
Professor of classical Greek, KA's tutor.

Franco, General Franciso
Spanish dictator

Frantzi, Andia
Taught with KA on Greece-USA exchange programme during seventies; witnessed one of his swimming mishaps.

Friche, Hélène
Nurse to KA and brother George, later to Mayer family.

Gallenkamp, Charles
Author and historian, RCA hagiographer.

Georgos (Prearis)
Fisherman and environmentalist, Diafani, island of Karpathos.

Glenn, Pat
Friend of KA, Yvette Borup, Chips Smallwood. Daughter of Constance and Heyward Cutting.

Gorky, Ashile
Armenian-born abstract expressionist painter; former husband of Magouche Fielding.

Granger, Walter
Member of RCA expeditions from 1922; sometime friend of Yvette Borup and RCA.

Gurdjieff, G. I.
Creator of The Fourth Way system of self-exploration and expression.

Hadzimichaelis, Vana
Athenian friend of KA

Hakkert, Adolf
Mysterious publisher, bookseller; published KA's *Greece in the Dark.*

Heller, Edmund
Zoologist, explorer, accompanied Yvette and RCA on early expeditions; became zookeeper.

Herring, Elizabeth Boleman
Author, journalist, close friend/lover of KA during last months of his life.

Howard, Brian
Dissolute son of Lura Chess and Tudie Howard, acquaintance of many British literary figures in

the thirties, appears in *Brideshead Revisited.*

Howe, Dr E. Graham
London psychoanalyst; treated KA.

Jellico, Lord
Commander of Special Boat Service, arrived in Athens on borrowed bicycle as Germans were leaving, friend of Patrick Leigh Fermor.

Kaplan, Robert D
American writer and journalist

Karras, Simon
Greek musician, friend of KA.

Kazantzakis, Nikos
Greek author of *Zorba the Greek.*

Keeley, Robert Vossler
Friend of KA 1956 – 89; US ambassador to Greece.

Kinsolving, Lucien
Diplomat, arabist, early friend of KA.

Kipling, Rudyard
British author and poet; close friend (possibly lover) of Perceval Landon.

Kostandis (not real name)
Right wing braggart and murderer; appears on front cover of final edition of *The Flight of Ikaros*

Krishnamurti, J
Religious teacher who emphasised meditation and spiritual aspects.

Kondorani family
From Samos; occupied cabin next to KA on his first visit to Greece

Laing, R. D.
Psychoanalyst, psychiatrist, existentialist.

Landon, Perceval
Imperialist, adventurer, journalist, author, lifelong friend of Rudyard Kipling, close friend (perhaps lover) of Yvette Borup, possibly KA's father.

Lindbergh, Charles
Made first solo transatlantic flight; two-year-old daughter later kidnapped and murdered.

Manolis (Papamanolis)
Bootmaker, Diafani, island of of Karpathos.

McCarthy, Joseph
American senator, conducted anti-Communist witch-hunts.

MacNiece, Louis
Poet, friend of KA. British Council Athens 1950-51.

MacDermot, Frank
Irish banker and politician; third husband of Elaine Orr, hence stepfather of Nancy Cummings

Makarezos, Brig. Stylianos Pattakos

Papalas, Anthony
Professor of classical history; author, expert on island of Ikaria.

Papandreou, Andreas
Economist, socialist, Greek prime minister. Son of George Papandreou.

Peary, Robert Edwin
American admiral, polar explorer, close friend of George Borup.

Pitkin, Dorothy
American author, friend of KA.

Powell, Dilys
Journalist, author, film critic.

Ritsos, Iannis
Writer, resistance fighter, member of Greek communist party KKE

Roberts, Field Marshall Lord
Imperialist, friend of Perceval Landon

Roosevelt, Willard
Son of Belle Wyatt Willard and Kermit Roosevelt I, grandson of US president Theodore Roosevelt. Pianist, composer, close friend of KA. Married Nancy Cummings (who later married KA); two children: Elizabeth, Simon.

Sarafis, Marian
English writer on modern Greece; wife of General Sarafis, wartime resistance leader.

Samiou, Domna
Member of refugee family from Asia Minor; fascinated by Greek folk music and eventually became its saviour. Anti-right wing/reactionary politics, close friend of KA.

Seferis, Georgos
Major twentieth century Greek poet, Nobel laureate, Greek ambassador to UK

Schliemann, Heinrich
Archaeologist; controversial excavator of Troy

Shackleford, James B
Photographer, member of RCA expeditions from 1922.

Skandalis family
Accommodated KA in Athens in late forties. Father was a general and cavalry commander in Greek army; two sons fought with ELAS, Greek army of resistance, and were interned in prison camps during and after civil war.

Smallwood, Harold St Clair (Chips; The Bounder), Captain, later Squadron Leader
Married to Margot, lover of Yvette, possibly KA's father.

Mayer, Cotton and Liza
Friends of KA; their nurse was Hélène Friche.

Mercouri, Melina
Actress, Greek minister of culture, resisted the Junta.

Miller, Henry
American author

Mims, Amy
Author, prize-winning translator of modern Greek literature, close friend of KA.

Minas, Papa
Priest in Diafani, island of Karpathos

Morehouse, Marion
Lover of E. E. Cummings.

Morgan, Vin
Managing director, The Grangers Papers Project covering work by American palaeontologist Walter Granger and his wife Anna.

Nikiphoros (real name Charalambos)
Met KA in hospital, Athens 1948; suffered from TB, nephritis and later leukaemia. Friendship and subsequent death recorded movingly in *The Flight of Ikaros.*

Norton, Sir Clifford and Lady Peter
Friends of KA and Yvette Borup; he was post-war British ambassador to Greece, she was KA's godmother

Olsen, George
Palaeontologist, member of RCA expeditions from 1922.

Orfanos, Nikos
Hotel owner and travel agent, Diafani, island of Karpathos

Orr, Elaine
Mother of Nancy Cummings. While married to Scofield Thayer had daughter, Nancy, with Thayer's friend, poet Edward Estlin Cummings. Later Elaine married EEC, divorced him, married Frank MacDermot and together they brought up Nancy.

Osborne, John
English playright and actor.

Osborn, Henry Fairfield
Director, American Museum of Natural History; friend of RCA and, later, of Yvette Borup.

Panagoulis, Alexander
Mathematician and Greek army officer. Attempted to assassinate Papadopoulos, captured, tortured, released, became member of parliament, murdered.

Papadopoulos, George
Head of military coup in Greece April 21 1967, leader of subsequent military government (the Junta, the Colonels) 1967 – 1974. Henchmen: Col. Nickolas

Spielberg, Steven
American film-maker.

Stratou, Dora
Helped re-create Greek traditional dancing in Athens;

Thayer, Scofield
Immensely rich, gay, first husband of Elaine Orr, mother of Nancy Cummings.

Theodorakis, Mikis
Popular Greek composer. Man of left despite brief sojourn with New Democracy; resisted the Junta.

Thomas, Dylan
Welsh poet and author; drank with KA in New York.

Tsanteris, Vangeli
Baker, *andartis (*partisan), close friend of KA on island of Ikaria.

US army friends of KA
Johnny van der Putte, Lornen Frank, Chuck Walro, Donald Pitkin.

Viktoria Luise Adelheid Mathilde Charlotte, Princess of Prussia, Duchess of Brunswick.
Only daughter of William II, the last German Kaiser, and his wife, Empress Augusta Victoria. Known as Sisi, lifelong friend of Yvette Borup.

Villagers – Olymbos and Diafani
Minas Prearis, Papa Iannis, Ilias Minatsis, Nikos Philipakis, Vassilis Protopapas, Nikos Meleissis, Nikos Orfanos, Vasillis Sofolis, Manolis Kritikos.

Watts, Alan
British philosopher.

Williamsen, Corinna
Daughter of KA and Ioanna Williamsen.

Williamsen, Ioanna
Early lover of KA; his landlady in Athens in 1949.

Wulsin, Janet
Explorer of Tibet, Mongolia and China during twenties.

Younghusband, Lieut. Col. Sir Francis
British army officer, explorer and spiritual writer; led 1905 British invasion of Tibet; friend of Perceval Landon

Young, John McKenzie
Canadian war hero, member of later RCA expedition, friend of Yvette Borup and RCA, favourite of George Borup.

ONE

The First Cemetery, Athens

In Mets a district of Athens close to the city centre, *Anapafseos* (Eternal rest) street passes shops selling flowers and other funerary odds and ends, and leads to *Proto Nekrotafio* or First Cemetery. This is one of Athens' hidden gems, with its baroque, rococo and neoclassical tombs and mausoleums. Among Greece's rich and famous are Heinrich Schliemann (excavator of Troy), Melina Mercouri (actress and Minister of Culture) and former prime minister Andreas Papandreou. Giorgos Seferis was buried here in September 1971 amid mass demonstrations dealt with later in this story. There is also a memorial commemorating the one hundred thousand Greeks, 40,000 from Athens, who starved to death during the 1940-1941 winter.

On September 8 1989 more than 200 people gathered to honour a modern-day Greek hero. Old and young, men and women, writers, journalists, artists, workers and neighbours. A grieving widow, distraught children and a redheaded woman with painted nails. Grief didn't prevent some jostling for position, some pushing and shoving and some unruly behaviour.

This book tells the story of the one they had come to bury, Kevin Andrews, author of *The Flight of Ikaros*, perhaps the greatest travel book ever written.

TWO

Roger's story

The story begins with my arrival in Diafani, a small Greek village on the northeast coast of Karpathos in the Dodecanese. Since then I have been going there for more than a quarter of a century. For half the year I live in my little pink house on the hill. From one window I see the harbour, from another the mountains. I speak a village Greek that is probably unique to Diafani. We miss out ds, gs and several other consonants and throw in a scattering of Doric and Turkish words so that Athenians and educated people find it difficult to follow.

I have a small fishing boat with an outboard motor and I keep bees on the wild island of Saria nearby. I regularly dive to spear fish, lay out my nets or go line fishing. I was taught this work by my friend Georgos, an expert fisherman. Most days I can if I wish eat fish but when the sea is too wild I walk in the forests and the mountains. Our priest, Papa Minas, used to be a shepherd and kept sheep before he took to caring for his human flock. He knows all the paths at this end of the island and showed me them years ago. When I come across an indentation in the pine leaves with broken twigs and bent blades of grass I know Papa Minas has lain there to escape from the parishioners and to gain comfort from the trees.

To check my bees or gather honey I take my boat and head north to Saria. I thread in and out of the rocks under the shelter of the cliffs, away from the strong winds and, where possible, away from the big waves. The sea is dangerous here. The weather can change in minutes – direction, strength and temperament. If this happens an hour or more from home it can be lonely. Coming back in the dark it can be very lonely. But the villagers are my friends. If I am going far I tell them. I make sure I am seen. If things get bad they will come and find me in a bigger boat. It has not happened yet. But perhaps...

In the mornings I have coffee in Anna's *cafeneion.* In the evening I drink *ouzo* there. I time my excursions to avoid the tourist boat since tourists always ask the same questions: When did you first come here? Where do you eat? Is this the best Greek island? How much does...? Why?

The only interesting question is: Why? But, they never listen to my answer. I try to answer it here because it reflects on the purpose of this book and the life of Kevin Andrews.

I was born in England in 1942. There was a war on, our flat had been bombed and we were homeless. My father, an orphan at the age of fourteen, was away in the army. My earliest recollections are of travelling with my mother and a suitcase. I remember buses, trains, lorries, occasional cars, but travelling, always travelling. A few days here, a week there, staying with friends and relatives who did not want us and, even if they did, had no room for us. Poverty in those days was having no food, no money and empty cupboards. Poverty was bad teeth, anger, depression and violence. My father returned from the war in 1946. He was a hero but turned down the offer of a Military Cross. On D-Day, June 6 1944, he landed on Gold beach at 11.25 am. His job was to lead the way for the invading armies, clear mines, cut wire, put up signs, kill the enemy - hard, difficult and dangerous work that occupied him until the surrender of Germany in May 1945. After D-Day there were the killing fields of Normandy, Arnhem, the Ardennes, crossing the Rhine under fire, relieving concentration camps. Then a victory of sorts. A job done.

When he returned home there was no home. Only a small boy frightened by this strange man he had never seen before and a wife scarred by poverty and homelessness. We lived in a one-bedroom tenement with a toilet in the scullery and an open fire to cook Spam and dried eggs. I remember stealing wood for the fire from the streets and the bombsites. I must have been five.

I try to imagine my father's longing for normality after the butchery of the war and his inability to express his feelings at what he had seen and done. And I remember my inarticulate mother clinging to the only bit of love she could understand. That of her only child.

My mother was mentally ill, agoraphobic. She was the youngest of four daughters with a younger brother, brought up in extreme poverty in a tenement block in Cable Street in the East End of London. One living room and one bedroom for a family of seven. The outside toilet was shared with three other families. Each child grew up with its own phobia: Aunt Lil, a large woman, was scared of spiders, with Rose it was dirt, Aunt Dorothy had problems with sex and Uncle Ted was alcoholic. They were nice people and they tried to cope but here was no help. My father dedicated his life to caring for my mother. She made his life a torment. She could not thank him.

I left home as soon as I could and travelled. As a child I walked in the country, at sixteen and seventeen I went everywhere by bike, at eighteen I was walking and hitchhiking, mainly to England's West Country. The grandmother I knew had lived in Salisbury in Wiltshire, where I was born, before she moved to Cable Street. Using a pony and trap she sold herbs from the forest and at the Sixpenny Fairs. My great grandfather had been a shepherd.

These were rural people, unknown, and romantic, touched on and described by Thomas Hardy. People I could identify with. The search for the pre-industrial life became my obsession. I had a folk memory of the days before telephones and mass entertainment, easy communication and monotone culture.

I sought different places and different eras. India, Morocco, Libya, Egypt, Iran, Turkey, East Africa, Mexico, Guatemala, Greece and, time and again, Spain. I was homesick everywhere, but for a home I never had. In Spain I met Socialists, Anarchists, Communists, workers and peasants seething under Franco and his indigenous army of occupation, the *Guardia Civile*. In the 1960s there were still parts of Spain straight out of Laurie Lee, pockets of life disconnected from the twentieth century, without roads, television or newspapers. I walked the old mule tracks, the paths of the iron hooves. In small villages or isolated inns I was made welcome by simple, innocent but suspicious people.

One scene is with me still. Somewhere in Andalusia, a day treking along a path in the hills, the sun hot and high, a white building across the fields, a cobbled road, horses. There'd been no food and little to drink. I entered the inn where they asked if I had a horse. I said I was walking. They fussed and tutted. There was cold water in a clay jar.

My room had a wooden bed, a straw mattress, an oil lamp, a nail in the wall and nothing else. The price, with evening meal and breakfast, was about 25 pesetas, say 20 cents. They showed me where to wash, after which I lay on my bed listening to life in the courtyard. I heard horses in the stable below my room. I smelt them as I dozed. A bell summoned me to supper. Fifteen of us sat on wooden benches around a large wooden table, helping ourselves to stew from a pot on the fire. And to wine. Young lads took me to a bar to drink cognac - six of us, three miners from Asturias, two bullfighters and me.

The miners were now *journaleros,* day workers in the vast fields of the south earning 100 pesetas or less. The coalfields of Asturias had been closed by strikes for six months or more, leading to pitched battles in the streets in the north with police and miners killed.

The bullfighters were not matadors but fifteen-sixteen-year-old apprentices, travelling from one village *corrida* to the next. They fought steers and difficult, unpredictable bulls that the big names would not touch. They showed me scars on their sides, by the kidneys, ugly, red marks 15 or 20 cm long. They got their money scrabbling in the bloody sand for pesetas thrown by the spectators after each fight. Sometimes they got nothing. After many drinks I said,

> I am *barracho*, drunk
> No, not *barracho,* only *tranquillo.*

In the morning they were gone. And I had a hangover. The courtyard was empty. There was cold coffee. I drank water, put fruit and dry bread in my pocket and set off across a vast, yellow landscape.

Gradually Spain modernised, joined the twentieth century. Tourists arrived, roads were built, Franco died and society changed. I needed to look elsewhere and I came to Greece. Crete attracted me for several years. I made friends in Zakros, a charming, small settlement at the eastern end of the island. I began to understand the Greeks' temperament, to appreciate their love for life, their hospitality, their faults and virtues. I kept on looking for remote, different places where the elements were important and had to be measured and assessed. I found Diafani and Olymbos.

For several years I'd wanted to understand the people and customs of northern Karpathos, drawn by photographs of women in traditional clothes and its strange, wild music. But the ferries were always a day early or late, or too expensive, or were cancelled due to bad weather. One day in 1981, with my family, I took the ferry from Pigadia in the south of Karpathos to Diafani in the north. It was late and the children fell asleep on the quayside. We carried them on board. In those days there was no harbour at Diafani. The large ferries stopped offshore and Nikos Orfanos came out in an open boat, six metres long and powered by an outboard motor. We arrived about 2 am in a calm sea. We stared into the blackness. A voice called out,

> Throw down the bags.

We lowered our rucksacks to Nikos who threw them to the bottom of his boat.

> Give me those others. Throw them down
> They are not bags, they are children.
> Oh. Pass them down carefully

We did. Then we were in the boat, alone at sea in the dark, heading in the gentle swell to a small light on the horizon. The ferry, a floating fairyland, shrank and disappeared. My small son woke up for a second and looked around.

> Are we going all the way in this?

Nikos looked carefully at the children. He said,

> You can stay with me.

For ten years we did just that. Now I have a house in the village and my granddaughter comes to stay.

We arrived at *to molo,* (the mole). Nikos brought the boat in carefully, tied up, unloaded the rucksacks, handed the children up to us. We carried them, still sleeping, ashore. A woman in the traditional black dress, the *cavai,* appeared. She balanced one bag on her head, carried the others. We followed her to her little *cafeneion.* This was Anna. She had been waiting for relatives from the south but they had not come. She made us coffee while Nikos got our rooms ready. She would not accept money for the coffee.

I did not know it but - more than two decades earlier - a famous man, Kevin Andrews, had made much the same trip. Seeking similar experiences, escaping similar pressures. Arriving at another Aegean island to the north, he used these words,

> It was paradise, oil lamps and donkeys.

By the time we got to Diafani electricity had arrived and most houses had at least one electric light. But the village was dark now and outside Anna's, tied to the village's only lamppost, there was a donkey.

I had arrived. For a while at least, I had found a home.

THREE

Manolis

Manolis is about eighty, a score or more years older than I am. He is a gentle man with good manners. A kind man with a sense of humour, well thought of by the villagers:

> He comes from a good family.

One of his pleasures is his granddaughter and that is how we became friends. One Easter I took black and white photographs of a young girl on her way to the village dance, proud in her festive clothes. I developed, printed and enlarged them, then showed them to Anna in the *cafeneion*. She said,

> *Manolis. To engoni tou Manolis*
>
> Manolis. It is the grandchild of Manolis.

He was sitting outside so I gave the prints to him. He wanted to pay. I said no. He offered me an ouzo and we became friends.

Manolis became a bootmaker many years ago; it is just possible he was taught by the first bootmaker on the island. His boots are soft leather with hard soles. Reaching just below the knee they are perfect for walking on hillsides covered in thorn and scrub. Bootmakers have status; they are thought to be wise. Manolis is wise. I seek his advice about my bees and he explains carefully and slowly. He doesn't hector me like the others, doesn't tell me I am a fool.

When life was hard in the early seventies he and his wife went to Baltimore where he worked in a restaurant, cooking and waiting on fellow Greeks, many of them his fellow villagers. I have a feeling he was not happy there. The eighties found him back in his proper place, in the village, making boots, farming a few terraces and keeping bees.

Although I regard myself as confident and well-informed my first conversation with Manolis shocked me. I had not even scratched the surface of this small village , which is my home.

> You are not the first tourist that came here.
> I know that.
> Kevy was here. Kevy Andrew.
> Who?
> Kevy. He used to sit there. In that place where you are sitting now. Kevy Andrew. *O Kevis.* An American.

I realised he was talking about the author of ***The Flight of Ikaros,*** a book I had read several times. It tells of the young Kevin walking through the wild places of Greece during the civil war. It is beautifully written by a man who clearly loved the Greek people.

> He was here? Kevin Andrews came to Diafani?
> You knew him?

And the story came out. Kevin Andrews came to the island several times in the sixties and early seventies. He stayed in Diafani and made friends with these people. He was here before the roads came and before the harbour was built. Sometimes he came by ferry, sometimes by *caique.* He was always alone except, once, with his daughter.

His Greek was so good he could write *mantinades,* rhyming couplets still composed for name days, celebrations and festivals. The rules are strict - each line has fifteen syllables - and a good *mantinada* is passed down by word of mouth from generation to generation sometimes over a hundred years. They may be spontaneous or - for special occasions like the celebration of someone's life – composed in advance and written down. Often they are collective efforts, the first line suggested by one person, others suggesting the rest.

Manolis wrote down a *mantinada*, which Kevin had created. Later that night another friend in another bar told me how it was written.

We were there in the *cafeneion,* he said, trying to help him choose the right words and then suddenly they came and we had a new *mantinada:*

Tora to apofasisa na ginw Olymbitis
Dioti emai sidero, kai topos sas magnitis

I have decided to be Olymbitic
Because I am iron and your place magnetic

The company went wild. The poem is good, the endings Olymbitic and magnetic have just the right resonance and dissonance in Greek. You cannot go wrong with such people if you write verses praising their homeland or *patrida*. Forty years later they still sing this *mantinada*. If I recite it in the *cafeneion* I sometimes earn myself an ouzo.

Olymbitis....magnitis.

Speaking to this gentle man I sensed the respect Manolis had for a foreigner, a *xenos,* he had not seen for forty years. Then he wrote me another Kevin Andrews *mantinada*. It was about the wind, the ever-present wind of Karpathos. Later that night I sat on the veranda at Gabriella's, a nearby restaurant, having my final drink of the evening and rather the worse for wear. Slowly I translated the words into English, copying them down carefully below the original. As I finished I sat back and a gust of wind took the piece of paper away, up, up, into the night, yellow against the black sky. Then it was over the sea and gone. I had no other copy. I have been too embarrassed to ask Manolis again. I have asked others but nobody else knows it. Never mind. There is poetry here – the wind taking away a *mantinada* about the wind – and Kevin would have approved.

Kevin Andrews was a prolific walker and knew all the footpaths. There were many more in those days. Some fanned out east of Olymbos to the beaches along the east coast, others followed the valley and up and over the ridge to Avlona and beyond. Tristomo, Vrakounda, Steno all had their paths, some paved and dating from

Minoan times. Some have been destroyed, for the people here have little respect for the historic landscape. Others have fallen into disuse and are overgrown by bushes, shrubs and trees. If you branch off the two or three routes known to tourists you are unlikely to meet anyone. But in Kevin's time these footpaths were thoroughfares, lifelines for remote communities. Donkeys, goats mules, sheep and people moved up and down, east and west, north and south. A shepherd with a flock, an old woman with fuel for the fire, children walking back and forth from Diafani to the school in Olymbos, ten kilometres each way. Kevin preferred walking alone but would have relished the brief company of these country people before striding ahead and leaving them behind.

Manolis made him a pair of boots. When I heard this I had to have a pair. Manolis asked,

> Just like Kevy?
> Yes, just like Kevy.

They are soft yellow suede, hand-sewn with thick soles. I wear them when I go to Saria where, apart from guarding my legs from thorns and thistles, they also protect me from my bees. A bee on the ground by your feet may climb up your shoes and up your leg. If your trousers are not tucked in it will continue climbing to a destination that can be painful or embarrassing or both. By tucking my trousers into Manolis' boots I can separate the bees from the parts of a man where a bee should not go.

My boots are strong round the ankle and the soles are made from the rubber tyres of an old truck. They will last me out, as Kevin's did. His daughter Ioanna told me she threw them away, black and travel-worn, just a couple of years ago.

Walking round the island Kevin wore an indigo cotton shirt of the kind that used to be made and worn locally. Sometimes while resting he played a *flogera,* a shepherd's flute. This was a strange sound to the villagers because the instrument is not indigenous to this part of Greece. But they liked the piping music.

There was a darker side to these excursions. Kevin was physically attractive and people even referred to him as a *palikari* (a brave man or a warrior). But he was also epileptic. He suffered badly, sometimes several seizures a day. He fought his illness, tried to ignore it. The consequences were bad but could have been disastrous. Several times villagers came across his inert or shaking body by the side of a path. Not understanding they tried to comfort him. They ignored the mess, put their arms around him, revived him with water, lifted him to his feet and took him back to the village. Kevin must have been devastated by the shame, the lack of control, the gossip.

He suffered terribly, they tell me. Terribly. But they did not know the half of it.

FOUR

Corinna's story

Searching libraries, newspapers and the internet revealed nothing about the life and whereabouts of Kevin Andrews. Then a friend noticed a reference in the preface of *The Flight of Ikaros* to his old college, the American School of Classical Studies in Athens. The librarian there provided a link with Kevin's daughter. I took the bold step of writing to her.

We met at Syntagma Square in Athens. Corinna is a pleasant, open-faced woman, middle-aged and friendly. I am the wrong daughter, she says, I am *exogamos.* Born out of wedlock. I have never been to Diafani. Never visited Karpathos.

You want the other daughter, Ioanna. Or his wife Nancy.

We only had an hour together but that was enough for Corinna to unroll a fascinating story. For the first time I heard of Nancy and Willard Roosevelt, of E. E. Cummings and Roy Chapman Andrews, Yvette Borup and her brother George. Some names meant nothing, some I knew a little about but they were all part of the tangle that formed the life of Kevin Andrews. Corinna's version of her father's life diverges from other parts of this narrative. It is a complicated story.

Corinna was born in 1950. Her mother, Ioanna, was Greek and already had four children, She rented out a room to Kevin Andrews in Athens. She was 46; he was 25, a student. Years later when Corinna asked, as daughters do, but mummy why…? her mother would only say,

> Oh, but you should have seen him. You should have seen him.

So the lonely youth far from his American home claimed a conquest more than twenty years his senior. As with much of Kevin's life there are many questions and few direct answers, only scattered clues. In the later edition of *The Flight of Ikaros,* amid the wild landscapes and the wild people engaged in a civil war, there is mention of assignations, assignments and love.

In those days Athens resembled a large village, run down and poor, battered by German occupation and then the civil war. Assassinations, disappearances, starvation and banditry were still commonplace. Kevin must have represented romance and glamour plus a hint of American luxury.

When Ioanna told her husband she was pregnant he agreed that, if the affair with Kevin was kept a secret, he would bring up Corinna as one of his own children provided Kevin renounced all rights to his daughter. As a result Corinna grew up in a happy, middle-class family of five children

But Kevin did not keep his distance. He visited Ioanna after dark when her husband was away. He argued, manipulated and inveigled his way back into his daughter's life. When Corinna was six she was sent to Switzerland to stay with a man and a family she did not know. Kevin promised not to reveal his fatherhood but of course he did. He was married now to Nancy, the daughter of E. E. Cummings, and Corinna joined a family of five. Nancy had two children from a previous marriage and a baby daughter by Kevin. The daughter was christened after his lover, Corinna's mother. She was and is Ioanna Andrews. When he met Corinna Kevin immediately blurted out,

> I am your father

She did not believe this at first. Then a few days later, while walking with Kevin on a mountain path, she ran ahead, tripped and tumbled down a steep incline. Kevin, petrified, ran after her, and pulled her to him and to safety. The look of horror on his face told her. Yes, this is my daddy.

So, the relationship was established. But it was not easy to maintain.

Corinna's life was changed by the encounter. Although she was welcome in both families she did not belong in either. She differed from her mother's children and was always the outsider with her father's. Not that she complained as she rattled through the story as fast as she could.

She told me about the books Kevin wrote. One about the Junta, another about Cyprus. She mentioned a novel.

When Kevin and Nancy broke up Nancy took the children to London while Kevin stayed behind, as he thought, to resist the Colonels. Corinna said his arm was broken by the police during that terrible time at the Polytechnic in Athens. She believed he was even locked up for a few days. A Greek prison, then or now, is not a good place for an epileptic.

He renounced his American nationality and became a Greek citizen, she said, in protest at American support for the Junta. In order to relinquish his American passport he had to make statements before a judge, explaining his decision. Few people have ever done such a thing.

Then Corinna told me how he died. Drowned, off the island of Kythira. She paused: some people think the CIA did it.

I knew I had to write this story.

FIVE

Ioanna's story

My letter to Ioanna Andrews was tentative: I am writing a series of short stories, one of them based on a conversation with Manolis the bootmaker in Diafani. He knew your father. He made a pair of boots for him. Did Kevin write anything about Diafani? I do not want to impose. If I could meet you, an hour would suffice.

I expected to be rejected but Ioanna said, yes, that's fine, it would be nice to meet you.

Finding myself in Rafina, not far from Athens, I was nervous. I had no obvious qualifications to go poking around in someone else's life. But Ioanna opened the door with smiles and embraces. And this is Sergio, she said. Sergio too was charming but less exuberant, less extrovert.

Inside I was given a glass of water and allowed to make friends with a large dog. Ioanna is striking, handsome, a mop of thick curly hair, a great smile, full of enthusiasm.

She handed me a copy of Kevin's first book, the classic study *Castles of the Morea*. Not a copy, *the* copy, Kevin's copy with his name written inside. I felt as if I was holding a Shakespeare First Folio. I was intimidated. It was his. His hands had turned the pages mine were turning. I wanted to own it. I handed it back.

Around the walls were paintings of Diafani women. Big acrylics done in a particular style, resembling photographs blown up so the grain becomes visible. Women sitting in a group, *aposperizo* as they say in the village. Women sitting in a circle, talking. The pictures are beautiful. Sergio painted them.

> So you have been to my island?
> No, never.
> Well how?
> From photographs. Kevin took many photographs and I did the pictures from them

And Ioanna took out a package of black and white photographs, very small, about 7 x 5 cm.

The little pictures were very good: a woman, a man on a hillside, a windmill. Wait, I said, feeling in my bag. I have an old Leica TT6. I love black and white. One of my 25 x 20 cm pictures was of the same windmill.

> Where did you get that?
> It's mine. I took it in October.
> But Kevin took it forty years ago.

We had taken the same photograph, standing in the same room at the same window at the same time of day - early morning. I had stayed in the room and so had he. Goose bumps.

Then more stories and more coincidences. I asked if Kevin wrote anything about Diafani. Ioanna waved an exercise book. After her father's death, she went through his notebooks and copied everything he wrote about Diafani and Olymbos. His thoughts as a writer, the mini verses, the questions about Greek light.

Why is there more light in Greece early morning than at midday? Why can you see more in the autumn than in summer? Because horizontal light is more interesting than vertical. It illuminates the boats in the harbour from below. At noon the midsummer sun pounds down, hiding detail and colour, making dull photographs.

Then it all came pouring out. Kevin's father was, well, Roy Chapman Andrews (or Indiana Jones though Spielberg denies it). He found dinosaur eggs in the Gobi desert. In fact he wasn't Kevin's father; Captain Smallwood was, or maybe Perceval Landon. The books say Smallwood and his mother, Yvette, confirmed this, albeit much later. I found no photographs of Landon, Ioanna tells me, so if you can find one... maybe we will know for sure.

Then there is the wife, Nancy. She moved to London after the marriage broke up. She'd been brought up believing her father was Scofield Thayer, her mother's husband at the time Nancy was born. But her real father was E. E. Cummings, the poet. This had been kept from her. And when Nancy met Cummings and found him attractive...

A swirl of photographs, cuttings, books, memories and coincidences. Kevin was born in Peking and here is a picture of him at the Summer Palace. By chance I'd been there recently. The film, *Indiana Jones,* was made at Angkor Wat. I was there too.

More names and more places and two hours had passed. Except for water, we had not paused for food or drink, nor even for breath. But I had a plane to catch. A taxi was called and we embraced. Excited and intimidated I tried to write notes. My short stories were becoming a book.

Back in Diafani I asked around. Many people knew about Kevin. Everybody liked him. He arrived speaking their language, he played the *flogera*, could write *mantinades,* seemed to know all about them. One statement, from the mouth of a villager, has the clarity of truth.

Itan exipno apo ton diabolo. Eikai calces apo ton diablo.

(He was smart from the devil. He had the devil's socks.)

In Greek it is difficult to distinguish between too smart and very smart. But here the meaning is clear. He was so smart it damaged him. He was smart from the devil.

His friends are listed: Minas Prearis, Papa Iannis, Ilias Minatsis, Nikos Philipakis, Vassilis Protopapas and on and on. He seemed to be close friends with half the village.

Aware of my limitations as a writer, and more so as a social being, I found Ioanna difficult to deal with. She is refreshingly naive and open and it would be easy to exploit her. Later I found others had attempted to do just that.

In the academic world there are honest scientists, dedicated historians, kindly profs, but there are also sharks and charlatans, distorting truth to fit theories, promoting their friends, and offering bribes to obtain papers for this archive or that centre of study. Ioanna met and dealt with such people. They got short shrift and were sent back to the USA. Yet she trusted me. When she opened my letter her reaction was: thank God somebody is interested.

At the time I met Ioanna I had a bad knee and my doctor told me to take exercise. It turned out he was wrong. A new path above the village starts at the cemetery, climbs up and over the mountain tops following the line of the coast. The views are spectacular, the path is safe and well made. My knee hurt but I reckoned I could walk it off.

Two hours out, no longer on the recognised path, I was in trouble. My knee was agony. I am not sure I was in danger but I had to rely on my own resources. These hills are big, there are few walkers and shepherds about, and I had told nobody where I was going. Kevin Andrews' problem was epilepsy; he was found unconscious on these paths. There would be nobody to find me. I decided to take a short-cut back. An old path led down some abandoned terraces. It was downhill, I could hobble, hop and jump. I was doing quite well until I found the track blocked by the branches of a large tree. I could see the path below but had to pass the tree. There is only one way. You throw yourself carefully into the upper branches and they lower you slowly and gently to the ground. It sounds silly but I had done it before. I submitted to the tree's embrace and there I was, on the ground, scratched and bleeding, covered with old leaves and dead insects, and pierced by the odd thorn. But I was intact and the path was now easy. I made it back down the mountain without problem.

At home I showered and lay down. Then the phone rang. It was Ioanna enquiring about my health and whether my knee was any better. I told her about the tree. If you throw yourself into the top the branches lower you to the ground, I said. There was a pause at the other end. Ioanna said, I have just been reading something my father wrote about walking in the mountains. He had hurt his knee. His descent was blocked by a tree and he was in pain. He describes throwing himself into the top branches and letting the branches do the lowering.

Now I paused. That's interesting, very interesting. Goose bumps again.

Ioanna continued. I know you are interested in my father in Diafani. He writes that he returned to Piraeus on a *caique* from the village. He was wearing *strivania,* the boots made by my friend

Manolis, the familiar blue cotton shirt, with a *tsoubali* (woollen bag) over his shoulder. *En route* to his house on Mount Lycabettus he was approached by a man:

> *Eisai apo ton chorio mas?* (Are you from our village?)
> No, but I have been visiting there.

Kevin must have been pleased to be taken for a local.

A day had passed and I had recovered from my adventure. The young doctor recommended I take it easy and that I take these anti-inflammatories.

I was sitting in my favourite place in the *cafeneion* with my back to the outhouse wall. I had ordered *elleniko sketo,* Greek coffee without sugar, and Georgos Koufardas, a small man, about sixty, grey hair, an inquisitive cheeky face, approached me. Sometimes I buy eggs from him. Sometimes I forget to pay him or he forgets to collect the money. His wife is more dynamic.

> *Ela re capitanos*. Hello captain.
>
> You have been asking about this man Kevy. *O Kevis Andrew*. I met him once. I was walking across Syntagma when I saw this tall foreigner wearing boots from the village and *blousa,* the old blue shirt that the men used to wear...

The wall behind my back seemed to move a little.

So Ioanna, Sergio and I became friends. We exchange emails and occasionally meet. Daughters of celebrated male writers often have problems: John Osborne denied that his daughter, fifteen at the time, even existed; he threw her out of his house and never spoke to her again. With Durrell, Dylan Thomas and others there are accusations of alcoholic behaviour and physical, even sexual, abuse. I interviewed dozens of people for this book and the more I learned about Kevin Andrews the more I realised what a difficult man – and difficult father - he was. To come to terms with the sudden death of a man like that cannot be easy. If you love him it is more difficult still.

SIX

Yvette Borup

She stands barefoot on the back of a horse, smiles and challenges the camera; young, seductive, coquettish, full of life. Even across 90 years of history it is possible to feel an attraction, to know she was a heartbreaker. A small voice tells me,

Be careful.

I am looking at a family album of Yvette Borup, sister of George Borup, the Arctic explorer. Yvette was once the wife of the adventurer, Roy Chapman Andrews. And loving mother of Kevin Andrews. This is a striking picture but there are others. In one she sits on the same horse, bareback and still barefoot. In another, also on horseback, she is grandly dressed in front of a line of cavalry, tunics bright, lances gleaming in the sun, a young girl seemingly commanding a squadron of the Kaiser's bodyguard.

In the Kevin Andrews story major and minor names tumble out as you turn the yellowing pages of old newspapers, search Google, or interview a charming lady in a French restaurant. To describe Kevin as a snob is probably harsh but he was certainly proud of his forebears and the celebrities he met. However, there is a confusion about his origins and his later years were dominated by an obsession with what he called his murky past.

Even though we know many facts about his mother she remains a mystery. Yvette Borup was born in France, February 28 1891 Her Danish grandfather migrated to America in the 1840s where he married Yvette's grandmother, half-Huguenot, half-Chippewa Indian. In later life Yvette had a family tree drawn up which showed, so she claimed, she was descended from William the Conqueror, via George Adlington Brandreth (born in Leeds 1828), Elkanah Watson (born Plymouth, Mass.1758), Governor Edward Winslow of *Mayflower* (1594), Sir Henry Percy (Harry Hotspur) killed at the battle of Shrewsbury 1403, Edward Plantagenet (1245) and Henry III (1216). Naturally the Borups, a prominent Connecticut family, considered themselves to be part of American and British aristocracy.

Yvette's father was Captain Henry T Borup, a West Point graduate who became the American military attaché accredited to Paris, London and St. Petersburg. The year of Yvette's birth Henry Borup climbed Mont Blanc. The next year Yvette's mother, dressed in a tight-fitting whalebone bodice and a skirt that was all loops and puffs, made the same ascent. In 1892 Henry was accused by thc French of being a spy and attempting to purchase the plans for the fortifications of the port of Toulon from a disgruntled employee of the French Ministry of Marine. Later these charges were dropped but Jefferson Coolidge, the American minister to France at the time, pointed out that Borup's action had been perfectly useless as not only was America at peace with France but the small American navy was incapable of attacking Toulon. However, Borup's behaviour was not totally irrational. America had recently embarked on a programme of upgrading its own coastal defences and Borup presumably believed this information would help. Borup also claimed he had instructions from his military superiors to sketch certain French fortifications. Whatever the truth he did the job well - too well - and was expelled. One of Yvette's earliest memories, probably at age two, was being hidden on the floor of a horse-drawn carriage as it drove through the streets of Paris while bystanders pelted it with stones. Yvette was to claim later that her father was somehow involved in the Dreyfus affair and was fleeing the mob. The family had to leave France and move to America. There they lived in the family home, Careswell, a large colonial building with porticoed pillars, dark corridors and huge rooms, overlooking the Hudson River. Careswell and, later, a Manchu palace in Peking were the only two places that Yvette looked on as home.

When Yvette was only six her mother died. Soon after, Henry Borup's duties took him away to the Spanish-American war. From then on, Aunt Julia brought up Yvette and George. The two children went to boarding school and Yvette became an independent, yet lonely girl.

Few people now alive remember Yvette and her voice emerges only through brief recollections, jottings and a rather grand, but sanitised, journal witten in 1937 and bequeathed to her two children.

Before the end of the nineteenth century Yvette moved with Aunt Julia to Berlin where they lived with a nurse in a pension near the zoo. Arriving on a Saturday Yvette started at Fräulein Krain's Höhere Töchter Schule the following Monday. Leisure for Yvette included boating on the zoo lake, riding in a horse-drawn Victoria carriage and travelling in the city's newly installed green trams. On January 5 1904, aged twelve, she began boarding at the Stiftschule, founded to house the children of German officers killed in the Franco-German war of 1870. It was supposedly the best school in Germany and the Kaiserin Augusta herself took a great interest in it. Dreadfully homesick for a while Yvette learnt to love this school where she was known as the ***kleine Amerikänerin***. One day the Kaiserin visited the school with her young daughter, HRH Viktoria Luise Adelheid Mathilde Charlotte, Princess of Prussia. Sisi, as she was sometimes known, spent the day playing with children of her own age, including Yvette. Being particularly high spirited and athletic Yvette excelled at a German version of cops and robbers. Days later Sisi invited

> the little American girl who could run

to tea at the palace. Yvette and handful of other girls were collected by a horse-drawn carriage with liveried footmen. Yvette taught Sisi to shin up poles and other gymnastic feats originally mastered in the garden at Careswell.

At the beginning of the century the European royal families were significant and serious institutions connected by political beliefs as well as marriage and family. A few weeks before Yvette's visit, an anarchist had thrown a bomb at the King of Spain and the royal families in Europe were tense and nervous. Oblivious, the young girls, out of sight of the Kaiserin in the games room, had fun re-enacting the attempted assassination with wooden bowling balls, blowing one another up and falling down dead amid squeals and giggles.

Sisi and Yvette became close friends. Without an established home Yvette was invited to spend holidays at the palace. She was known to the Kaiser as *Yvettchen* and mixed easily with the German nobility, adding to her confidence in her looks and ability. At school Yvette learned French, German and English, was poor at mathematics but loved the dance classes. Learning the minuet, gavotte, old Francaise and the Lancers served her in good stead when she later attended balls and court dances. Yvette was a romantic child and dreamed of becoming a professional dancer, wanting

> to descend from above and float across the stage.

But boarding schools are lonely, often strict, places. One young girl could not cope with the Spartan environment and on All Saints Day, November 26 1905, attempted suicide by throwing herself out of an upstairs window, badly damaging her hip and leaving her crippled for life. The girl left the school and was never seen again, but fourteen-year-old Yvette was profoundly impressed. In later life she learnt to throw tantrums to get her own way. In her teens she became an accomplished drama queen and longed to be a legitimate actress. Aged seventeen, and living in Paris she was spotted by the newly arrived Sarah Bernhardt who invited Yvette to join her company. Perhaps wary of Bernhardt's reputation as a lesbian Yvette's father would not allow this and she was sent back to Berlin to attend court balls as the partner of Prince Joachim, one of the Kaiser's sons. Later she was even presented at the German Royal Court. Encouraged by her father, she began to study photography and, at twenty-one, worked with Rudolph Duhrkoop a leader in the new art form of taking portraits with a camera. Duhrkoop suggested Yvette find some models and follow suit. Without thinking, Yvette sent out invitations to the people she knew; the *Kommandant* of Berlin, colonels of crack regiments, débutantes and minor princes and princesses. Acceptances poured in and she took dozens of pictures, creating a huge furore in upper class German circles.

Soon after, Yvette returned to 313 York Street, New Haven, Connecticut, to housekeep for her brother George. She was proud of his exploits. He worked at the American Museum of Natural History (AMNH), was an intimate of Admiral Peary and took part in the 1908-9 expedition to the North Pole. George invited Yvette with several friends to an outdoor, but comfortable, holiday on Crescent Beach, Long Island. Her role would be to make beds and, if someone could show her how, wash dishes. She would not have to do the catering as George's special friend, Winship Case, was a superlative cook. One day while canoeing they commented on how cold the water was and wondered how long a man would survive at that temperature. That night, in the same ocean, the *Titanic* struck an iceberg and sank. Two weeks later George went back to Crescent Beach. Yvette expected to be invited but this time George wanted to be alone with Winship Case. Again they went canoeing in the cold Atlantic. A mere 100 yards from the shore the canoe turned over and the two went missing. Yvette was summoned for the rescue operation, joined in the search and was there when the bodies were found. They took George back to Careswell where somebody cut a lock from Yvette's hair and placed it in the dead hand of her beloved brother.

Yvette was devastated. George's body lay in the great music room and Yvette stayed with him all night. Peary and Henry Fairfield Osborn, the AMNH director, attended the funeral as did Roy Chapman Andrews the explorer and adventurer. The service was led by George's old headmaster. At Yvette's request *Nearer My God To Thee*, supposedly played as the *Titanic* sank, was sung by the congregation.

Yvette felt that everything worth living for had been lost with George's death. Aunt Julia came back from France to comfort her and she visited the grave daily. Her father arranged for a Greenland boulder to be set at the head of the grave; the *SS Roosevelt's* bell, which had sounded the watches during Peary's polar expedition, was placed at the foot.

Soon after the funeral Yvette's aunt received a letter from Roy Chapman Andrews (RCA). He had been a friend of George Borup and wanted to meet his dead friend's sister. He too had suffered a similar loss. At college in 1905 he was boating on Rock River with a close friend, Monty White, a professor. The boat overturned and White drowned. Suddenly there was a new man in Yvette's life, someone who was part of her history, someone who had known her brother and shared his ambitions and hopes. Six weeks later Yvette and RCA were engaged. Yvette says,

> I don't know how it happened.

Ninety years later we cannot be sure how it happened either. We do know that Andrews was ambitious and that his best friend, Henry Fairfield Osborn, had suggested the meeting. Osborn, was an arch operator. He knew the Borups and perhaps saw Yvette as distraught, rich and beautiful, someone RCA, a real man, could rescue. Or acquire as a trophy. We do know that Yvette's family had their doubts and that her father and Aunt Julia both opposed the engagement, believing

> Yvette was not to marry anyone at the moment and certainly never, no never, Roy Chapman Andrews

Soon Yvette was studying photography in Newark with the famous and influential Clarence White. She wanted to learn his techniques because White had taken a heroic photograph of George. But Europe was not forgotten and a year later Yvette travelled across the Atlantic to Germany to attend Sisi's wedding to Ernst August, the Duke of Cumberland. In a press interview Princess Lichnowsky, the wife of the German Ambassador to London, explained why Yvette was invited:

> Her brightness is contagious, her wit sparkling and she has a laugh which rings out like silver bells, so musical that men have fallen in love with it.

Yvette was overwhelmed by the etiquette, the clothes and the grandeur of the occasion - one of the last great gatherings of the small family of people that made up Europe's royal families before the upheavals of World War One. Faded black and white photographs still convey the power and arrogance of this tiny ruling class. Yvette's youth, beauty and proximity to the bride turned heads and attracted suitors. She was pursued by kings and princes. In her journal Yvette describes the heavy, gleaming uniforms, the jewels burning in the May afternoon sunlight and the huge dress trains. The *New York Herald*, in late May 1913, carried a wedding photograph, which includes the bride and groom, the Emperor, the German Crown Prince, the King and Queen of England and little Yvette.

Leaving for her honeymoon the bride threw a garter to the guests. Yvette could not retrieve the talisman in the scrum that followed but she did catch her dress on a medal of a fellow guest. Red-faced with embarrassment the man apologised as he tore her dress unhooking himself. The out-of-breath old gentleman with the piece of taffeta hanging from his Order of the Black Star of Russia was the Czar of all the Russias!

SEVEN

Roy Chapman Andrews

Born in Beloit, Wisconsin, in January 1884 Roy Chapman Andrews was driven by a desire for adventure. After college he claimed to have forced himself into employment at the American Museum of Natural History (AMNH) in New York City. He swept floors, tidied up, mixed clay, made *papier maché* models of animals and became a skilled taxidermist. Later he developed an interest in whales. He photographed them at sea, was the first Western naturalist to record whales mating and the first to see them giving birth. He rediscovered the American grey whale then thought to be extinct.

Slender, with slightly sloping shoulders, Andrews was hardly impressive at 5 ft 10 in. and 180 lb. although photographs, many taken by Yvette, often show him in heroic and impressive poses. America loves its explorers whereas Europe, having absorbed its colonialism and acknowledged a multicultural future, has reevaluated the past. The casual violence, the slaughter, slavery and banditry are now recognised for what they were, and attempts have been made to own up to the casual racism of those days. In America, however, explorers are still revered. Few questions are asked about what was being explored, and why, and at what cost to the environment and indigenous populations. Perhaps the American Frontier and its myths are to blame. Penny dreadfuls, national self-promotion and early films have combined with the myths to disguise the truth that America itself was a country mercilessly pacified, its native population and fauna slaughtered. Buffalo Bill was still alive when Roy Chapman Andrews ventured abroad looking for distant frontiers to conquer and opportunities to prove himself the new American hero.

Roy Chapman Andrews was a more controversial figure than his hagiographers would have us believe, and many of his stories are clearly exaggerations. During field work in Indonesia he was said to have been attacked by a 20 ft python that he shot dead. At other times there were bandits and tigers. While working on a Japanese whaler (supposedly studying the whaling industry) he claims to have ended up in the sea attacked by sharks. The harpoonist on the whaler, a man called Johnson whom RCA thought was insane, harpooned a whale but did not kill it. The order was given to pursue the animal in a small boat and Andrews went along as an oarsman. Other members of the crew included the first mate and a Japanese soldier. The mate took another harpoon and thrust it into the whale, which smashed the boat with its tail. As the men clung to the wreckage, sharks attracted by the whale's blood circled around. The men kicked and punched at the predators and RCA claimed he even shoved a wood beam down a shark's throat. The Japanese soldier had his leg bitten off. Johnson, pausing briefly to pick up the men, continued to chase the whale but it escaped. Andrews said he was furious about Johnson's behaviour and for years regretted he had never punched him in the mouth. But none of this is true. In 1918 Edward B Pettet, a whaler for some forty years or more, wrote to Andrews and challenged this tale. Andrews was forced to concede he had never harpooned any whales though he had killed (ironed, in contemporary jargon) a few porpoises. Nevertheless the story is still circulated.

The wild adventurer and the beautiful Yvette became a celebrity couple with an adoring and fascinated public. They married on October 7 1914 at the Trinity Episcopal Church, Ossining, NY. Yvette's father avoided the wedding by going to Canada, Aunt Julia stayed in Careswell but was absent from the ceremony, which was attended by only a few relatives and close friends. Another aunt, a Mrs Hartley, gave Yvette away. Miles Slocum was the best man and his wife, Yvette's cousin and golfing partner, was the matron of honour. Yvette wore the white satin and chiffon she had worn to Sisi's wedding and carried white roses and lilies of the valley. Yvette's journal sometimes throws up sharp statements that would delight Freudian sleuths. In a rather sad passage she wryly states that the night before the wedding the sexton had oiled the floor of the church and it was still moist. So she walked down the aisle

> quite unaware that the glittering white of my train was being marred for all time.

After a honeymoon spent shooting deer in the Adirondacks the couple moved to the exclusive estate of Lawrence Park, Bronxville. Roy and Yvette spent the first few months of their marriage poring over maps of Asia, concentrating on the unmapped white bits where Roy might satisfy his ambitions as a naturalist. He had been to Japan, Korea and Borneo and was seeking somewhere new. Between them they decided on Yunnan province in southern China where no western trained zoologist had ever been. Later their trip was described rather grandly as an expedition although today it would be regarded as a safari. The local US newspaper summed it up in the headline: *Bride off to Hidden China on a Hunting Honeymoon.*

On March 26 1916 they left New York and did not return to the USA for eighteen months. Yvette notes, sadly, she never saw her father nor Aunt Julia again. Both died during her absence.

Yunnan province was in revolt against the central Chinese government and it took time to obtain visas. The situation was precarious and sometimes dangerous, though the Andrews were rarely far from telegraphic and other communications and for the most part travelled in luxury. Besides tents they took beds and tables, a bath, white tablecloths and full sets of cutlery. Given Yvette's background this was still quite an adventure and she took to it without complaint. She was designated the expedition's official photographer and was equipped with a portable, rubber darkroom. When she wanted to develop a plate she simply flung this device over a tree branch, near a suitable source of water. She even managed to take and process coloured photographs - a difficult task under the best of conditions.

First stop was Foochow where they stayed with a missionary couple too poor to afford ice even in this tropical heat.

Then they were invited up river by Harry Caldwell, another missionary with a penchant for hunting. Roy wanted to shoot a blue tiger supposedly sighted by Caldwell. Many weeks were spent tracking their prey but they never saw a tiger, blue or otherwise, though Roy, who suffered from nightmares, scared everyone once by rushing out with gun in hand in the middle of the night. After innumerable train journeys they found themselves on the caravan route to Talifu in northwest China on the Tibetan border.

On September 9 1916 they set off with Edmund Heller, a well known and competent zoologist, entering what the West considered to be unexplored country. Covering up to thirty kilometres a day on horseback and accompanied by numerous servants and porters, they camped out at night or stayed in temples. At Likiang they stayed with Pentecostal missionaries, Mr and Mrs Kok, who had not seen a white woman for four years. Here they began to collect small mammals for the museum before moving north. They camped at 12,000 ft and started shooting everything that moved and some things that didn't. They shot wild goats and sheep as they ascended to 16,000 ft before descending to the banks of the Yangste where they shot geese, ducks and cranes. When Roy and Heller were not shooting animals they were trapping them and when doing neither they came close to shooting one another. Once Heller, hidden by undergrowth, discovered he was being stalked by Andrews and only saved himself by shouting,

Don't shoot it is only me.

Heller had been on notorious expeditions with Theodore Roosevelt in Africa and had seen plenty of slaughter. Nevertheless he was heard to wonder whether Andrews had lost it. On another occasion Roy was shaken to find he was stalking his wife whom he had mistaken for a monkey. She claimed to be amused by this.

Less serious, but perhaps just as typical, is the story of a squirrel Yvette had adopted as a pet. It slept in her sleeping bag and travelled on horseback and in vehicles. One day Roy – not the most careful of men - sat down heavily and squashed the creature. By New Year's Day 1917 they were back in Talifu reading their mail before returning south, shooting monkeys and gibbons as they approached the Burmese border. They crossed the border by mistake and were kept as guests of His Britannic Majesty's Government while waiting for permission to leave. In subsequent travels they added peacocks and black monkeys to their collection.

After nine months, of which 115 days were on horseback, Yvette and Roy returned to Peking in September 1917. They had covered more than 3000 kilometres and had shot or trapped more than 2000 mammals and 800 birds, many still on show in the AMNH in New York. Yvette was pregnant and wanted a Christmas baby but George, named after her late brother, was born on Boxing Day (December 26) 1917. The family of three travelled by boat along the Irrawaddy to Rangoon and then across India before catching a liner from Bombay to New York. They were accompanied by a baby Tibetan bear bought in Tenghueh. Searching Yvette's name on the internet reveals a charming picture of Yvette playing with the bear. She looks like a child, a female Christopher Robin, rather than the hardened explorer she had become.

A book written jointly by RCA and Yvette, *Camps and Trails in China. A narrative of Exploration, Adventure and Sport in little known China*, was published in 1918 and dedicated to the president of the AMNH, Henry Fairfield Osborn, as an expression of gratitude and admiration. The object of the book was said to

> present a popular narrative of the Asiatic Zoological Expedition of the American Museum of Natural History to China in 1916-17.

It sold thousands. Quoting *The Call of the Wild* by poet Robert Service its style aims to exploit the contemporary romantic passion for the outdoors:

> Let us probe the silent places, let us seek what luck betide us;
>
> Let us journey to a lonely land I know.
>
> There's a whisper on the night-wind, there's a star agleam to guide us,
>
> And the Wild is calling, calling ... let us go.

Back in America Yvette and Roy sought funds for the next trip. This was time-consuming and it was not until June 29 1918 that Roy set sail for China from San Francisco on *SS Ecuador*. Yvette followed, taking George and his newly appointed nurse, Hélène Friche.

Andrews carried two contracts: one an 18-month expedition agreement with the American Museum of Natural History, the other a year-long agreement with the Office of Naval Intelligence. He was to scour around China and the Mongolias under the guise of doing AMNH fieldwork and provide written reports to Commander I. V Gillis, the U.S. naval attaché in Peking. Roy was a spy, codenamed Reynolds, occasionally using secret ink made from lemon and sugar. At $8 a day his pay was twice the going rate and he also claimed costs and expenses. Up to April 1919 he was entirely occupied by Bureau of Naval Intelligence work. This happy state of affairs ended when the U.S. Government opened one of Yvette's letters home and found it too revealing. She told friends her husband was working for U.S. Naval Intelligence. It might seem strange that the daughter of a military attaché should behave in this way since she must surely have understood the need for discretion. In the event Roy Chapman Andrews' work was compromised and the contract terminated. In May the couple set off on the grandly titled Second Asiatic Zoological Expedition. Leaving George in Peking with an amah and Hélène they crossed Mongolia by motor car with three Chinese assistants, arriving at Urga, the capital. Urga was chosen as the base of operations because it is at the junction of the Siberian and Central Asian ecosystems. From June 1 until the middle of July they collected fauna, shooting ibex and sheep, antelope and gazelle and horses, covering over 2000 kilometres on horseback, including the Gobi desert. After returning to Urga they worked in the forests north of the city for another two months acquiring a totally different range of fauna. Yvette, returning home alone one evening by pony, was attacked by wild dogs that attempted to drag her from the saddle. In contrast to her husband's tendency to over-dramatise she made very little of this terrifying incident.

As the photographer Yvette shot about five hundred pictures and three thousand feet of motion picture film, providing a record of the Mongolians and their life and costumes. These can still be seen in books and in museums in the USA, Mongolia and China. On their return to Peking they were met at the station by George with the amah. George was quite a grown-up two-year-old, fairly indifferent to his mother and father. He offered his cheek to be kissed by Yvette then turned to the amah to talk excitedly in Chinese about the locomotives.

Yvette was more than just a photographer; in many ways she was the joint leader. On their voyage back to the USA she and Roy began to develop a broader vision of exploration. They planned to lead large-scale expeditions with geologists, anthropologists, palaeontologists and so on. They also needed another zoologist as Roy was barely qualified. The glamorous couple presented their plans to the AMNH and others. Roy's marketing skills and Yvette's vitality and beauty clearly worked their spell on Osborn as they were granted massive funds, mostly by the AMNH. Yvette described Osborn later as being

> like a god to us.

The new funds paid for another expedition and also maintained the couple's lavish lifestyle. They were now celebrities with an adoring public, discussed at dinner parties throughout the world and regularly photographed by the tabloids.

By April 1921 they were back in China again. Their house, No 2 Kung Hsien Hutung, in Peking, was a Manchu Palace, having once belonged to an important prince. Contemporary descriptions list 47 rooms, eight courtyards, a large garden with trees and a rock garden, stables, a laboratory, a dark room and ten permanent staff. Yvette's bedroom was some distance away from Roy's quarters. Some rooms were large and cool, a blessing in the hot Peking summers. Constance and Heyward Cutting, American friends of Roy and Yvette, were passing through Peking on their honeymoon that year and Yvette enlisted Constance, an interior designer, to assist in the decoration of the palace. This was completed during the autumn. Subsequent visitors included Douglas Fairbanks and Noel Coward.

According to Yvette the amah who looked after George was a gem. They believed her to be 40 - 60 years old but, significantly, knew little else about her, not even her name. The head of the household staff was Lo and, in the subtle racism of the times, was known as Number One Boy. Lo was a gracious and skilled diplomat and a fixer whom the young George Andrews grew to revere. He remembered Lo as rather tall and kindly. While the house at

Kung Hsien Kutung was an enclave of western life the practicalities of Peking were not far away. Squeals from the pig market would be heard on the hot afternoon wind and convicted criminals were beheaded nearby. For a while Roy and Yvette also rented the Temple of the High Spirited Insects, in the hills to the west of the city, which they used at weekends and on holidays when the city was too hot. There they could relax while Buddhist monks moved quietly around, seemingly unmoved by this invasion of aliens.

In 1922 Yvette accompanied RCA to Mongolia for the last time. George was left behind once again, this time in the care of Hélène. A close friend and financial advisor to the Andrews, Captain Harold St Clair (Chips) Smallwood, moved into the palace to keep Hélène company. Smallwood and the Andrews were part of a syndicate that rented the appropriately named Temple of Hopeful Fecundity. Sometimes known as The Bounder, Smallwood was a fascinating man. Born in 1883 he ran away from an alcoholic and physically abusive father and an invalid mother at the age of 14. He joined the Imperial Yeomanry in 1901 and fought in the Boer War with the Transvaal Horse Artillery earning himself the Queens Medal with five clasps. Then it was India and Burma until, on the outbreak of World War One, he enrolled in the 15th Bengal Lancers and served in Mesopotamia. Seconded to the Royal Flying Corps and then its successor, the RAF, he flew a variety of aircraft until a plane crash in which he fell from 30 m fractured his skull causing severe concussion. After the war he was transferred to China working as an aeronautical advisor to the Chinese Government Air Service. Reputedly he sold Vickers machine guns to warlords as well as pioneering the air route from Peking to Ulan Bator. He was the local correspondent of the London newspaper *The Daily Telegraph* and had a profound impact on Kevin's life.

In the Yunnan days Roy and Yvette travelled with only one qualified scientist, Heller. The 1922 expedition included the palaeontologist, Walter Granger, two geologists and a zoologist, together with assistants and over twenty local porters and servants. The group travelled in five vehicles – two Fulton lorries, two Dodge delivery wagons and a Dodge car - and used more than 150 camels to transport food and petrol. The team also included James B. Shackleford, the official photographer. Shack had spent the previous year in Tahiti as a cinematographer working for the William Randolph Hearst motion picture company. Yvette records, a little sadly, there was

> little use now for me, the former official photographer

The first permanent çamp was Iren Dabasu just inside the Inner Mongolia border, along the main caravan road from Kalgan to Urga. On April 24 fossilised bones were discovered. Strangely Roy and Yvette seemed unmoved by the find and, a day or so later, left for Urga to deal with passports for Outer Mongolia and so that Yvette could photograph the area. When Yvette returned she was accompanied by Davidson Black, professor of anatomy at Peking Union Medical College and a friend of the Andrews. Yvette went on to Kalgan and Peking while RCA stayed in Urga until the main party eventually met up with him to the south of the city. While the Andrews were absent from Iren Dabasu Granger and his assistants excavated more than 50 lb of fossils including dinosaur bones (the first north of the Himalayas) and the teeth of a titanothene. Much later in the summer, as the party was returning to Kalgan, Walter Granger discovered what he thought to be an eggshell fragment at a place named Flaming Cliffs. Prior to the early 1920s dinosaurs were believed to lay eggs although there was no absolute proof. Walter was a consummate and painstaking scientist and sent the fragments off to be analysed. Later that winter his hypothesis was confirmed. Flaming Cliff was to prove one of the most exciting locations in the history of palaeontology. RCA played only a minor role in the scientific excavation of these sites but was relentless in using the discoveries to enhance his personal reputation.

Meanwhile, amid these developments, Roy's attitude towards Yvette was changing. Despite their joint successes, he believed

> Women are simply inferior as explorers and scientists… especially so in the isolated wilds of expedition fieldwork.

Yvette did not go on another expedition and, from now on, her behaviour changed dramatically. She began to party, so much so that the scandalised white population of Peking gave her a new nickname - Merry Andrews. Being replaced as official photographer by Shackleford may have sparked this reaction.

George Andrews recalled years later,

> success had a bittersweet taste. Roy's total dedication to his work came at a high personal cost. During the years 1922-1930, he put exploration ahead of everything, including family.

Writing about his mother he says,

> She was popular, petite and beautiful, in demand and courted by the French and British and American gentlemen who found her witty, charming and mostly alone.

In different ways Roy and Yvette were living on the edge. While Yvette partied Roy began hunting without any pretensions to sportsmanship. Using a high powered rifle with silencer he started shooting wild asses, not singly but in dozens. Approaching these docile creatures by car he took aim from as close as fifty metres, breaking legs and skulls and splattering the desert with blood, guts and brains.

Andrews was a skilful self-publicist but his macho image reveals something hollow, something not quite right. The accounts of his exploits were both exaggerated and boastful and sometimes he lied. Emotionally cold he had a vile temper and enjoyed animal slaughter.

Living with such a boor could not have been easy for the lively and cultured Yvette. Now, as the expeditions she had dreamed of grew larger and more successful, she found herself sidelined. Contemporary female explorers were still exploring. Her friend, Anna Granger, twenty years older than Yvette, was about to accompany her husband, Walter, on his next expedition to the Yangtze while Yvette was forced to stay at home. Her father and her brother had treated her as a housekeeper and now her husband was doing the same. But she was older now, a renowned beauty, more confident and more willing to take risks. She had found other interests.

Yvette once described the year in Peking as:

> March to May racing, May to October polo, October to March hunting.

An enthusiastic and skilful horsewoman she took full advantage of this calendar She danced all night on the roof garden of the Peking Hotel, slept through most of the long, hot days and, at dusk, rode into the Temple of Heaven. Sometimes she accompanied friends to Shan Hai Kuan village where transportation to the beach was by a hand cart on a single-track railway line. There she was happy, swimming at all hours even in the moonlight. Later, young George, then six, sometimes stayed with a Mrs Goodrich at Pei-Ta-Ho. With George in this seaside resort, an hour by car from Peking, Yvette was free to enjoy herself.

There were more than 2000 expatriates living in Peking at the time - missionaries and bankers, diplomats and dealers - the majority of them men far from women of their own social standing. Yvette began to flirt, to turn heads, to invite comment. There was talk of a scandal involving a Japanese magician. This narrow, closed community did not approve. Soon there was another man in her life; to be more precise, there were other men. Yvette made little effort to cover up her liaisons She was considered to be a loose woman.

In the spring of 1923 Roy lead an expedition back to Flaming Cliffs, leaving Yvette in Peking. On July, 10 Roy's assistant paleontologist, George Olsen, unearthed a major find - complete dinosaur eggs with nests. Eggs and nests, surrounded by bones, provided the required evidence that dinosaurs were reptiles. In retrospect what is surprising is the apparent lack of excitement at this discovery. Walter Granger merely notes:

> Olsen found this morning a group of fossil eggs, dinosaurs presumably…

The hapless Andrews set out hunting on the very morning of the discovery and was either not told about the find or did not recognise its significance However, when he realised what *had* happened he used his media links to create and further promote his own image. Because he had sole contact with the press it was he who became famous. Even today he is erroneously credited with discovering dinosaur eggs.

The news provoked intense interest in the outside world. There were headlines in daily newspapers in the USA and William Randolph Hearst is said to have offered $250,000 for the exclusive story. Roy Chapman Andrew's fame grew and Yvette's earlier photographs assisted this process. He is shown as a strong man in khaki with boots and a Mountie-type hat complete with feather. Alternatively holding a rifle, standing in the desert, staring into the distance. Later RCA, Yvette and a group of colleagues are seen camping out or crossing the Gobi in a convoy of Dodge cars. RCA looks every bit the role model for Indiana Jones, a suggestion repeatedly denied by his progenitors, Spielberg and Lucas, but encouraged by those with a vested interest in promoting RCA as an untarnished American hero...

EIGHT

Kevin is born

Yvette was deliberate and thoughtful, not spontaneous. She once described her life as a series of enjoyable chapters, which she could close down with an iron curtain before the next chapter began. An iron curtain separated the death of her brother and now another was about to fall.

In 1923 she became pregnant again. The new child was conceived between late April and mid-May. For some of that time Roy was in Peking attending the races, which lasted for two weeks, so he could have been the father. Contemporary diaries and notebooks show Roy and Yvette acting as a dutiful couple but say nothing about Yvette's condition. The Osborns were visiting Peking at the time and on September 29 Anna Granger writes:

Mr and Mrs Andrews gave a big party for Osborn and his wife for their wedding anniversary. On the same date Walter Granger wrote to his father:

> Osborn and Andrews will sail for the States on October 16. Andrews is to spend the winter lecturing and trying to raise more money for the continuance of the work; he expects to return to Peking in late spring or early summer

Neither Anna nor Walter mentions the pregnancy, which must have been noticeable in the diminutive Yvette. Nor do they comment on Roy's plan to leave his wife alone in Peking for six months when, with a looming civil war, many foreigners were leaving and those that did stay were sending their wives home to Europe and the USA.

When the Grangers left Peking in December a now heavily pregnant Yvette took George down to the port to say goodbye but the Grangers record nothing about her condition. Were they embarrassed by some scandal, restrained by local gossip or just confused? There is no obvious reason, nor is there one that explains why Roy did not wait for the birth of the new baby.

One person who does allude to Yvette's condition is Chips Smallwood. At the end of November, when Yvette was seven months pregnant, he starts a letter:

> Dear Old Roy.

Wishing Roy A Merry Christmas he adds:

> Yvette looks amazingly well... her face is rosy and she looks the picture of health.

He describes RCA's financial position which is

> as rosy as Yvette's complexion. She is really wonderful well and blooming.

He concludes:

> All success to you and love from us all. Yours ever, Chips

Janet Wulsin, another traveller and photographer, was a close friend of the Andrews though she considered them

> rather worldly.

She had missed all the gossip as she had been on a nine-month expedition in Mongolia. When she returned in early January 1924 she wrote to her mother:

> Roy Chapman Andrews has gone home for a four-month lecture tour at $35,000 for five lectures a week.... She is here having a baby.

On January 20 1924 the birth started at 4 am and at 6.30 am Kevin was born. At dawn Yvette heard the doctor say,

> Bad luck it's a boy.
> Bad luck nothing,

she thought, and turned to see

> my beautiful son.

A few hours after the birth, George was led in but was not impressed. He had been promised a sister and much preferred to play with a new drum left for him by his father. Yvette thought her new son was

> a most adorable little man, with the bluest of blue eyes.

After months of correspondence between Roy, Yvette and, surprisingly, Osborn, the new arrival was named Roy Kevin Victor Andrews. The formulation was deliberate. Yvette wanted him to be a winner and leave his mark on the world. Later in life Kevin found this burden difficult to bear. He dropped Victor and, for different reasons, Roy.

Roy Chapman Andrews did not return to Peking until July 4 1924, nearly seven months later. He was to claim that Yvette was flirtatious and warmly welcomed him. He thought Kevin to be

> of the merriest disposition.

But something was wrong. Yvette could barely tolerate her husband near her new son. She was extremely possessive and endowed with a seemingly fanatical desire to govern Kevin's body, soul and mind

It is reasonable to suppose Roy believed Kevin was his child. He could have been and behaved as if he was. But there are two other contenders.

Perceval Landon was a noted imperialist, a close friend of Rudyard Kipling and of Lord Roberts. A journalist in the Boer War he was a prominent player in the Great Game, alerting the British government to, what he called, the threat from Russia and urging the pre-emptive conquest of Tibet. When Tibet was duly invaded Landon went along as the special correspondent for *The Times* (of London). This punitive invasion, led by Francis Younghusband, was completely unprovoked and resulted in the massacre of unprepared Tibetans armed only with muzzle loaders. Newspaper photographs show wide, barren landscapes covered with Tibetan dead and shackled prisoners in the background. Landon reported the massacres and the victorious march into Lhasa with glee. The invasion led to some very unequal treaties between Britain and Tibet, opening the way for China to do much the same in more recent times. In 1906 Landon wrote ***Lhasa: An Account of the Country and People of Central Tibet***, still cited as one of the earliest and most lyrical first-hand foreign accounts of The Forbidden Land. Later he wrote several other works, some about India, as well as the renowned ghost story, ***Thurnley Abbey***.

In 1922 Landon, in his mid-fifties, was living in Peking this time as special correspondent for ***The Daily Mail*** of London, then as now a paper with imperialistic inclinations. He knew Roy Chapman Andrews and Yvette had caught his eye. He wrote to her suggesting breakfast at the Peking Hotel roof garden, adding,

> I have something to show you.

That something was a ringside seat of the bombing raids against rebel forces on the outskirts of the city. Presumably Landon's connections had leaked to him that this assault was going to happen and, presumably, RCA was out of town. Yvette and Landon watched modern warfare from an opulent roof garden commanding lovely views of The Forbidden City, the Legation quarter where the foreigners lived, and well over 100 square kilometres of surrounding countryside. The couple sat in luxury watching aircraft kill and maim bandits and rebels. Despite this odd form of entertainment they became close. They spent days exploring Peking and its surrounds, photographing the sights including the famous ***stupa*** (Buddhist tower) at the Yellow Temple. Both were photographers and Yvette records they spent hours together in the darkroom having great fun.

She describes Landon as having silver hair, dark-eyes, glasses on top of a high bridged nose and small hands. What impressed her most about this urbane, well-connected and well-travelled man was:

> his simplicity.

Landon was an amateur artist and gave Yvette a small crayon sketch of the Spirit Gateway to the Manchu palace at dusk. Standing in the gateway, in the dark, is a romantic figure of a woman. Beyond her, inside the garden, a fire burns. Landon told her:

> You see, I have painted you haunting your own house.

I have held this picture. It conveys sadness, a sense of loss, a different time, a feel for what might have been. Yvette kept this picture, together with chalk and crayon drawings of Kevin as a baby, throughout her life. All appear to be by the same hand. They could have been drawn by Landon. One is inscribed:

> Yvette in respect of your spirit.

Clearly Landon and Yvette had strong feelings for one another. Whether they were lovers is less certain though one close friend I interviewed told me Yvette believed Landon would have loved to have had a child by her.

The couple could only snatch brief periods together since Landon's work took him to Turkestan, the North-West Frontier, the Chinese city of Wo T'a Su and, in 1926, Nepal. Their last day together was at the Hall of the Classics, a favourite haunt. Yvette says Landon knew he would never return to Peking, knew they would never meet again. But he kept this to himself. Instead, as they walked under the dark cypress tree, he said,

> Don't come back here without me, will you?

Yvette promised this and she never returned. The words tell us this was no casual relationship. Soon after, Landon left Peking for Europe. One quiet afternoon, several months later, Hélène, the children's nurse, read aloud from a local newspaper to Yvette,

> *Que c'est dommage, madame, ce pauvre monsieur est mort*

In her journal Yvette supposes she

> looked at the paper because I can still see the cold little boxed cable at the head of the page, which meant the end.

Tough and resolute Yvette continues coldly and crisply,

> Turning on my heel, I walked back to my room and closed the door.

An iron curtain comes down. The journal never mentions Landon again.

Landon died on January 23 1927, the cause unknown. He was buried four days later. He was 57 and had never married. Yvette was not specific about her relationship with him but there are clues. In her picture albums several photographs are cut in half. Kevin as a baby, Kevin as a young child, and the shadow of an adult. But never the adult. Landon was a close friend yet there are no photographs of him. Is this a case of The Dog That Did Not Bark? Was Yvette sanitising history for her new son? Trying to protect him? But from what? There is some evidence that Landon was a Spiritualist. In later life Yvette went to séances and it is possible, just possible, she was trying to contact him. She kept his letters all her life; the iron curtain was not impenetrable.

Among the albums there are several photographs of the other paternal contender: Captain Smallwood who helped look after George when Yvette went to Mongolia in 1922 . Smallwood and his wife were members of the Andrews' inner circle of friends. Could such an unassuming, thoroughly decent man, knowing the situation, write to Roy about Yvette:

> She is really wonderful well and blooming.

Perhaps he did not know at the time or maybe he was not the father. It is said that the morning Kevin was born Yvette phoned Smallwood, who already had two sons (William and John) and was a skilled horseman, to tell him,

> You have a hand for polo.

Supposedly he cried. A few days later, accompanied by his wife, Margot, he saw the boy for the first time.

The year Kevin was born Margot Smallwood returned to England. Captain Smallwood stayed on in China but visited England frequently until the 1930s when he returned permanently.

When Roy Andrews finally returned to Peking he continued to plan for expeditions but could only dream. The political situation was dire. Yvette led a separate life, leaving her children in the care of Hélène and others. She was out and about with Landon and with Smallwood, scandalizing the white population of Peking and tormenting and confusing her husband. These were dangerous times in Peking and Roy was often away: in America raising funds for the Andrews' lavish lifestyle and for expeditions that never took place, or up-country preparing for these ill-fated expeditions. The relationship deteriorated over the next three years and in 1927 Yvette and Roy separated. RCA wrote begging her not to leave him. He professed undying love:

> If only you would be frank with me, but you have shut me out of the life of my child and out of your life.

Later he begged her to stay:

> We are standing on the verge of worldwide, lasting fame.

Perhaps that line tells us more about Roy Chapman Andrews than any book, newspaper or hagiography. His darling wife is leaving him. He is heartbroken but can only offer worldwide, lasting fame. The letter was written in 1927 and, months later, Yvette and the children left Peking. RCA remained for a further two years. Unaware of the full story, he wrote to Osborn:

> It has definitely been decided for Yvette to take the children and go to England. It is the wisest course we both know.... I've played the game according to the rules, and, after all, we can't do more!

Contemporary press releases state that, in 1922-1930, Andrews put exploration ahead of everything, including family. Although the family shared the same home in Peking, he hardly saw them between expeditions. He was always busy and his son George remembered

> he was almost indifferent to children and family.

It is impossible to say now whether Yvette's behaviour led to this indifference or stemmed from it. Either way, Yvette was tired of Andrews and the birth of Kevin blew the marriage apart

Over a decade was to pass before Yvette told RCA he was not Kevin's father although, by then, this was probably not news to him. She did not tell Kevin until the eve of his thirtieth birthday.

NINE

Pictures in a library

I am hunched over a magnifying glass looking back 100 years. The photograph shows a squat man from a different age, a man from an imperial past, standing adjacent to a strange object. Perceval Landon, author, correspondent for *The Times* and *The Daily Mail*, friend of Rudyard Kipling, friend, perhaps lover, of Yvette Borup Andrews and, maybe, the father of Kevin Andrews.

Photograph 1083/13(204) is labelled: Golden Ornament on roof of Palkhor Choide Monastery [Gyantse], with Times correspondent Landon. The Bailey collection, Tibet 1903-4, FMB Vol 2. I am within the inner sanctum of the British Library and I have permission to examine archive material of the India Office. I am entitled to be here but I do not belong. I try to look like a researcher, an academic, but all I want to know is, does this man look like Kevin Andrews? I sketch the face. I record in my notebook: stocky man with short, broad face, low ears sticking out, dark moustache.

The library assistant waits expectantly. I look again. Was he Kevin's father?

On a whim I ask if the library has any pictures of Captain Smallwood.

The assistant comes back, wearing gloves, with a box containing a leather album. A label reads: Bourne & Shepherd. Photographers to their Excellencies the Viceroy and Commander-in-Chief, Simla,

Calcutta & Bombay. I am not allowed to touch the album; the assistant opens it to the right page. A long, somewhat faded photograph is marked: Delhi Durbar. 1903. Delhi. Some 200 military men, empire builders, in three or four rows, sitting or standing to attention, stare at the camera. Landon is near the front. At the back, on the left, one man, partially obscured, is not looking straight at the camera. A slight, balding man. Captain Smallwood. The Bounder.

What have I seen? These two men mixed in the same circles and knew each other for more than twenty years. One or both were Yvette's lovers. If anything, Landon looks like the younger Kevin Andrews. But Yvette claimed Smallwood was the father.

Why did Roy Chapman Andrews accept the outward responsibility of fatherhood? Surely he could count months as well as any husband. And why did his son, George, insist that Kevin resembled RCA and was his full brother?

One of these three men was Kevin Andrews' father. But which ?

Does it matter? In the preface to the Penguin edition of *The Flight of Ikaros* Kevin Andrews, the man I am trying to understand, describes himself as being of

> multiracial ancestry, a shrouded origin in an outlandish birthplace, a divided heritage, and a mistaken belief in my natural right to a quiet surname...

So it mattered to him.

TEN

Leaving Peking

Kevin Andrews was brought up by an amah unnamed in any of the records. Having lost her own child she was Kevin's wet nurse and totally adored him. She took him on daily excursions, on visits to her family, on shopping trips to Peking's marketplaces. Perhaps it was the smoky fires, the one-pot cooking, the animals and the peasant life that formed the basis of Kevin's empathy for the Homeric men and women of the Greek mountains.

Not only did Yvette avoid breast-feeding her child for a while she even found it difficult to hold him. When Kevin was christened, the amah, not his mother, took him to the font. Yvette looked after her children one or two days a month and then, in Kevin's own words, took to her bed to recuperate. Was this the result of passion for Landon, shame at her liaison with Smallwood, uncertainty about the father of her second son, or post-natal depression? Or did cushioned colonialists find it difficult to take care of their children in a normal relationship?

One thing is certain, Yvette continued to amuse herself. Expatriate society in Peking lived well and every night there was a dance in the Peking Hotel attended by diplomats, White Russians, adventurers, counts, explorers - the flotsam of early twentieth century colonial life. Yvette enjoyed going to balls and parties and visiting Yi He Yuan known to tourists as The Summer Palace. This cool, impressive, lakeside enclave on the edge of Peking was the playground of the pampered white population of that great city, a place where they could convince themselves they were special people chosen to rule China.

As breast-feeding ended the amah had served her purpose and was replaced by Hélène. Kevin's first language, from the amah, was Chinese, his second was French which, together with his elder brother George, he learnt from Hélène. She also taught them what was quaintly known as deportment which, these days, would probably be called good manners.

At the time, China was subject to unrest and upheaval and even Peking was not immune. In 1926 the capital was sealed off from unruly soldiers and arrangements were made for Yvette, Kevin and George to take refuge within the American Legation. Roy Chapman Andrews planned to defend his compound with sandbags and machine guns but the uprising was subdued and life returned to strained normality.

Even in times of comparative peace Peking was a lawless place. George recalls in his journal riding in the back seat of a Dodge open sedan with his father:

> Our car was stopped in the narrow, crowded street by a mob crowding around a merchant's open-air stall. Apparently he had given false weight, or committed a crime that enraged the mob. The terrified man was dragged out by his pigtails and, there being no handy execution block available, the front wheel of the Dodge was used as a block, and his head chopped off by a local policeman.

Apart from such dramatic interludes the lifestyle was regal. In his detached way George says his mother

> was riding a wave of good times, indulged by the legation culture. ...there were grand dinner parties, some so large that silverware and plates would be exchanged from one house to another. At a legation dinner, my mother might encounter her own knives and forks and wine glasses.

The disjointed relationships in the Andrews household continued: the husband, supposedly still in love with the beautiful Yvette, is away for extended periods while Yvette cements her relationship with Smallwood, believing perhaps that he would one day leave his wife.

By late 1927 the marriage had foundered. Yvette later explained:

> We had reached an impasse. It was time for George to be educated. The little boys and I would have to go.

Yvette made arrangements to go to England but there was one more drama. On an excursion to the Great Wall, some three hours drive from Peking, Kevin was bitten by a monkey. Fortunately there was a nurse nearby and she sucked the wound clean. Fearful of infection a German doctor cauterised the wound with a red-hot poker. Kevin was three at the time.

In those days the preferred form of travel for the rich was the Trans-Siberian Express, a service which, though modified, still connects travellers from Peking to St Pancras station in London. Upheavals in China and the imposition of Soviet rule in Russia and its component states meant that the journey was not easy. The railway line had only recently been reopened. Yvette's heavy luggage was sent via Suez but there were still eighteen suitcases to accompany them on the train. Yvette and the children were leaving for good. Leaving not only her husband but her home, her friends and a life of wealth, happiness and fun. She kept to hand the sketch by Landon of the Spirit Gateway. She remembered his words:

> I have painted you haunting your own house.

Desperately she tried to preserve

> the memory of the velvet green hills, pink temple walls and a well loved figure (Landon?) silhouetted against the sparkling North China sky.

But Landon was dead; he would never return to Peking and she wanted to be close to Smallwood.

Despite the scandals and the gossip Yvette was a popular woman and many friends came to see her off. The platform was crowded with men in uniform or Savile Row suits and women with astrakhan hats and fur coats. Among the fuss, the crowds, the noise, the steam and the turmoil of putting the luggage on the train, Yvette said goodbye to Peking:

> George is aboard and all the luggage. Somebody hands me a fat little bundle. It is Kevin. I had almost forgotten him. I can't bear it any longer; I turn away and bury my face in my hands.

And then there's this unexplained observation. Yvette became aware of a Frenchman who shared the carriage. She cannot remember his name. But something strange happened or maybe not. Kevin wanted to go to the toilet and the Frenchman offered to help, saying he:

> could manage the buttons.

Maybe it was unimportant but Yvette usually concentrated on significant events:

> He was in his way the kindest Frenchman I have ever known.

Perhaps we read too much into such simple words. But they hint at a Victorian melodrama. Was there something more?

It was now deep winter and the seventeen-day journey across the Russias and Europe continued. Russian and Chinese track gauges differ so, at Harbin in north-east China, the passengers transferred to a Russian train. At 4 am in the freezing cold intrepid Yvette, with two small children and a heap of suitcases, dealt with customs officials, bureaucrats and the Soviet Army. George Andrews says:

> On a cold railway platform, under the yellow light of a gas lamp, she marched off to attend to the unknown, leaving me in charge of the three year old Kevin. My orders were not to move and to defend Kevin and the baggage at all costs.

And the ten-year-old George did just that until Yvette returned, papers in hand, passports stamped and two porters in tow.... talking rapidly in English, French, Chinese and German. Soon Yvette, Kevin, the calm, brave George, and the suitcases were on the new train. Distracted by Yvette's beauty the guards failed to detect the jewellery and furs she was smuggling to help start her new life. The next day they arrived in Tarskaya where they connected to the Trans-Siberian line between Moscow and Vladivostok. Then, south of Lake Baikal, to Irkutsk, Omsk, Tomsk, and eight days later to Moscow.

At either end of the passenger car there was a Russian soldier in a fur cap, fur coat and black boots, armed with a rifle and a pistol. George went over to make friends with these big men and they, with an eye on his mother, wanted to make friends with him. George's account of these events eight decades ago is dispassionate, inquisitive and amusing. But he was ten. It is more difficult to assess their impact on Kevin.

Picture a blank screen, white to light grey. On the right-hand side a third of the way up is a dot. The dot passes from right to left. It gets bigger, a line emerges, then smoke, then the noise of the train as it passes through this dead, cold landscape. From one carriage a small face is pressed against the window.

He had left behind his father, his home, his amah and his nurse. Now, in a crowded carriage of strangers, the child was being transported through a vast landscape to the other side of the world. He had nobody to turn to except an older brother and his stressed mother.

There was little or no food on the train, only samovars of steaming tea. Occasionally there were stops at small, isolated villages and passengers leapt out to buy produce. Yvette bargained for simple foodstuffs, milk for the children, vegetable stew and occasionally meat. Yvette says Master Kevin ate borscht three times a day.

From Moscow they changed train again, travelling on to Poland and Germany until they arrived at Ostend. On this stretch of the line there were social encounters. The wealthy people Yvette had known in Germany, now scattered and impoverished by the social upheaval of World War One and its aftermath, kept an eye on the list of travellers on the Siberian railway. Some - the Cerrutis in Moscow, Udi Lagow in Poland - arranged to meet Yvette and her children as they crossed Europe, exchanging gifts and gossip, hugs and farewells.

Arriving in London the family were met by friends of theirs from Peking: the O'Malleys, Marjorie Turner and.... Margot Smallwood.

A measure of the stress this journey entailed is revealed when Yvette admitted to being reassured by the sight of a London policemen. Although she had to bribe her way across some frontiers she had managed to keep most of the jewellery and furs. The little family checked in at the Grosvenor Hotel, then as now, a temporary home for celebrities.

Poor George was soon made aware of their reduced circumstances when Yvette told him off for leaving his clothes on the floor. There was no amah to tidy up after him, no nurse. He was shocked by the news.

ELEVEN

Life in England

After a few days at the Grosvenor, Yvette, George and Kevin moved in with - of all people! - the Smallwoods. The nature of this ménage is unknown but surely Margot Smallwood could hardly have ignored the vibrations between her husband and Yvette, vibrations that would have resonated beyond the one known relationship, that Chips was Kevin's godfather. Yvette and the children stayed with the Smallwoods for six months, paying rent throughout, before moving not far away to Courtesy Cottage in the Oxfordshire village of Islip. They lived there for three years, sometimes sharing the house with a French nurse, her husband and their two children.

Yvette did not manage to bring down a curtain entirely on her China days. Landon was still on her mind. He was dead but soon after her return to England she visited Landon's closest friend, Rudyard Kipling. Staying with the family of Sir Francis Anglin, former head of customs in China, she discussed with Kipling the man who had moved her so much. There are no records of their conversation though Yvette says she thought Kipling wanted to tell her something but was prevented by the presence of his wife. He would not talk openly in front of her.

The close relationship between Yvette and Smallwood continued. Yvette used to claim Smallwood wanted to marry her but she told him to think of his wife and children. So, in a constrained and very English manner, probably with the full knowledge of Margot, they carried on a liaison that lasted more than 30 years. With the allowance she received from RCA she even paid for William, one of Smallwood's sons, to attend a good English public school, Wellington. Her own son, George, was sent to Dragon's School, Oxford, while Kevin went to Ripley Court and later to Dragon's.

Islip, on the western edge of the fens of Otmoor, on the River Ray, is a quintessential English village. Its peace and tranquillity were a direct contrast to Peking's bustle. Yvette says the house, with its great open fireplace, gave her a kindly welcome. Courtesy Cottage was three hundred years old, slate roofed and with a thatched extension added two centuries later. A large garden at the back sloped down to a river. Nearby was an old lady who made and sold toffee. The children were happy there but Yvette wasn't. Writing to a friend in China she talks about her attractive house but complains about the weather:

> I have got an enclosed coupé which I can drive all over the place. It's dashed lonely often, but then I can crash off and see friends and it isn't quite so bad and the wireless helps a lot in the evenings. Kevin's English is getting fluent but he refers to that revolting dish tapioca pudding as *du tapioque,* so Hélène's influence still prevails. We are all quite happy when the sun shines!! Enjoy Peking sun. Whenever I think of Peking I think of light and colour, and I have to stop short - I feel too dashed homesick.

No hint of scandal, no explanation about her present way of life, just the muted voice of a privileged woman living alone with her children in difficult circumstances. While it was common knowledge among their social circle that Roy and Yvette had separated the reason was concealed. John McKenzie Young, a Canadian war hero and one-time expedition member, was a friend of the Andrews and a great favourite of George. Writing to Roy from his Chelsea address in London on November 25 1929 he reveals the preoccupations of the Peking set, discusses the possibility of further expeditions with Roy then moves on to polo:

> I hear you have been going great guns for the Peking side this year but have not yet heard the result of the Inter Port Match

and mutual friends

> Gordon Verekers was home for the summer also the Rougetels. I have not seen anything of Smallwood for some months but believe he is something now in the City... the O'Malleys we see occasionally..

Suddenly Yvette steps right into our story and some 80 years later we even know her mood

> As I am writing this letter Yvette has just sailed up in her car. She is lunching with us ......I am quite sure that Yvette is not happy and really it hurts to see two such great pals of us being miserable. More specifically when there are two such ripping children in the family as well ...Is it too much to hope that you and Yvette might join up again?

Yvette was more than unhappy, sometimes she was desperate, even suicidal. Around this time she was so distraught she climbed the parapet of Battersea bridge over the Thames. Holding Kevin, she was preparing to throw herself and him into the river when a passing stranger grabbed her and pulled them back.

She was not yet forty but had lost her mother, her brother, the aunt who had brought her up and her father. She had been an explorer, a pioneering photographer and a renowned celebrity married to a famous but driven man. She had fallen in love with Perceval Landon. He died. Her involvement with Smallwood was going nowhere and now she was bringing up her children alone in a strange land and the strain was beginning to show. There were also financial problems. RCA lost nearly all his investments on October 28 1929, the infamous Black Monday during the Wall Street Crash. He could no longer provide the same support for his wife and children. Yvette was under pressure, pressure that was to have its impact on the young Kevin who was close to his mother throughout her life. George, being older and always a detached observer of Yvette, and at times close to his father, escaped many of these strains.

Roy, dividing his time between China and the USA, reluctantly accepted the time had come to divorce. Facing up to a failed marriage and explaining this to the children is not easy. It was even more difficult for Yvette whose children believed they were full brothers and that they shared a father. Keeping up the pretence,

Yvette says in the calm prose of her journal, written for Kevin and George,

> one does not end the life we had shared of high adventure in many lands, gaily and hopefully undertaken, without regret.

Delicate negotiations took place; they were still celebrities and the press had to be handled carefully. There was also the matter of the financial settlement: the time for large scale expeditions into China had passed and Roy could no longer raise the fees he once commanded. American and European élite couples habitually used the French courts to terminate marriages and so did Roy and Yvette. The divorce took two years to arrange. Yvette stayed with Kevin in an apartment in Paris, 10 Rue Andinot on the Left Bank, while Andrews stayed in rooms nearby. Andrews made a final bid for reconciliation but Yvette would have none of it. George travelled over to visit his father but Kevin became ill with lung trouble and Yvette took both children off to Switzerland to aid recovery. RCA's description of Kevin at the time is heartbreaking:

> Kevin is too sweet for words.......I can look at him from a detached standpoint, as I have seen him so little, and I have never seen a better mannered or generally desirable little chap in all my life.

From then on, Yvette filled Kevin's horizon, tragically suffocating him with her worship and flattery.

> I did nothing without the thought of her, was as much in love with her as an emotionally infantile person could be...

By the time Yvette and the children returned from Switzerland the details were settled. Roy Chapman Andrews sailed to the US on the *Mauretania* and, on March 30 1931, using the fabrication that RCA had deserted Yvette they were divorced. The split was not a quiet affair. These were glamorous and famous people. The newspapers carried many sensational accounts. A typical headline:

> ....whose Romance was so Beautiful.. The most Devoted Couple in Exploration because they faced Death so often in China.

The press blamed the divorce mainly on the strains of being an explorer's wife, explaining how difficult it must have been for the diminutive Yvette, who was used to the Paris salons. Yvette was quoted as bemoaning the fact that RCA insisted on keeping a pet vulture in the house. No newspaper came near the sensational truth. Yvette's secret was safe for a while longer.

TWELVE

Courts, camps and counters

After the divorce an accommodation was reached. In autumn 1931 Yvette and the children moved from England to a rented apartment in a fashionable area of New York at 333 East 68th Street. Occasionally the children stayed with Roy. He was not flush but nevertheless paid for the two boys' school fees. Short of money, Yvette took a job. Having flirted with the proprietor, Jay Milldorf, at a dinner party she began work as a glorified sales assistant (Gift Secretary for Men) at his exclusive Manhattan shop. She was good at advising rich and nearly-rich American males what to buy their wives, girlfriends and mistresses and made money. There is no hint of complaint about this, no self-pity, no reference to a fall from grace in having to care for two children and being forced to lead what she called a humdrum life.

Roy had returned to the USA from Peking via Paris after leading his final so-called expedition in 1930. Ostensibly he'd been mapping remote areas of Mongolia as a contribution to scholarly research; in fact he'd been gaining strategic information on behalf of America and its ally Britain. At least two of his topographers worked for the American and British armies. Hilariously the team was also infiltrated by Soviet spies and Andrews found himself accused of being a spy, plotting with the American and British governments to take over Mongolia. However the American newspapers never let truth get in the way of a good story and RCA continued to be treated as a serious scientist. In 1933 he became temporary director of the American Museum of Natural History and was confirmed as permanent director in 1934. His earlier financial embarrassments were put behind him since his salary allowed him to move into a luxury penthouse at Hotel des Artistes, West 67th Street. Nevertheless he was far from happy in his work and became a heroic whisky drinker.

George felt more at home with his father than in Yvette's cramped apartment. Having moved in with Roy he found himself acting as a messenger between the adults. Surprisingly he believed Yvette wanted to rekindle her relationship with Roy. Because she did not like to use the telephone George went back and forth carrying verbal or written messages. All to no avail. RCA had a new love, a 28-year-old, twice-married beauty, the splendidly named Wilhelmina Anderson Christmas, also known as Billie. George boarded at St Paul's school, staying with his father in the holidays. The family divisions were beginning to spread to the children and George was to say that he and Kevin were brothers

> vastly different in temperament and separated by geography for many years. We were not close but we were not distant either.

If Yvette was really trying to win back Roy lack of a permanent home and emotional support must have made her desperate. Billie and Roy married, honeymooned in early spring 1935 and stayed together till RCA died in 1960.

There were other problems for Yvette. Sledging in early winter 1935 Kevin hit a stone wall and required substantial plastic surgery on his face. The surgery was successful but his nose had changed shape. George was also in the wars. Driving his mother's Model T Ford he went through the windscreen and spent six weeks in hospital.

RCA's improved finances meant Yvette was able to leave Milldorf and devote herself to writing her journal, grandly titled *Camps, Courts and Counters*. Supposedly on a whim, she bought three tickets at Thomas Cook, New York, for a cheap return trip to Europe. Perhaps there was a major reason for this upheaval. Charles Gallenkamp, a biographer of RCA, claims that on one occasion (Gallenkamp says 1937 but his dates are unreliable) something strange occurred at RCA's residence. Kevin was staying there and Yvette appeared unexpectedly, there was a huge row behind closed doors and Yvette left taking Kevin with her. Whether or not the row developed from revelations about Kevin's paternity is unclear but around this time RCA was told he was not Kevin's father and that must have led to perturbations. Whatever the reason New York in 1935 had lost its attraction for Yvette and it was time to go. She and the boys were on the move again.

THIRTEEN

England and America

On their return to England the three of them moved to Tudor Cottage in Witley, Surrey, the heart of what the middle classes call the Home Counties. Tudor Cottage was so small that the postman could deliver letters through the first-floor bedroom window. Half-timbered walls and uneven floors made it resemble a fairy story illustration, according to Yvette. Now in her forties she spent her time in the garden and sitting by the open hearth at night, writing her journal and reading. Tudor Cottage was part of an estate owned by Lura Chess, an American friend, and Yvette soon started work for Lura in her Mayfair shop, selling expensive cosmetics. What she earned supplemented the payments from RCA and allowed her to continue shopping at Harrods and Selfridges. George stayed there for two summers when he wasn't at St Paul's School or with his father in the USA.

Kevin went to boarding school at Ripley Court in Surrey. He was bright and popular, did well in exams, scored goals in what he referred to as soccer, went for walks and bike rides and spent money at the tuck shop. Innocent and sensitive he bore no resemblance to the tormented man he became. He was extremely close to Yvette with whom he exchanged letters two or three times a week. Smallwood also wrote and sometimes he and Yvette wrote a joint letter. Kevin also corresponded with Lura and Sisi his mother's school friend, now the Duchess of Brunswick. During the holidays Kevin cared for Yvette when she was ill, helped her with her writing and got the garden under control. He was taken out for treats by Yvette or by Smallwood, and sometimes both, although he still had no idea of their real relationship.

Despite a maid and a canary Yvette led a lonely existence even though Smallwood occasionally managed to get away from his family and stay the weekend. Later the money from Lura's shop allowed Yvette to take a small flat in London and the couple met there several times a month. They even took a short trip to Italy. Yvette gave him money from articles she wrote for stylish magazines and some of the alimony from RCA. But their emotional life wasn't easy. Being torn between love and duty was unbearable for Smallwood. Once Yvette had been confident enough of her lover to recommend he thought of his family as well as her. Now - perhaps through growing insecurity - she taunted him for fearing his wife. The ménage continued.

Yvette's life may have seemed compromised and grubby but she still had Kevin and the days of glamour had not entirely faded. In 1937 her relationship with Sisi resumed when they met in Holland at Clingendaal, the house of Yvette's cousin Mrs Grenville Emmet, wife of the US representative to the Netherlands. The old feelings returned as Sisi and Yvette compared the way their lives had changed since the heady days of 1913. As Sisi was leaving she told Yvette that the (ex) Kaiser sent his love and invited her to pay him a visit at the palace of Doorn where, since his abdication, he was now a guest of Queen Wilhemina of the Netherlands. At the end of July Yvette visited Doorn with an extremely excited Kevin. President Wilson described the Kaiser as an autocratic, militaristic warlord, but Yvette saw only

> parchment skin drawn taut over his cheek bones, snow white hair and beard. Only the eyes were the same, the very bright blue eyes of the Hohenzollerns.

It has been a long time since we met, he said, kissing her hand and presenting her with a large bouquet of flowers.

Kevin was introduced to the family after lunch then he and Yvette drove to Germany to stay with Sisi. Later they took advantage of the newly constructed autobahns and drove to Berlin where Kevin met his old nurse Hélène and was introduced to her new employers the Mayer family which included the two sisters, Cotton and Liza (see Chapter 14).

That autumn Kevin moved from Ripley Court to what he later called one of England's hellish public schools, Stowe. Writing in 1989 he claimed that he was conditioned by

> the stout-hearted and persecuting ethos of an imperial Herrenfolk.

While he did not relish Stowe his life there was not that bad. His mother visited regularly at weekends and sometimes took him to stay at Sezincote, the magnificent home of John Dugdale, journalist, politician and later minister in the post-war Atlee government. Dugdale was an old friend from Peking and Sezincote became a second home to Yvette and Kevin. In 1937 they spent Christmas there.

In January 1938 Yvette returned to America for a few weeks, possibly to secure RCA's agreement about keeping Kevin's origins a secret.

Brother George also travelled several times back and forth across the Atlantic, sometimes working his passage as a Merchant Navy deckhand chipping paint and washing dishes. On one visit he and Kevin tackled Helvellyn's tricky Striding Edge in the Lake District. Wordsworth climbed this mountain regularly and George educated Kevin about him, Coleridge and the other Lake Poets. Nearly four decades later Kevin not only recalled this walk but also that his brother used the occasion to tell him the facts of life.

By now Kevin was quite the young beau as he escorted his mother to art galleries, the cinema, theatres and concerts. Back at school he worked hard and kept out of trouble, hated rugger but enjoyed squash, went on runs and walks, drew and read voraciously. Cakes arrived from Mummy and Lura, presents from Smallwood but nothing from RCA until a letter in the summer of 1939. As a result, with war looming in Europe, Kevin sailed for America in August. He was met in New York by Roy, introduced to Billie and went to stay with the couple at their new home Pondwood Farm on the edge of the Berkshires in Connecticut - bought with Billie's money.

Once the European war broke out Kevin realised he would not return to England for a long time.

Soon he followed George to St Paul's school in New Hampshire. Homesick for England, he missed his mother but found other interests. His young friend Liza Mayer arrived in the USA soon after and, by October, Yvette was also in New York. By now, Kevin was reading *Elektra*, his first recorded exposure to Greek culture.

Soon, the pattern at Stowe was repeated. Yvette wrote several times a week and visited every two or three weekends. Kevin lived with Yvette during the holidays in a two-room apartment on E 79th street in New York. He had the bedroom while she slept on a camp bed in the living room. Once again she took a job, this time selling glass at the Steuben store. Whether Gallenkamp's account of the blazing row was true or not, Yvette and Roy behaved civilly to one another, Kevin spending Christmas Day 1939 with mummy and taking tea on Boxing Day (December 26) with Roy and Billie

Teenagers have awkward lives, whether their parents are divorced or not, but Kevin hardly suffered. He was growing to be an outward-looking young man, although certainly close to his mother. Like most youths he was insecure and took himself too seriously, but he was generally happy. Life at home or school revolved around long walks, listening to, or playing, music and reading, reading, reading. The war in Europe rarely intruded though he was aware of events and wished he was back,

> in a familiar England,

where he dreamt of having his finest hour in the Blitz.

In neutral America Kevin stood out with his Limey accent and a vocabulary scattered with English epithets: walks were wonderful, fellows splendid, concerts magnificent and tea delightful.

He tried acting at school, visited Billie and Roy occasionally and shopped at Bloomingdales with his mother. He even tried smoking a pipe. In the manner of the American upper classes who like to dance he bought a tuxedo.

More significantly, his allotted seat in the dining hall at St Paul's was next to that of Walter Adams, an enthusiastic student of ancient Greek. So positive was Adams about this dead language that the next year, and at the last minute, Kevin asked William Flint, the Greek teacher, if he could join his class. From then on his fate was set.

With the exception of this apocalyptic encounter with ancient Greece, 1941 was much the same: tea dances with his friend Pat Glenn, words of wisdom from Liza, skiing, swimming, study, letters from Cotton (Liza's sister), Hélène , Lura, Chips and, inevitably, Yvette.

On December 7, along with the rest of America, he became aware that Japan had attacked the USA and that, finally, his country was at war.

Kevin was quite religious, discussed God with his mother, went to Mass and read the Bible aloud. By the end of 1941 he

> thanked God for five happy years.

But perceptions change. Fifty years later the 65-year-old Kevin Andrews described his move to America in a high-flown manner as

> being sent on a diplomatic mission to a long-lost father.

The purpose was made clear enough:

> to soothe another generation's wounds and charm away an ancient wrong...

The truth is less noble. Yvette, Kevin and many other Americans of their class were escaping the war.

By the time Kevin enrolled briefly at Harvard in 1942 RCA was increasingly cold and distant. He had turned against his putative son and it hurt. Kevin later wrote that the confusion over his parenthood:

> was as known and unforgiving by the Wisconsin father as it had once been known and tasty to Peking's languid little foreign set in 1924. (However, he) the injured party, only spoke of the matter in public, never privately to me.

Kevin goes on,

> Justice sufficient was his sustained, uncordial dislike - he was not one for the finer explanations, and he had been kicked in the guts.

RCA's state of mind can be guessed from a memoir, *Under a Lucky Star. A Lifetime of Adventure,* he wrote in 1942 – 3 in which he fails to mention Yvette, Kevin or George.

Yvette's behaviour made matters worse. The mother who wasn't able to hold her son at the font became obsessively loving, smothering him with affection. Isolated in the USA and far from Smallwood, perhaps she realised how alone she was and how dependent on alimony. Having lived a carefree, even scandalous, life in China she was now obsessed with money and, most of all, keeping up appearances.

Kevin tried to distance himself from her but she was a strong and determined woman. In any case there was no alternative and their lives were tightly bound together. He felt suffocated.

FOURTEEN

Liza and Cotton

What makes fiction writing exciting is when characters take off, invent their own dialogue, draw the author towards unplanned, even unknown, places and scenes. Biography can be much the same. Stalking your central character you open letters, check library archives, and trawl the web, all the standard stuff. If you are lucky there are people to interview. If you are very lucky these people have a good tale to tell and you enjoy their company.

I found myself in a Parisian restaurant across the table from Liza Mayer, a tall, grey-haired perceptive woman. Her name came from a chance acquaintance. I traced it on the web but failed to recognise an obvious clue. Liza is the founder member and leading light of the Pan Theatre in Paris. We exchanged emails, spent two delightful evenings talking of Kevin Andrews and became friends. Her sister, enchantingly called Cotton, helped. Between them they told me about Nana (Hélène Friche) and about Kevin. Perhaps I could have recast what they said and claimed it as my own but I am trying to catch the man, not write a thesis. The following words of Cotton and Liza are lightly edited and – for the sake of continuity – I have not corrected some minor details which differ from other sources. What is important is the way Kevin Andrews emerges as troubled but not yet obsessed by later demons. There are also clues about the haunted and contrary man he became.

Liza and Cotton first met Kevin in the late 1930s but had heard of him before. That they wanted to talk about him says something about the man himself.

Extracts from emails

To Liza Mayer. From Roger Jinkinson. October 23 2005

I live for six months of the year on the Greek island of Karpathos. I understand from an old friend of yours you were friendly with Kevin Andrews. Kevin came to my island several times in the seventies ***(Later I discovered he arrived in the sixties. RAJ)***. We have a mutual friend, a local bootmaker, and I have written a story, recently published in ***Tales from a Greek Island,*** about life in the village. I am now writing a book about Kevin. I met his two daughters and wonder if you could spare the time to meet me early in 2006. I would of course come to France.

Ioanna, his daughter, believes that one of the keys to Kevin's remarkable ability to communicate with peasants and working class Greeks arises from his relationship with his Swiss nurse. I understand you shared the same nurse, so your testimony could be very important to me. I am not interested in sensationalising his life. If you could spare the time to see me I would be very grateful.

To Roger Jinkinson. From Liza Mayer. October 24 2005

Many thanks for your message - Kind of amazing, and out of the blue! Yes, I'd be happy to meet you early next year. I'll be in Paris then,

To Roger Jinkinson. From Liza Mayer. October 24 2005

I'll be in Paris from mid-November until the end of March - I'm a voice teacher and am busiest in January/February, but basically free evenings and weekends. I'd like to send your original email to my sister in Canada if that's all right? She was closer in age to Kevin and I'm sure would be interested in hearing about your book and in writing you

To Roger Jinkinson. From Liza Mayer. October 25 2005

My parents met Kevin's out in China, and the nurse we shared was Swiss - a dear soul, who adored Kevin, as we all did. I'm also glad to hear that you've been in touch with Kevin's daughters - I hope they're well. I met Ioanna and Corinna a couple of times in the 80s and again in Athens, shortly after Kevin's death. We were in touch for awhile and then life moved on in different directions.

To Roger Jinkinson. From Cotton Aimers. October 25, 2005.
My sister, Lisa Mayer, sent on your emails and I am very interested that finally someone is writing a book (biography?) about one of the extraordinary men of my generation. Kevin was a heroic person in our family – mainly, perhaps, because of the stories of his perfection told by the Swiss nurse who cared for him and then came straight on to our family in Peking when his parents' marriage dissolved and his family left China. Also because he was an older, handsome, kind young man, etc. We kept in touch more or less and saw each other in Greece in the 80s. As you probably also know our parents were great friends - his mother came to my wedding - she too was larger than life... Would you care to have my recollections? Katharine Aimers (I am known by my nickname: Cotton)

To Cotton Aimers. From Roger Jinkinson. October 25 2005
Cotton - what a lovely name! I would love to have your recollections. Write down anything you want and as much as you want. I will take it from there. I will respond with questions and a few comments. The information I have is from his children and the people on my island and of course what little there is published about Kevin as well as information from the web.....

The stuff from Karpathos is incredible in that everyone remembers him and speaks highly of him. There is one question I need to ask. A local man, supposedly Kevin's best friend, told me that Kevin attempted suicide, cut his wrists and wrote in blood on the pavement: Save my papers. This would have been 1988/89 *(In fact it was much earlier. RAJ)*. Do you think this is true? I know there was a fuss about his papers after he died...

Nearly everything about Kevin's life could be sensationalised. It reads more like a film script than a book. I do not want to do this but I do need to get the facts right. I am interested in a number of things. What made him such a good writer? How did he understand the Greeks so well? Why did he not write more?

I have no idea why the marriage broke up. I hear that Kevin was frustrated in not being able to live from his writing. Did her having money cause problems?

Both he and Nancy had three potential fathers. Did this inhibit his writing? Did it drive him to be such a good writer? What happened to his mother? What was her name? Enough. I want to write a good but honest story about the man. We are alike in a number of ways though he was a better writer and walker than me and much more of an intellectual. But we both love Greece. If you ever come to Europe let me know. Roger

To Roger Jinkinson. From Cotton Aimers. October 25, 2005,
You sound like a thoughtful person. Kevin had many demons but he was an honourable, deeply intellectual and great hearted person of huge enthusiasms (Hence the liberation of Greece from the Colonels and his Greek citizenship). He went to the same school in England which my husband attended and adored, Stowe, and had the same classical education there. Think he too was taught and influenced by the great Timothy White (T. E. White, *The Sword in the Stone*). My husband and I spent an evening with Corinna and her husband after Kevin died. Good evening, Cotton. (My brother couldn't say Katharine properly)
Later......
Nana's name was Hélène Friche. She was from a tiny little farming hamlet called St-Prex, French-Swiss, child of unwed mother, who lived on a farm with people she called uncle and aunt and was fairly harshly treated. At 15 she left school... She was also a devoted churchgoer, Protestant, and a believer which I am sure sustained her. Perhaps my sister could add or has added to this. Kevin was such a beguiling young man that he must have been twice as loveable as a child.

To Roger Jinkinson. From Cotton Aimers. January 10, 2006
Kevin Andrews was our hero - hero to three young girls, sisters, who had worshipped him, from as long as they could remember, the perfect little boy in their nurse's stories. I don't know when we first actually met this paragon but my first clear memory is of a boy, almost man, of 15 or 16 - very muscular, vigorous and strongly built, very confident, with a lot of curly dark brown hair,

dark eyes and an infinite capacity to amuse, by story and verse and conundrum, and on and on. We laughed and sang and worshipped every kind gentle word and kept these in our hearts until my recently fading memory tricks me and I have forgotten what we used to shout out: these questions and answers to each other for years to come.

There was our friend, our young god, but the messenger was our beloved nurse, Hélène Friche, called Nana in our family (and Hélène, rather shrilly, by my parents and their friends and of course by Yvette Andrews, Kevin's mother. I think Kevin also called her Hélène.)

Our Swiss nurse told us over and over stories of Kevin's goodness, stoic nature, kind heart. It's amazing that we didn't hate him as it was always clear Kevin was everything we were not. She never, in my memory, spoke of his older brother George. Perhaps because she had looked after Kevin from the time he was a baby while George was perhaps two or three *(In fact he was six. RAJ)* when she joined the Andrews in Peking.

Nana was born in Switzerland to a single mother in the rural village of St Prex my sister Looloo and I once visited. Nana grew up on a cousin's farm with many hardships and little or no education. But luck and hard work, and an obvious desire for adventure, flung this small person from one mythic family to another, and across the ocean, to Brooklyn (where she had to learn English to survive) and into a nurses' course at the then famous Baby's Hospital in New York City. There I think was where the Andrews found her. China was the next stop.

Roy Chapman Andrews was already the icon of his generation - probably as famous as Lindbergh. But from what little my parents and Nana said his fame covered a distant, cold, self-centered personality. In any case Nana had full charge of the children in a totally strange country and gave her complete devotion to the younger one. Soon there were rumours of Yvette carrying on - a twenties euphemism for having affairs - and one of the British colony was said to be not only her lover but Kevin's father. Nobody liked him (Smallwood). He went back to England. My mother became pregnant. The Andrews marriage collapsed. Yvette took Kevin to England - to follow her lover? My parents inherited Nana, as we always called her, this extraordinary person who brought up my brother and myself and my two sisters, in China, across Europe, in Haiti, in Washington and finally in the depths of Vermont.

Continued...

To go to such lengths about Nana is to explain Kevin. He and his mother were in England in the thirties. Kevin had been sent to Stowe....

Roy took George when Yvette took Kevin and went to England at the time of their divorce, 1927, (***Cotton is mistaken here.*** ***RAJ***) the year Nana moved into my parents' Peking house and took over their new baby, John Duer Mayer. I suppose (Kevin and George) saw each other again, although years later I asked Kevin if he ever saw his brother. He said no - with no emotion. I urged him to get in touch and wonder if he ever did. This break at such a young age must have been traumatic. And at the same time Nana's favouritism? And did he ever see his father again as a child? (*Yes. RAJ*)

Perhaps all this explains the deeply bitter man Kevin became. The golden boy, the adventurer, the outdoors man, poet, scholar of his Harvard years (one of the brains of his generation, the books say) became the hermit I saw again in Greece three times in the seventies and eighties - an ageing man who, when invited out for dinner and asked to choose a place to eat, led us to a mean little restaurant on the side of a street full of rubble where we drank sour wine. An old friend who took me for the day (Jeff, my husband, had a date with the Acropolis) to see Daphne's Spring and walked home with me through fields and alleys as blithely as the young man in Vermont, but wouldn't enter our hotel, the George V. A savant and a hermit who walked us around the Acropolis on another occasion and couldn't speak - barely bothering to point out one cornice. The only American to receive Greece's highest honour - to be made a citizen of Athens?

Did his whole life bend to the devotion of his Swiss nurse? - I wonder. Nana, after retiring from my parents' house, ended her long career by working for two world-famous ballerinas . She couldn't take retirement in staid, old-fashioned Lausanne! So moved back to New York and eventually to Park Avenue and the ballerinas - they knew something about devotion - and ended up being torn away from the second of these charges when the parents realised their child's life had grown around only one person - Nana.

Nana died aged 100. As far as I know they never saw each other again after several weekends in Vermont half a century ago - never communicated. But the stories of the perfect little boy and the young hero and the old hermit are part of the myth as is the tale of the brave little person who connected us all together and brought me up and my sisters and my brother and is part of my heart.

To Cotton Aimers. From Roger Jinkinson. January 18, 2006
You have touched on some of the issues that I am trying to explore. He seemed to be such a gifted man: good looking, kind, rugged, intelligent. A great writer but he became so bitter. He wrote so little. I am the same age as KA was when he died, but I feel none of the anger that he clearly felt. Some of this may be to do with his epilepsy. I am told he was ashamed of this, but he also seemed to have problems with his murky past. Did he mention any of this to you?

To Roger Jinkinson. From Cotton Aimers. January 19, 2006
Kevin never mentioned any family or health issues to me. He was very proud as well as bitter and withdrawn (by then). However it seems to me his miseries were more based on abandonment - by his father and brother, by Hélène, his and our nurse, and by the difficult paternity problem. It was Smallwood who our nurse always said was his father. Do not know those other names. ***(I had mentioned Landon. RAJ)*** However, as you know, Yvette was said to have many liaisons. Two other points also keep coming back: his mother's character and his father's fame. Both of these, in my mind, cannot be underestimated.

Yvette considered herself American aristocracy. She too was v proud, a tiny (under 5 feet), very intense, almost fierce person who also always wanted to be the centre of attention. A person of physical courage. She was, as you probably know, on several expeditions with Roy, one at least as official photographer. She and Kevin used to take long walks and precipitous hikes together. This closeness perhaps didn't help his relations with women of his own age as I think when young he seemed to worship his mother (after all she alone stood by him...)

And I think my mother thought Yvette was immoral. All this may give you a clearer picture.

As for RCA, I also can't underline more strongly what a mythical figure he was to my and the earlier generation. That is why I compared him to Lindbergh. He was immortalised by the dinosaur egg find. That tall handsome commanding image. This must have been overpowering for a small child and an intolerable burden to carry as he went through life as not quite the son of...

These were burdens, like epilepsy, to be deeply ashamed of in that era. Hence his flight to Greece. Far from the American or British establishment.

He loomed so large in our lives and I know in mine because of Hélène and because of the contrast between the golden boy and the sad old man. And the dinosaur myth. PS. Kevin was v musical - he used to carry a small flute in his pocket. He sang and taught us songs as well as conundrums and songs and puzzles.

To Roger Jinkinson. From Liza Mayer. January 21 2006
Re KA, you can be sure that his father was Smallwood. Two stories here: our nurse, Nana, told me that she heard Yvette Andrews playing with Kevin when he was a small baby, calling him (out of earshot - except Nana's!): Kevin Smallwood, Kevin Smallwood, Kevin Smallwood... Kevin told me that he was told very early on that Smallwood was his godfather. He knew something wasn't right somewhere. Andrews wasn't very nice to him, didn't pay much attention to him, etc, and one day, when Kevin was in his twenties, he was shaving and suddenly the penny dropped. He looked at his face in the mirror and said to himself: This is Smallwood's face. He also told me that Yvette told Nancy about Smallwood, and that Smallwood was Kevin's father. By this time Kevin was in his early thirties, late in the day to hear about who your real father is. Nancy then told Kevin. *(There is another version. RAJ)*

To Liza Mayer. From Roger Jinkinson. January 21 2006
I arrive in Paris Saturday February 25, 17.23, Gare du Nord. Unfortunately I have to leave Monday February 27 on the 10.19 train. I have to hurry back in order to pick my granddaughter up from school. Could you choose a time for us to meet up. I think we would need around two hours before one, or both of us, gets

tired. I find everything about KA very confusing. So many names crowding into the story.

If you could reserve me a room at the Garden Hotel or any other small, quiet place I would be grateful. I will be alone and want the simplest room available. I am impoverished by grandchildren.

To Roger Jinkinson. From Lizabeth Mayer. February 28, 2006
Another contact that I remembered is a book by an English woman, Patience Grey, *Honey From a Weed.* The book is delightful. Patience Grey wrote articles about food and cooking for English mags and newspapers. She married a Belgian sculptor and they went to live near stone quarries in the Mediterranean. Her book is about the recipes and people that she met in villages and cities, literally learning about weeds and honey and people, and all. She met Kevin and there's a recipe he gave her there.

The words, more or less, of two sisters who knew Kevin and liked him. A portrait from two gentle, kind women showing a young god declining into a bitter recluse. There is one more thing. I recently saw a photograph of one of my correspondents, I will not say which. It is black and white and shows a pretty, blonde young girl sitting on a lawn with other young people. I was told some words of the young Kevin Andrews:

> She loved me and I loved her but neither of us said anything and so nothing happened.

FIFTEEN

Kevin goes to war

Nineteen-year-old Kevin enlisted on February 16 1943 in New York as Roy Kevin Victor Andrews, place of birth China, probably Mongolia, and was given the Army serial number 32807003. Having reported for duty at Camp Hale on March 6 he joined the 10th Mountain Division engaged in winter training. Probably he chose this demanding unit to suit his love of the outdoors but it was an honour to be selected and he would have had to convince the army he had the necessary qualities.

Yvette, being fluent in German and French and knowledgeable about the German upper classes, joined the US Censorship Bureau, reading mail from prisoners of war and US businessmen. Her proclivity for conspiracies stood her in good stead when she came across a letter from a first cousin who was secretly exporting steel from the USA to Germany via Brazil. Later that day she was his guest at a cocktail party. She continued to monitor his letters for two years.

By April 1943 Kevin was serving with the 86th Infantry Regiment. On July 8 he was promoted to Private First Class and transferred a week later into the 10th Mountain Cavalry reconnaissance troop. By December he was receiving advanced training with the Army Specialised Training Program and, on his return, was assigned to the 87th Regiment.

Brother George married his long-time sweetheart Mary Nancy (both brothers were to marry a Nancy) in autumn 1944 in Texas. Neither parent attended the wedding; Roy and Billie did not want to if Yvette was likely to show up, while Yvette's excuse was that, at the time, Kevin would be home on leave before leaving for Europe. There was even a notice in *The New York Times:* Double Event for Mother, in which Yvette wished she could be twins to attend both events. This is disingenuous. Whichever way she chose to dress it up, and however polite and kind she was to George, there was only one son in her life and that was Kevin.

In the winter of 1944 Kevin was sent to a remote region in Northern Italy where, for many months, he volunteered as a scout in combat with the reconnaissance platoon of the 87th. US scouts worked in advance of the main force, patrolling, reconnoitring, liaising with local irregulars and gathering intelligence. Lightly armed and mobile, scouts also acted as spotters for aircraft and artillery. The work was lonely and dangerous.

Unknown to Kevin another young man, whom he later believed to be his half-brother, had been similarly engaged a few weeks earlier and only a few kilometres away. Major Bill Smallwood, son of Yvette's lover, Chips Smallwood, was working with the partisans. Crossing the hills from Forni to the German-speaking area of Sauris he fell, breaking his arm and damaging his leg so badly he could not walk. As he was carried down the mountain his band was spotted by a German patrol, Smallwood was captured, taken to hospital in Udine and sent to a German prison camp. Kevin, who managed discreetly to tell all his army friends that his father was Roy Chapman Andrews, was of course still unaware this might not be true and that he had brothers other than George.

On February 28 1945, during the 10th's first major offensive against the Germans, Kevin was awarded a Bronze Star for his actions near Abetaia, Italy. On that day his platoon was pinned down by German mortar fire, his friends Johnny Van de Putte and Lornen Frank were killed, and Kevin and another friend, Chuck Walro, spent two hours in an observation post on a ridge under intense fire during which their foxhole was obliterated

The terrain was wild and hostile, much of it at 5000 feet or more, and rain, snow and ice were regular features. Later he was to write about the rigours of war in the Apennines:

> The hours in foxholes shaking under the whine of German mortar shells, the crunch of snow crust underfoot behind enemy lines at night, and the sight of gutted towns and hilltop villages still exquisite in their ruin.

Kevin was quietly proud he had volunteered for this work. He learned one valuable lesson about moving cross-country which he frequently repeated in later life:

> Never gain unnecessary height.

An ironic thought given the title of his best- known book.

In a photograph taken at the time he is standing by a small tent on a mountainside. His arm is inserted casually through a coil of climbing rope and an ice axe is carefully placed alongside the tent. Kevin looks away from the camera but knows it is there. He is posing.

Yvette followed Kevin's military service and kept newspaper cuttings about the Italian campaign. The only other relic is a long short story written by the young PFC in December 1944. The tone is that of a sensitive adolescent, pretentious and naive. But there is also a self-critical streak and an understanding of literary techniques and styles.

Following combat, Kevin Andrews was granted leave in Venice from June 16 - 21 1945. On July 2 1945 he was transferred to the 2675th Regiment, then attached to the Fifth Army (parent of the 10th Mountain Division), where he was involved in the military government of Italy during the American occupation. It was a time of massive confusion as vast groups moved across the landscapes of Europe, jostling for power between - and within - the military blocs formed by the victorious allies. Italian partisans struggled to be recognised as legitimate liberators of their country, and armed bands of communists and democrats from neighbouring countries attempted to take power. Kevin describes,

> the incomprehensible atmosphere in Italy's NE border province of Venezia Giulia, where no passage was allowed across a bristling frontier into an allied Yugoslavia.

Kevin was stationed at Bolzano and Merano. He was a popular soldier but always slightly apart. While others drank coffee, wine and grappa he insisted on tea. He didn't smoke. He talked occasionally of Roy Chapman Andrews but was not considered to be a typical young American. His British accent was thought strange and he is remembered playing European tunes on a wooden recorder and singing Celtic and other antique songs, one of them *My Lagan Love.*

His cultural interests extended beyond folk songs. A fellow soldier, Robert Johnson, the same age as Kevin, recalls they were both given an unexpected day off in February 1945. They borrowed a jeep and headed into Florence.

> Roy had one goal in mind: to see the Masaccio frescoes in the Brancacci Chapel of the Chiesa del Carmine.

A reluctant priest acted as guide and, from the glow of one bare light bulb, together with daylight piercing the narrow slits from the bricked up window,

> they drank in the early 15th century visual manifestations of the Renaissance.

Now well into his eighties, Robert Johnson is still grateful to the young Kevin Andrews, an innocent young man, one of the

> minds of the century.

Like many veterans Kevin rarely spoke about combat afterwards. When he did he remained modest, mentioning only that he was scared and hated the danger and discomfort. Sitting in a foxhole, under fire, his only comfort seemed to be in reading the collected works of Henry James. His daughter Ioanna recalls sitting with him at his desk in their house in Athens when she was about five, discussing the nature of courage. He explained what a burden the name Victor had been, that he'd always felt he was a sissy at school and had been terrified in the army.

In another memory Kevin sang to Ioanna when she was sad. The Italian love song, *Amaryllis,* was so beautiful it made her cry. His eyes also filled with tears at the refrain,

> *Apri il mio petto i vedrai scritto in cuore.*
> *Amarylli e il mio amore*
> (Open my chest and you will see written in my heart
> Amaryllis is my love)

Asked why he cried, he explained that in the army in Italy he met a girl called Laura, the daughter of a countess. She lived in a great stone palazzo in Venice hung with tapestries and ancestral portraits. He got to know her family and was often a guest there, even going AWOL to do so. They were in love, he said, but then he returned to the USA and did not see her for many years. He had learnt the song in Venice and presumably sung it to Laura.

This story has a strange, perhaps sad, coda. Some twenty years after the war Kevin visited Venice to see Laura and her family. The countess was cold and the count ailing. Laura was married, though open and friendly. The naive Kevin Andrews clearly expected more and wondered at the lack of closeness between the family and himself. Later Laura wrote hoping they would remain friends but Kevin never answered the letter. Of course, *angst*-ridden as he was, he couldn't leave it at that and later wondered at his detachment and callousness.

This experience gave substance to Kevin's love of Italian music: Neapolitan songs, operas by Puccini, Monteverdi and Verdi, all of which he learned by heart. Years later, at moments when he felt good, he would burst into song and fill the space around him with what he had learned.

SIXTEEN

Kevin on fire

After release from the army in 1946 Kevin went back to Harvard to cram two years' study into one. He studied under John Finlay,

> the most electrifying Greek professor on the Eastern Seaboard.

Under Finlay's tutelage he produced a thesis on the Prometheus-element in Aeschylus and Melville. This earned him a one-year fellowship with the American School of Archaeology in Athens. Andrews was to claim that nobody else applied. The school had been closed during World War Two and took no students during 1946. In 1947-48 five students were enrolled including Mabel Lang and Hazel Palmer who, along with Kevin, made their mark in archaeological and classic studies.

Prior to leaving the USA Kevin spent time with his friends who included Willard Roosevelt, Robbie Cabot and Robert V. Keeley, later US Ambassador to Greece. All three stood by Kevin throughout his troubled life. Like most men who have survived a war he liked to drink, sing and play music. Above all he liked the open air and walking in the mountains. He was, however, still sexually inexperienced and shy with girls. A mini-portrait just before Kevin left for Greece in the summer of 1947 sees him as

> a very dashing and attractive young man; athletic, curly haired.

The above admirer was helping out at the Appalachian Mountain Club Pinkham Notch hut. She was too shy to speak to Kevin, but recalls him

> striding along the ridges in the waning evening light, making spine-tingling music

on his favoured instrument at the time, the bagpipes. Over sixty years later the sound is with her still, as is the belief that this man, with his abundant charm and *joie de vivre,*

> could have anything he wanted.

Down the years many women thought the same. All were mistaken.

In autumn 1947, at the age of 23, Kevin Andrews…

> as ignorant about my own origins as (I) was naive about contemporary Greek history…

set out for Greece aboard a passenger liner. On arrival he was gripped in a spell which would last the rest of his life, a spell which led him to write compelling, sensual prose. Prose based on simple elegant phrases that conveyed Greece's brilliance: the colours, smells, shades and shadows, the wide overarching sky and the ever-changing sea.

Describing two lovers on deck of the ship in Greek territorial waters, he writes of the:

> tingling, granulated texture of the moonlight that, like a sunrise or a bath of honey, both engulfed the lovers and gave life to the dun colour of the deckboards.

And:

> With the first daylight I saw the long, bare southern scarp of Hydra plunging its sable cliff-shadows into the glaze of a waveless sea.

And (his first sight of Athens):

> through the pellucid air the Acropolis was a lone, delicate incision above two separate towns of red-tiled roofs....... The light was deceptive only in its invitation to enumerate the leaves and tiles as effortlessly as the pebbles on the surrounding mountains.

He had an immediate grasp of his new environment. Writing forty or more years later, but using notes scribbled at the time, he describes passengers disembarking into the all too familiar Greek bureaucracy:

> We were rowed ashore in open boats through an outsize reed-bed of mastheads to the customs house. Pandemonium was in swing there.

As it is to this day. Families lose luggage... everyone who should be responsible claims at the top of their voices that they are not.

Kevin is driven through the car-free streets to the suburb where he is to stay. He is open mouthed at the bullet-pocked walls, the broken and blank windows, the beggars and the amputees. Later he discovers the dry water taps and toilets, and the electric light switches with no electricity.

Wherever you looked in Athens, says Kevin,

> there was something missing.

He was impressed by the friendliness in the streets and among the poor people; less so by the isolation and almost total ignorance of his fellow countrymen. They were, he says,

> as welcoming as an exhibit of surgical instruments or an application of dry ice.

In a sentence which is chilling in its accuracy about academics, then as now, he refers to the teachers around him as knowing frighteningly much about virtually nothing. Knowledge was what counted, he says,

> but in concentration, saturation, density - not in breadth, not for any bearing on today.

He was, nevertheless, grateful to his teachers for being hard taskmasters and stretching his talents if not his horizons. He was learning to be a scholar. The day after his arrival in Piraeus the romantic Kevin was put in his place by the assistant to the director of the school. There was no chance that he would be allowed to do what many visitors to Greece dreamed of: reading the classics against the landscape they describe:

> Hesiod in Boeoetia, Aeschylus in the Argolid, Plato by the banks of the Illisos. And you are not going to be able to read the *Bachae* in the forests of Macedonia either….Because… there's a war going on .... and we don't take that kind of risk.

Instead he would learn archaeology, a process which meant confining himself to the sites referred to in the college library. He had come to Greece to hear the voices of the ancients but was offered instead 100-year-old excavation reports, annotated pottery shards and numbered stones by the ton. Fellow students asked:

> Where do you want to teach when you go back to the States?
> Here. I couldn't give even the wrong answer.

Within a week Kevin was off to the island of Paros, crossing the Aegean to stay with the Kondorani family who had occupied a cabin close to his during the Atlantic crossing. The matriarch,

> a grizzled woman with a sun-baked face,

adopted Kevin immediately. She had left Greece thirty years before to run a grocery in Brooklyn and was returning with her children to an island they had never seen. Travel to Greece today, go to the islands by ferry boat and you will meet similar people. A description of his arrival by ferry at the island opens *The Flight of Ikaros* (Penguin):

> Daylight burned red on the eyelids – tar-smell hot in the nostrils from deckboards throbbing under my cheekbone. Beyond the railings grey-brown rocks sped past between a race of water and a heaven deep with sun.

His eye for colour and smell transports readers to that place at that time. His description is exact.

Absent from the school for too long, Kevin was summoned back by telegram and during his return encountered the darker side of Greek reality. At the port of Hermoupolis on Syros prisoners with shaven heads and pathetic bundles were shepherded aboard the ferry by armed guards, *en route* from one prison camp to another. This was Kevin's first experience of the defeated in the civil war. He talked to the prisoners and, for the first time, learned about what he later called the massacre of 28 peaceful and unarmed demonstrators in Syntagma Square on December 3 1944. The demonstrators were *andartes* – trades unionists and other leftists - who had fought and defeated the Italian invaders and the German occupiers. Apart from the dead there were many wounded. Kevin writes that those who did the shooting were the Athens police,

> virtually unchanged since the Metaxas dictatorship and the Nazi occupation.

Greece, as always, suffered from a surfeit of interest by major powers. Churchill proposed to Stalin in Moscow on October 9 1944 that the Soviets would assume 90 percent influence in eastern and Balkan Europe while the west would have 10 percent. In return the British would have 90 percent influence in Greece with the Soviets taking the remainder. Stalin signified his acceptance with a neat tick on a hastily prepared scrap of paper. The *Wehrmacht* left Athens on October 12 . The demonstration in December aimed to celebrate freedom and to put down a marker for the establishment of democracy. The subsequent massacre led to a four-year civil war. Kevin studied this period as he matured. He believed Britain and, later, America deliberately and cruelly repressed the left who had fought hardest against the Germans. He was shocked to read Churchill's order to the commander of the British Expeditionary Force which could not have been clearer:

> We have to hold and dominate Athens, with bloodshed if necessary.

Having recognised this small country's sufferings Kevin later saw the civil war as a war of national liberation against collaborators, royalists and foreign interference.

In World War Two more Greeks were killed than Americans – yet America had twenty times Greece's population. Between 1940 and 1948 Greece lost a tenth of its population to fighting, famine and disease.

Kevin knew little of this at the time. It was that conversation with the prisoners on the ferry - eventually broken up by the guards - which launched the naïve young man's political education.

In contrast with the ship decks, small islands and *cafeneia,* where Kevin learned about modern Greek life, the American

School of Archaeology was an ideal place to study more sublime matters. Located in the quiet area of Kolonaki,

> high up under the pine-scented slopes of Lykavittos,

Kevin sat in the library or walked through the gardens with their enormous conifers, quiet benches and pergolas. Such a place can be idyllic in Athens, even in the high summer, and he appreciated its location even though he was not by conventional standards a good student. He had crossed the ocean to meet the people of ancient Greece that Finlay and others had enthused about. Occupying a Spartan room at the Loring Hall Annexe, staring at the brown-painted metal furniture, he felt he might go mad. Hopelessly romantic, he

> quickly developed a talent for making myself scarce when potsherds or foundation-stones were on the unsmiling agenda.

He had expected archaeology to be

> a blaze of revelations, art-works, insights into how the ancients really spoke their athletic and pulsating language.

What he got was academic dust. So it is not surprising that when permission was obtained to visit the approved sites he was not impressed. They were dead places, without echoes of the heroes he longed to meet. Instead what he heard was:

> the soughing of the pines, with a notable view between them… across a hot blue strip of sea to... the Makronissos prison camp.

What he enjoyed was:

> a stolen plunge into the sea or... laughing encounters with fishermen in the evening.

What he did was to climb the high mountains of Attica.

Kevin was beginning to fall in love with Greece. Not some wishy-washy, liberal Greece with ancient myths, sing-song peasants, blue seas and quaint white villages, but civil war Greece where the left were losing and the common people were suffering, Greece with cold winters, snow in the mountains and rain in the valleys, the Greece of starvation, brutality, blood, crime and treachery. But, simultaneously, a Greece where loyalty, generosity and warmth of heart were abundantly available. Naturally he responded to the beauties of the landscape and seascapes and recognised the unique nature of light, but it was the people he was infatuated with. It was their wisdom and stories he sought, preferably in some shady vineyard, *taverna, cafeneion* or olive grove. Over the years he found solace from these people and alienation from his own kind whatever that might be.

At the beginning Kevin had support in Athens. There was the school of course with its well-meaning, but ignorant, staff and students, and there were the introductions furnished by his well-connected mother. One of these consisted of a letter addressed simply: Her Majesty the Queen, Athens.

Yvette was still cashing in on her childhood friendship with Sisi whom she had not seen since 1937. Kevin's godmother had become a Nazi, believing Hitler might put one of her sons on to a restored imperial throne. When this became unlikely, in 1938 she married her daughter, Frederika, to her own first cousin, Crown Prince Paul, who in 1947 became King Paul the First of the Hellenes.

Kevin was totally out of his depth when required to respond to the Consort Frederika's question:

> I understand you know my mother?
> But the Royal Highness is my godmother.

And, after meaningless small talk:

> It must be very interesting to study archaeology… if you should need anything….

Kevin was ushered out.

Another contact, from a different part of the political spectrum, occurred at 22 rue de Marseilles an address Kevin himself inhabited three years later. It took some time to locate this crumbling mansion with flaking walls and windows sealed with wrapping paper against the cold. His knock was answered by a silver-haired woman who had known Yvette in the 1890s. Her story, told in Edwardian English, astonished the young American who it must be remembered had fought in World War Two for what he believed to be a democratic future. This gentle lady had married General Skandalis, a cavalry commander in the Greek Army who, after the 1922 invasion of Turkey and the subsequent retreat and massacres, had been a member of the military court that sentenced to death the six military leaders supposedly responsible for the debacle. In 1935 Skandalis took part in the revolt against the Monarchists under Metaxas and was sent to Akronafplia Prison. The old couple had four children, now around Kevin's age. Two sons were persuaded to join ELAS, the Greek army of resistance, by its leader Sarafis. They had fought with the *andartes* in World War Two and, after the counter-revolution and the civil war, they were sent to Ikaria and held in exile. Later one of them was sent to the prison island of Makronissos.

Kevin Andrews continued to learn about prison camps that still held guerrillas and wartime resistance fighters as well as artists and writers with left-wing leanings. The White Terror of torture and killings that still continued was shocking enough. Even more shocking was his fellow students' ignorance of the nightly roundups, mass arrests, military courts and executions not far from their quiet library and umbrageous compound.

Kevin's immersion in the cauldron of the Greek civil war had begun. But he was not yet done with the royal family. He was invited back for lunch at the luxurious summer palace of Tatoi on the wooded southeast-facing slope of Mount Parnitha. There was much laughter at the previous confusion, the consort admitting she had not believed that her mother could be Kevin's godmother. The family talked openly about the civil war. Kevin had the good sense to keep his mouth closed on this topic and records that Queen Frederika spoke of her gratitude to President Truman for sending a White House doctor to tend her husband during his recent illness. Meanwhile King Paul reassured his in-laws about the permanence of the dynasty while

> the six-year-old heir to this vagrant throne sat at one end of the table.

For Kevin the conversation recalled Hitler's verdict on the royal couple's uncle and grandfather:

> *Uber den Wilhelm ll gibt es nichts, oder negativisch oder positivisch, zu sagen.*
> Regarding Wilhelm II there is nothing, positive or negative, to say.

Away from this quaint backwater Kevin set out on the twin paths of learning. One was an academic study of the castles of the Morea which led him to the mountainous and remote areas of Greece. The other, unsupervised and unexpected, changed his life totally. By absorbing the political and social conditions of a country riven by civil war, he learnt to love a sometimes wild, exotic and generous people and, like them, to curse the country he believed to be his own, the USA.

In January 1948 fate cruelly intervened. He became ill with what he described as an obscure nervous disorder and was bedridden for several weeks. Meanwhile, Yvette, still living and working in New York, was planning a visit to Europe. She wanted to see Chips Smallwood and to visit her beloved son. Kevin wrote early in February, giving news of his birthday and a list of things to take to Greece. She wrote to Smallwood and other pals from her London days, arranged appointments, assignations and engagements and, on May 31, packed her bags and flew to England the next day. She stayed three weeks in London, dining at the Dorchester, lunching at Fortnum's, meeting the old crowd and of course her long-term and long-distance lover, Smallwood. At the end of June she met Kevin in Rome. He was working on translations of the newly revealed seventeenth-century fortification plans included in the Grimani Codex. Kevin had been granted another year's scholarship to complete his study of the castles of the Morea. In July 1948 Kevin and Yvette took the train to Athens where Kevin had permission from the Ministry of Public Order valid for

> many journeys throughout Hellas.

Soon mother and son were exploring Kevin's new country. They visited the sites of Athens, Corinth, Delphi, Argos, Mystras, Sparta and Crete, all at the height of the civil war when the Communist and other left-wing forces were at the zenith of their power, controlling large parts of the country. Outside Athens mainland Greece was unsafe for travellers after dark, roads were mined and kidnapping and banditry were rife. Travelling by bus and train, as well as on foot, they slept in inns and hostels though sometimes Kevin slept alone in the open air. During the day they ate in *tavernas* and bars or picnicked and dozed in olive groves, a simple life marred by Kevin's sickness which was now thought to be malaria. Kevin took many photographs and made extensive notes which formed the basis of both *Castles of the Morea* and, a few years later, *The Flight of Ikaros*. The former is an academic study in elegant but simple prose celebrating some of Greece's most striking and, until then, least studied architectural monuments. Sixteen of the larger medieval fortresses in the Peloponnese are described, especially those built by the Venetians who occupied the region for three decades from 1685. Until this pioneering work the era and its artefacts had been largely ignored by Greek and foreign scholars alike. Greece was classical Greece and nothing else. Kevin recognised medieval and Byzantine history as legitimate areas of study and Mystras and its environs as interesting places to visit.

The Flight of Ikaros, which appeared in several forms over the next thirty-five years, is a tale of adventure in a wild and war-torn landscape which amusingly fails to mention that he was accompanied, for some of the time, by his fifty-six-year-old mother.

Yvette returned to London at the end of July and then on to New York. Kevin remained in Greece for what was to be a year of solitude. He often took to the mountains alone, sleeping outside or in scarred ruins, dodging Government forces and militiamen while sketching and photographing cathedrals, churches and castles, particularly those of Mystras, the last capital of Byzantine Greece. In his rucksack he carried numerous Byzantine histories and even books of medieval verse which helped him identify and date the buildings he was studying. Local people took him to be a spy, or said they did, but they were charmed when he spoke their language, played music with them, sang their songs and ate their simple food. The dialogues in *The Flight of Ikaros* consist of individual voices within a framework of Greek peasants and workers and convey the essence of Greekness which he was drawn to. However a disturbing trait emerges. Kevin is seen to be attracted to bullies and hard men with guns. He revels in his friendship with the braggart Kostandis (not his real name) who takes him in with a boast of having killed 500 men – almost certainly an exaggeration. Kevin was determined to record and not to judge but *The Flight of Ikaros* shows he was attracted to this man however many Greeks he had murdered.

Kevin's obscure sickness was now diagnosed as epilepsy. At the time he did not understand its full gravity, and merely told his fellow students that at least the illness gave him a point of reference, a definition of who he was and where he had come from. His friends took the illness more seriously. Some thought it would be fatal. In any case, it came in two forms: *petit mal*, which resulted in immobilisation for a shortish period, and *grand mal*, where unconsciousness, falling and vomiting might occur. These attacks were bad enough but there was more. The medication greatly affected all aspects of Kevin's life and may even have caused his death. He was also told to give up coffee, tea and strong drink and to avoid sharp corners on furniture, driving cars, irregular meals and worrying. Cliff edges, insomnia, long swims and marathon walks over empty landscapes were supposedly prohibited but Kevin ignored some of this advice and could not avoid the rest.

In autumn 1948 he spent two months in a small hospital in Patissia, a quiet quarter of Athens. There he became friends with the irrepressible prankster Nikiphoros (real name Charalambos), suffering from TB, nephritis and later leukaemia, whose subsequent death affected him so much and which he wrote about so eloquently in *The Flight of Ikaros*. After leaving hospital Kevin maintained his friendship with Nikiphoros visiting him and his family in Pangrati, a working class rookery of Athens. The patient lay in bed, month after month, playing Kevin emotionally in a way that only Greeks know. Despite his illness he was a vibrant and fascinating man with a great lust for life. In early 1950, on the day of the national elections, Kevin met his agitated friend at home, dressed in a suit and tie and shouting the odds about society and socialism. By this time he was very weak and needed Kevin's help to get in and out of his chair. When the two met again in the autumn of 1951, Kevin understood that the illness was terminal. With other interests, other friendships and with journeys to make, Kevin, in the way of young people, began avoiding his dying friend.

His contemporaries at the American School had returned to the USA in 1948 to pursue their careers in famous or obscure departments of classical studies or perhaps to follow daddy into Wall Street. Kevin had been granted yet another year's scholarship to complete his study of the castles of the Morea. The school was

> very impressed with (his) work.

he was thought to be

> well suited to his chosen field of study.

However, while staff rated him

> serious, intelligent and independent

at least one academic thought Kevin wasn't even the best student. Despite this he continued to receive funding until 1951. But by then the ASCS had a new head, J L Caskey, a war hero who served with the OSS and occasionally acted for the CIA. Caskey did not approve of students consorting with the school's Greek workforce particularly if the latter were left-wing - not surprising since he was a royalist who enjoyed taking scholars to meet Queen Frederika. Perhaps it galled him that Kevin already knew the Queen. Perhaps he was upset by the younger man's irreverence. An antipathy developed between them and Kevin became estranged from the school. He was beginning to go native. An inkling of Caskey's politics appears in the preface to the first edition of *Castles of the Morea* where Kevin mentions

> an era when ξενοσ αρχυολογοσ (foreign archaeologist) has become almost synonymous with προπαγανδιστησ (propagandist)

There is only a gentle hint in *The Flight of Ikaros* about the next major event:

> At last, one long, reckless and intolerable happiness.

He met Ioanna in early 1949 when looking for somewhere to live. He was twenty-five and she was twenty years older, had four children and was married to a Greek academic who was away from home at the time. Ioanna was stunningly attractive. Even today people describe her as a darling, charming, the love of Kevin's life. Kevin moved into Ioanna's attic and in a few days they were in bed together.

Nearly forty years later Kevin's daughter Ioanna talked to him about her namesake. Echoing a phrase once used to describe Yvette she likened her laughter to the sound of silver bells. Kevin was working at his lathe and there was a silence. He did not look up. Ioanna could see her father's eyes had filled with tears.

His lover Ioanna may not have planned more children but she wanted one with Kevin and soon she was pregnant. Kevin was to claim later that his first epileptic attack occurred while making love to Ioanna. Sometimes he varied the story, preferring to say that it happened while holding his daughter for the first time. He was not present when his daughter was born and several days passed before he saw her. Supposedly he played the *flogera* in the alley below Ioanna's hospital window, experiencing ecstasy and joyful numbness. But – perhaps characteristically - no sense of responsibility. Kevin told his mother about Ioanna but Yvette's reaction to the prospect of acquiring a grandchild whose mother was closer in age to her than to Kevin is not known. She did not seem unduly perturbed about the pregnancy, merely noting in her diary:

> March 4th. News of the birth of my grandchild.

She sent a cable to Kevin and greetings to Ioanna with whom she exchanged letters over the next few years. The daughter was christened Corinna.

Like many a young man Kevin wanted his freedom and did not consider the financial or long term aspects of their situation, thinking only that the baby need not know he was the father. In any case this was a much older woman in a foreign land and he was intending to return to New York. Soon he was off on another field trip. When he returned the lovers could only manage a few hours together somewhere in the suburbs of Athens.

Kevin's field trips mainly involved the castles he was meticulously studying. He travelled by boat, donkey, lorry and bus, exploring the Mani and the Taygetos mountain.

In the spring of 1950 he took a bus to Megara, walked 18 km further south and then inland into the Yerania mountains There he again met Andonis, a shepherd and resin gatherer, a man of the mountains, who dreamed of a better life but was content to share the one he had with a different kind of dreamer. He asked Kevin if he would become godfather to his remaining unbaptised son. Thus Kevin famously became *koumbaros* which, in Greek rural society, represents an invitation to take responsibilities and become part of the family. Kevin felt honoured and took a full part in the ceremony, carefully following the customs and providing the right gifts. All this was later described in *The Flight of Ikaros* - the preparation, the baptism, the naming (*Nikolaos*), the sealing of the child's nine orifices, the oil and water, the lock of wet hair lopped off and dropped into the font, and the subsequent feast.

Shortly after, Andonis's family requested that a cow be sent to them in Yerania – from their viewpoint a simple request. Greece is the centre of the world, America was the land of plenty, Kevin must be rich and it would be an easy thing for him to accomplish. The ensuing project lasted many months during which Kevin became increasingly entangled in the labyrinthine bureaucracy of sending a real live cow from the USA. Despite costing Kevin a lot of money the animal never reached its destination.

Later that summer Kevin was back in Sparta and Mystras, this time in the company of the less savoury Kostandis, described as having

> chestnut eyes with a warmth and humour that flickered intermittently like a snake's tongue around the edge of something else, deeper inside him with nothing gentle about it.

By the autumn of 1951 Kevin was planning to return to the USA. He visited his *koumbaros* to say good-bye. Nobody can milk a farewell more than a Greek and Kevin was truly torn at the parting.

Back in Athens he bought his tickets and packed his bags. He attempted to visit Nikophoros in Pangrati but found him away. Kevin never saw him again.

With only a few days left there was a sudden improvement in the autumn weather. Mild weather traditionally associated with the feast of Saint Demetrios provided Kevin with the opportunity to climb Mount Olympos for the first time. Having overcome the bureaucracy to get the necessary permissions he travelled by train and then on foot, careful to avoid guards and checkpoints. Typically he got lost and found himself in a mist on the edge of a cliff on the wrong summit. He retrieved the situation by edging along a path in the dark and, when further progress seemed impossible, jumped into tree branches which lowered him gently to the ground, repeating this several times until he was safe The next day Kevin reached the real summit, an epileptic alone on the highest mountain in Greece

Kevin's involvement with Greece was not as neutral as he made out in *The Flight of Ikaros*. In January 1947 a United Nations Special Commission on the Balkans (UNSCOB) arrived in Athens to report on the civil war then breaking out. In May 1950 the commission was still present. Kevin had been staying with the Skandalis family and wrote to the commission concerning a planned fact-finding visit to the prison island of Makronissos. His letter highlighted the illegal imprisonment and torture of some of the inmates, notably one of Skandalis' sons in whose room Kevin was sleeping at the time. UNSCOB simply covered up what had happened.

Kevin wrote again in November. In a visit to the US Embassy's political section he was told,

> We're very sorry, but you know these people are Communists.

Kevin persisted but got nowhere. Pressing the British Ambassador, Sir Clifford Norton, a friend of his mother's, he was told,

> A country gets the government it deserves.

Angered, he challenged Peter Norton, Sir Clifford's wife, at a social occasion. She responded,

> Communist guerillas are Communist guerillas; what happens to them in prison is their own responsibility.

Kevin was beginning to understand the self-serving role that western governments were playing in the democratic process, a subject he tackled extensively as a writer in the eighties.

But it wasn't all work. He took full advantage of his natural gifts. At a party in 1950 or 1951, at the American School, Kevin is described dancing with a girl named Rebecca with splendid Pre-Raphaelite red hair flowing down her back. Mesmerised by this beautiful young couple and their easy movements, everyone stopped to watch. More than fifty years later a bystander told me simply,

> It was electrifying.

Another description dates back to the summer of 1951:

> A broad, high valley near Sparta in the midst of the largest *panigyri* (village festival) with hundreds dancing upon the

> grassy stage. An exotically beautiful woman admired a man in *foustanella*, the traditional Greek dress, dancing with abandon; she had a way of attracting attention and the man came over. He had a reddish-brown moustache, a wonderful smile, sweat on his brow from dancing. He took the woman by the hand and they danced the *ballos*.

The man was Kevin Andrews. Like his mother he was a heart-breaker.

He was also a soft man and, in impossible circumstances, tried to be a good father, sneaking into the house when Ioanna's husband was away to put Corinna to bed.

At the end of the year he sailed for New York. A yellow cab took him home to Yvette He resumed his acquaintances with his friends and colleagues. But his heart was still in the hills and the mountains of Greece with his daughter and her mother. He thought of Kostandis and Andonis and, of course, Nikiphoros. He wrote to them. One day a letter arrived. Kevin did not recognise the handwriting. It was from Kallirhoi, telling of the death of his friend and the gratitude they all felt for the time Kevin had spent with him and the gifts he had sent. With the letter was another in Nikiphoros's handwriting. After wishing Kevin good luck he describes the beauty of Athens in the springtime, the flowers and the joy of the Attic earth. He adds,

> I am avoiding something that I think is drowning me, is making me burst and makes my breathing difficult, and I am trying to cast myself out into the light, into the air, into life, that I may hold onto something, and control myself and resist and not fall into chaos, but stand somewhere still, and find tranquillity quiet calm release.

The letter was unsigned and unfinished. Kevin had lost his friend.

SEVENTEEN

Nancy's story

Nancy Cummings – always her preferred surname - agreed to be interviewed by me, then changed her mind, explaining,

> I am old and I am sick. I do not want to talk about that man particularly.

She died as I was writing this book. Her story is integral to the life of Kevin Andrews and an understanding of her background is essential.

Books and magazines have carried versions of her story but only one (*Dreams in the Mirror: A Biography of E. E. Cummings,* Richard S. Kennedy) is based on extensive personal interviews. Some of the material here was reported by Nancy to friends whom I interviewed. This chapter looks at her as Kevin's future wife and mother of two of his children. If Kevin's origins are complicated, Nancy's are labyrinthine.

Nancy's mother, Elaine Orr, was the daughter of an immensely rich paper mill owner and was stunningly beautiful. During World War One and afterwards she entered into a *ménage à trois.* The second part of the triangle was Scofield Thayer from a family of wealthy wool mill owners in Massachusetts, while the third part was his close friend the poet Edward Estlin Cummings, better known later as E. E. Cummings. In 1915 Scofield was living in New

York at a spacious apartment in a bachelors-only building. When Thayer met Elaine he described her as

> soft-spoken, refined and gorgeous — a lovely creature with chestnut hair, pale skin, and large brown eyes.

Thayer was a serious art collector and clearly wanted to add her to his collection. Elaine and Thayer were married in New York on June 21 1916. She was 19, he was 25 and E. E. Cummings was commissioned to write a poem for the occasion. However the marriage bed Cummings referred to in his poem remained unused. Thayer was a repressed gay man, attracted to adolescent boys. On return from their honeymoon the couple continued to live in their separate apartments.

Thayer was often away and Cummings and Elaine went out together. Far from being jealous Thayer encouraged the relationship, even sending Cummings a cheque for

> the time, energy and other things you have expended upon Elaine.

In time Cummings and Elaine fell in love and by 1919 she was pregnant by him. Both Thayer and Cummings pressed her to have an abortion but she refused and on December 20 gave birth to Nancy. Thayer agreed to accept legal responsibility for the child and her birth certificate cites him as father. The pretence suited all three and Thayer and Cummings remained friends. Unsurprisingly Thayer had emotionally related illnesses during the pregnancy and underwent psychoanalysis.

After Nancy's birth Cummings kept his distance and Elaine relied more and more on Thayer who was supportive and caring. Cummings found it difficult to come to terms with Elaine as a mother and, at times, strongly resented his child. They rowed. Cummings, a vicious and cryptic man, wrote to Thayer:

> And by the way is Elaine angry, or merely dead?

Later Cummings wrote that he,

> bitterly resented Nancy. Now Nancy becomes my rival, I suppress my real hatred. I cannot love E only as a prostitute… as a mother E has less sexual appeal but because she is the mother of my child I refuse to admit it.

These resentments and jealousies, though searingly honest, are startling coming from a modern man considered by some to be a socialist.

To Cummings' credit his feelings of jealousy subsided once he saw his child. However a note written a few years later reveals immaturity rather than a readiness to take on parental responsibility:

> After Mopsy's [Nancy's] birth — Idealisation
> extended: includes Motherhood
> so mysterious to me that Elaine, so slender, so young, could be
> a mother
> she does everything for Mopsy—my child. I don't feel her
> efforts appreciate
> i sit back, do nothing to help—never ask her
> to marry me
> i don't really want to participate in my own child!
> assume responsibility of *ménage*!
> be husband, with Elaine as my wife!"
> I prefer the lover-mistress arrangement: more freedom my
> work
> Puella Mea....sexual; at its strongest
> (idealization: strongest at same time)

As Cummings became more involved in his daughter's life Thayer withdrew, having taken up with the writer, Lays Gregory, whom he had hired as an editorial assistant at *Dial*, the literary magazine that was his obsession.

Since Cummings and Elaine were both madly in love again Elaine and Thayer decided to seek a divorce in Paris with Thayer providing grounds based on desertion. Cummings went along for the trip. As part of the settlement, Thayer provided a trust fund worth $100,000 (about $10 million today) for Nancy's support, maintenance and education.

After Paris, Thayer moved on to stay two years in Vienna, being psychoanalysed by Freud. Cummings and Elaine returned from Paris to the US. Thayer was in and out of mental hospitals for several years until in 1929 he was finally institutionalised and remained inside for the rest of his life. He died in 1982 aged 93.

On March 19 1924, Cummings and Elaine Orr were married by Cummings' father, a pastor of the South Congregational Church, in Cambridge, Massachusetts. Again, a cryptic note by Cummings enhances this bizarre story:

> Freud tells Thayer I should marry E[laine].

A month later, with legal and financial assistance from Thayer, Cummings adopted his own daughter, though five-year-old Nancy was told nothing and did not discover about the adoption until she was in her fifties. From then on she took the surname Cummings.

But this is not the end of the to-ing and fro-ing. Married happiness proved short-lived. In May, with Cummings' agreement, Elaine and Nancy sailed for Paris supposedly to help recover from the death of Elaine's sister, Constance. On the boat Elaine fell in love with a wealthy Irishman, Frank MacDermot and, within three months of marrying Cummings, she wrote to him from Europe asking for a divorce.

The merry-go-round continued. Devastated, feeling his manhood challenged, Cummings headed for Paris where he pleaded with Elaine, begged her, threatened violence, threatened suicide with a gun and, according to some reports, even raped her. To no avail. He returned to the USA to the increasingly unstable Thayer who was sympathetic but of no help at all. In fact Thayer collapsed, leaving Cummings in a worse state than before.

On December 4 1924, Elaine appeared in the same Paris courtroom she had entered just three years earlier when she divorced Thayer. The grounds prepared by her lawyers were the same as before: desertion.

On the back of an envelope Cummings wrote a note to Mopsy:

> Good-bye dear & next time when I feel a little better we'll ride
> on the donkeys & next time on the pigs maybe or you will bi-
> cycle & i will ride a swan & next time when my heart is all
> mended again with snow & repainted with bright new paint
> we'll ride you & I ...

The rich and politically powerful MacDermot made sure Cummings did not see his daughter for another fifteen years. Nancy was brought up in Ireland by a succession of trained nurses before being enrolled in boarding schools in France and England. Believing her real father, Thayer, was dead she forgot about Cummings.

But there's more. In 1940, Nancy, aged twenty and strikingly good looking, decided it would be more fun to live in America than wartime Ireland. Before she left, Elaine told her that her father, Thayer, was not dead but had suffered a mental breakdown and was under private care. Elaine urged Nancy not to try to see Thayer. But Nancy was curious. She contacted Thayer's lawyer, Hermann Riccius, saying that if Thayer needed anything she would be willing to help. She also asked Riccius not to inform Elaine about this. She tried to visit Thayer but Riccius refused to allow it.

In the USA on January 3 1943 Nancy married Joseph Willard Roosevelt, a naval officer who had served in the South Pacific. He was the son of Kermit Roosevelt and grandson of Theodore. Nancy and Willard's first child, Simon, was born September 17 1945. Elizabeth followed soon after.

Willard was a close friend of Kevin Andrews!

Nancy pressed her mother about her family history and in 1946 Elaine MacDermot casually mentioned she had been married to the poet E. E.Cummings but refused to answer any awkward questions. Nancy had pretensions to being a poet and was determined to meet Cummings. They were introduced by Henry James' nephew, William. The first time she heard Cummings' voice Nancy says she felt eerie and her hands shook:

> His voice seemed like a bell, like something from afar, almost echoing,

When others joined them, Nancy was

> left with no place to put this feeling as the afternoon was consumed in chit-chat and pleasantries

Late in 1947 she called on Cummings at his New York apartment. Cummings was an accomplished artist and asked his daughter if she would sit for a portrait. By then she had two small children and was unable to take up Cummings' offer until the following May. Nancy felt strangely attracted to Cummings but could not locate her feelings. Her marriage with Willard was already in difficulties and, wanting to avoid further strains, she decided to break off with Cummings when the portrait was completed. The poet was reluctant to talk about her mother or Thayer, whom she still presumed to be her father, so Nancy asked Elaine why she had parted from Cummings who was such an attractive man. Her mother only repeated:

> You must ask Estlin.

What happened next is a matter of dispute but Nancy told a close friend she was falling in love with Cummings. She confessed to him

> I feel there is a natural affinity between us

Supposedly, after a long pause, Cummings asked:

> Did anyone ever tell you I was your father?
> You cannot mean it.
> You don't have to choose between us.

before calling out to Marion Morehouse, his lover

> We have something to celebrate.

Marion came into the room and sensing the stillness and tension she asked what was happening. We know who we are, answered Cummings – a line that resonates through this narrative.

Nancy at 27 was devastated. Even though there was a striking family resemblance she did not at first accept Cummings as her father. Matters were not helped by Marion Morehouse who did her best to keep father and daughter apart. For a year or so they maintained a cordial but fairly distant relationship. Nancy did not tell her mother she knew Cummings was her father. She did however, on the few occasions she saw Cummings, explore the Thayer-Cummings-Elaine *ménage à trois*. Cummings handed over a bundle of correspondence to Nancy in which she found a card from Thayer. It had accompanied a cheque to Cummings and read simply:

> For value received.

She confronted Cummings, asking what the note meant. Feigning ignorance, innocence, or both, Cummings tried to pass over the subject until a furious Nancy shouted,

> Look at the date! Do you know when that was?
> No.
> The day after I was born.

Thayer had paid off Cummings for her birth. Worse, her father had accepted the money. The disgusted Nancy handed back the bundle of letters. She had learned enough.

Nancy had to stay with Cummings another night before taking the train back to New York. He tried to help her with her luggage but, as the train was leaving, he simply dumped the bag on the first available seat and left. Later he wrote:

> I turned to glimpse a gentle pitying look on my child's face... I almost didn't stand & wait for her car to pass - almost but not quite.

Given the turmoil in her life - three fathers to chose from, a beautiful mother who had lied to her, two babies – it's hardly surprising there were strains on her marriage with Willard. But they struggled on until, on October 3 1952, Nancy took the children off to Austria for a holiday and to clear her head. Returning four months later she found Willard was otherwise engaged and the marriage was over. Soon she too became involved with someone else.

EIGHTEEN

New York

The impact Greece had on Kevin cannot be simply ascribed to any individual, event or physical entity. Somehow the unique and shattering light of Greek seascapes and landscapes melded with his epilepsy causing electric shocks to pass through his brain, unleashing a fierce and compelling love of the country and its people. .

When he left the USA in the summer of 1947 he was a bright, innocent young man full of hope and expectation. When he returned four years later he was so depressed, angry, sad and confused he spent a year in almost total hibernation. He no longer belonged in the USA and yearned to be back in Greece with the people he cared for.

> In the crystalline air, on the edge... with the men of the mountains

Kevin wrote to the friends he had left behind and sent them parcels. There were responses from Ioanna, from the musician Domna Samiou, Andonis, an innkeeper in Monemvasia, a shepherd from Mount Olymbos and, in early 1952, the sad news from Kallirhoi. He went to Greek parties and festivals and on occasion met visitors from Greece. These included Dora Stratou and Simon Karras, old friends he played music with in Athens. In autumn 1953 he accompanied Yvette when King Paul and his wife Frederika paid a state visit to New York.

The affair between Kevin and Ioanna lasted three years and contemporaries have suggested their feelings for each other never died. In January 1950 their daughter Corinna was born but despite this Kevin decided to return to New York to complete his studies and write *Castles of the Morea.* Ioanna's marriage was shattered. She had five children and knew there was no future with someone so much younger, unemployed, with no money and living on a different continent.

After what Kevin called

> their ultimate farewell

Ioanna realised she needed security. By the time she and Kevin met again she had remarried.

Kevin longed to be back in Greece but needed an income. In Athens he tried to pull strings to find employment with an American government agency; in Washington he went from office to office seeking a post. He spent a month trying to fulfil a naive ambition to help distribute aid equably to the Greek rural population, but to no avail. One insider told him the failure was due to his illness but there could be another cause. His idealistic politics may have been the problem. America's involvement with Greece was not without self-interest and an informed source told me Kevin was blackballed by ASCS director Caskey.

After this he never applied for another post. Having stuck his neck out standing up for prisoners of the Government while in Greece, he found himself alone, without political support and deterred by the potential consequences of dissent in the USA. Senator McCarthy was in his pomp and Kevin was once visited in New York by the FBI, checking on the politics of one of his artist friends in Greece. For the next two decades Kevin avoided antagonising the US government.

In the summer of 1952 he returned briefly to Britain and went walking with his mother in Scotland. She was paying one of her regular trips to Europe and was dividing her time between her son and Smallwood. Perhaps Kevin suspected something between the pair of them; Liza Mayer confirms this but he said nothing. His major concern was his health. He suffered regular epileptic attacks. Mainly *petits mals* they did not usually last long but their frequency - up to ten a day - left him exhausted. For a minute or two, occasionally longer, he trembled and appeared absent. Afterwards he would look round puzzled, even ashamed, and then try to resume whatever he had been doing. The medication he was initially prescribed was phenobarbital and epanutin. Their side effects made him appear nervous while insomnia, nausea and vomiting added to his difficulties. Worst of all was the intermittent and unpredictable impotency. As a man gets older impotency tends to be understood, accepted and sometimes welcomed. For the young and insecure Kevin Andrews the sense of failure and self-loathing was devastating. He described the medicines as

> crude sedation, strong enough to knock out a horse.

Living from one bout of nausea and hallucination to another his days were disjointed. He tried to write, took a siesta, wrote again, went to bed late, could not sleep, lay awake or dozed until dawn, then started all over again. Physically fit, with his mind buzzing, he walked round Central Park or ran long distances through the canyons of Manhattan to tire himself . He suffered massive mood swings and had an identifiable but unrecognised and untreated bipolar affliction that sent him ricocheting off walls. Yvette's apartment was tiny and the pressure was enormous. Sometimes he lost control and once he went berserk, wrecking the place, breaking furniture and smashing mirrors and photographs. No doubt he suffered remorse and then guilt but it is easy to imagine Yvette's pain. Her situation compared unfavorably with the plush life of RCA her ex-husband. In addition to Pondwood Farm he and his young wife Billie lived in a luxury apartment in the old Pulitzer building at 11 East 73rd Street with a bedroom overlooking Central Park.

Some years before, RCA's views on women had caused a row with the renowned aviator Amelia Earhart. She knew RCA and Yvette and chastised the former for his unscientific approach:

> Why not come right out and say you just don't want women on expeditions?

Yvette, who shared difficult times and gruelling expeditions with RCA, only to find herself cut out of the limelight, grew bitter at her treatment, openly describing RCA as conceited, pompous and boring. She called him a long drink of water (that's the polite version) and mocked his achievements as an explorer and a scientist by referring to him as an expedition caterer.

Her son George was attracted to life in the limelight with Billie and Roy

> like a moth to a flame.

He never understood the mystery of Yvette and rarely saw her or his brother. Kevin on the other hand, taking the cue from his mother, could not bear to be near RCA.

Approaching thirty, hamstrung by indecision, bordering on the feckless and living off his mother, Kevin believed his mission was to become

> an American writer,

but was aware of his limitations.

> I wasn't butch like Hemingway; I was no burnt-out gem-like flame - a Scott Fitzgerald; I couldn't write simple sentences as recommended by Gertrude Stein.

Nevertheless he somehow managed to write and, in January 1953, to complete *Castles of the Morea*. By early 1953 the proofs were corrected and the book, dedicated to Simon Karras, went off to the printer. Kevin's feelings for the Greeks is expressed clearly in the introduction

> ....during a civil war, at a time when communication and accommodation barely existed, one could do no more than throw oneself on the forbearance of the people of the country, who know only one word for stranger and guest (*xenos. RAJ*) and where hospitality, generosity and trust provide a more valuable education than may be found in histories or monuments.

Castles of the Morea was generally well reviewed. His old teacher John Finlay thought it to be a work of finish and beauty with a burning intuition of the authentic Greece. But the accolades were not universal. Jock Anderson, also of the ASCS, was particularly critical of the schema and scope of the book while failing to mention the quality of the prose. More interesting is a review in the *Royal Institute of British Architects Journal* in March 1956 , which neatly and precisely identifies Kevin's prevarications and insecurities.

> its method of presentation is perhaps over-systematic; even the author's speculations are subdivided into periods and types.

Castles of the Morea is an accomplished work of scholarship and has recently been reprinted. In the spring of 1953 Kevin started another book destined to be his masterpiece. Based on his travels through Greece it is much more personal. He wrote and rewrote what came to be called *The Flight of Ikaros* for three decades before he was satisfied. Lacking confidence as a man and unsure about his judgement, his only answer was to apply scholarship and intellect to record his love of the country. It was hard, slow work. Some days he achieved nothing, others he dithered between a full stop or a comma. Chronically unable to make his mind up he wrote, analysed, crossed out, panicked, shouted, and threw a tantrum before starting again at the top of a blank page.

Talking to a renowned Hellenophile and a friend of Kevin Andrews for nearly five decades, I was told:

> He could not write for toffee.

When I ventured he was a great writer I was put down with:

> Tell it to the marines.

As I learnt more about Kevin Andrews I realised she was right. He was not a natural writer. He wrote several superb books but they cost him dear.

Occasionally there was light relief. While in Athens Kevin had become friendly with Louis MacNiece, then head of the British Council, and his wife Mary. The couple had separated and Mary moved to the US while Louis lived in England. Their son Dan moved to America to be with his mother and to avoid National Service in Britain. Louis believed him to have been kidnapped and in early 1953 MacNiece asked Kevin to check on the boy, thought to be living with his mother on a chicken farm in upstate New York. First Kevin was advised to seek background information from MacNiece's friend W. H. Auden who lived in a large loft in the lower reaches of Seventh Avenue. Auden never replaced books on shelves and Kevin sat there among piles of them scattered over every dusty surface. After discussing the seedy details of the MacNiece marriage Auden related a series of anecdotes about their mutual friend. One concerned a confrontation between MacNiece and the poet Roy Campbell who were on opposite sides in the Spanish Civil War. Some time in the 1940s, Campbell, a renowned macho man, had been holding forth in a bar among a group of fellow writers. Describing how he had floored someone with one punch he was interrupted by MacNiece who asked innocently,

> How hard did you hit him?

Campbell feinted a punch to which MacNiece responded,

> Are you sure it wasn't this hard?

clubbing Campbell on the jaw and knocking him out.

Attracted by celebrity and fascinated by violence and men of action Kevin continued to tell the story down the years even in MacNiece's obituary. Against Mary MacNiece's wishes, Kevin made the complicated and lengthy journey to her home. He stayed two nights and later described the farm as being festooned with cobwebs and having sagging ceilings. Mary insisted that Dan give up his bed for Kevin and this led to Dan moving into his mother's bedroom. Always interested in sex and scandal Kevin sneaked upstairs and saw there was just one double bed. He reported all this joyfully to MacNiece, but it is unclear how much this helped the poet. Dan returned to England in 1953 but following a lurid legal battle between his parents he returned to the USA to live with his mother.

NINETEEN

Kevin and Nancy

Some psychiatrists say we fall in love with our mirror image. Hoping against hope we long for a reflected self capable of salving our hurt and remedying the unfinished business of childhood. Kevin and Nancy could serve as prime examples. Both were confused about their fathers' identity and both had beautiful, powerful mothers who misled them. Neither had experienced their biological fathers behaving as such. Intelligent and magnificently egocentric they lacked empathy for those close to them. Kevin, always the actor, always outgoing, used charm and good looks to find casual acquaintances and friends then, employing every trick, placed himself central to the relationship. Nancy, attractive though outwardly cold, dressed down as much as she could. Described by friends as severe, she deliberately avoided intimacy but saw the world through her own prism: What Greece did to me. What Kevin said to me. How my children affected me.

It is doubtful that Belle Roosevelt, matriarch of the powerful Roosevelt family, thought of Kevin and Nancy as a couple when compiling the guest list for a dinner party in New York some time in 1952. After all Nancy was a mother of two married to her son Willard, while Kevin was Willard's close friend. To this trio must be added Yvette, Kevin's mother, E. E. Cummings, Nancy's father, and Cummings' lover, Marion. The party would have been deemed a success: glittering guests, sophisticated conversation, good food and plenty of wine. Yet Nancy felt uncomfortable. In the company of her husband, her father and her in-laws she was attracted to the man with piercing blue eyes who spoke so animatedly about his time in Greece.

Yvette knew the marriage between Nancy and Willard was failing and soon had Nancy marked out as a suitable wife for her beloved son. She eagerly tested Kevin's views about the poet's daughter who was also an heiress. Through Willard, Nancy had been aware of Kevin for some time but hadn't really noticed him. Now as Willard withdrew from the marriage she confided more and more in the younger man. He was exciting and amusing, playing tricks and telling jokes. The picture he painted of Greece was so compelling and enticing she was tempted to share the dream.

Nancy was an independent and strong woman with the kind of looks that last. Like many insecure men Kevin was impressed by physical beauty but he was inexperienced and terribly naive about sex and relationships. Friends from those days recall him asking questions about their sex lives, what they did, how they did it, what were their fantasies. Approaching thirty, affected by epilepsy and the side-effects of his medication, living with – and off - his mother he remained emotionally adolescent. Perhaps Nancy found this attractive in a man four years her junior, perhaps Kevin sought the security of an older, controlled, woman. They became lovers. Soon Nancy and Willard were living apart and there was talk of a divorce.

Kevin and Nancy took full advantage of New York's social life. Often accompanied by Yvette and sometimes by Cummings they went to concerts, exhibitions, poetry readings and the cinema. From the beginning, Nancy was willing to adapt to Kevin's life and sacrifice herself to his wishes. A city girl she even went camping with her lover. But there were complications. As the mutual attraction grew they felt in their different way they were betraying Willard. Kevin carried feelings of guilt for several decades. It cannot have been easy to write to a close friend and say you intend to marry his wife but Kevin somehow managed it. Supposedly they even met to discuss the situation. There were no raised voices, Nancy and Willard were determined the children must come first. Everyone was frightfully civilised.

When the pressure grew too much Kevin took to the hills. Notwithstanding his epilepsy, he was fit and healthy though always pushing himself to the limit, often to the point of recklessness. In August 1953 he was hiking in Maine on Mount Kathadin (now called Baxter State Park) when there was a bad storm. In his cavalier fashion Kevin failed to phone either his mother or Nancy to let them know he was safe. They feared the worst and it wasn't until he turned up outside Yvette's flat playing the *flogera* she realised her son was still alive. Hoorah, she shouted, hoorah. But the relief she felt must have been tempered by her reaction to his thoughtlessness. There were other distractions. Old army friends took him drinking or for a hike. Invariably he brought his bagpipes. Once, helping the author, Dorothy Pitkin, look for a house to buy the pair toured around in her car. As she concentrated on her driving Kevin sat alongside letting out a piercing wail on the pipes when a suitable property came into view. This was the public side of Kevin Andrews. The one the outside world was allowed to see.

In autumn 1953 Dylan Thomas came to New York. He met E. E. Cummings who admired him greatly. Yvette and Kevin watched Thomas perform on several occasions and after one reading Kevin introduced himself and invited him to go drinking with friends. The company was amused by Dylan's Welsh accent and stories of his marriage to Caitlin. Famously the couple were said to communicate by throwing crockery:

> we fight of course,

Thomas explained.

> Jealous, both of us.... good reason to be.

There was heavy rain that night and they got soaked as they went from bar to bar amused by Dylan's inventive language:

> shit and damnation.... lust and fornication... big Jesus

In the early hours they poured the Welshman back into the Hotel Chelsea in Manhattan. He developed what appeared to be a heavy cold A few days later he felt ill while drinking at the nearby White Horse Tavern. He returned to his room at the Chelsea and a doctor was called . His condition was not recognised and the doctor administered a large and, given his breathing complications, potentially lethal dose of morphine sulphate. The poet did not recover and on Monday November 9 at St Vincent's Hospital he died. In Thomas's *Under Milk Wood* a character reflects on the ignominy of dying from drink and agriculture. With Thomas it was pneumonia and incompetence, but the drink did not help.

By the end of 1953 Nancy's divorce from Willard had been decided and marriage to Kevin was planned. Nancy's history was well known in the upper echelons of New York society. Yvette felt close and the two confided. Forcing Nancy to promise secrecy Yvette revealed her relationship with Smallwood and asked whether Kevin should be told that Smallwood was his father. Nancy said he should. But the situation was complicated further as Yvette sought permission from the man himself. The strain on Nancy must have been intense as she waited for Smallwood to agree. It is difficult to imagine that Kevin did not notice something amiss with his mother and his lover. And what if Smallwood said no? But Smallwood said yes leaving Yvette to explain to her son that Smallwood was rather more than a godfather. We do not know how Yvette managed but the deed was done over tea during the 1953 Christmas holidays. Years later Kevin explained he had asked his mother how he resembled his new father and she had replied,

> The cut of the jib, the way your head sits on your neck.

So Kevin Andrews, a man estranged from the world famous Roy Chapman Andrews the person he thought of as his father, suddenly discovers a new identity. He has a new father Group Captain Harold St Clair (Chips) Smallwood. The Bounder. And now the man's suit that used to hang in his mother's wardrobe suddenly means something, as do photographs in old albums, vague memories of Peking, the past catching up with the present. Smallwood had always been part of his life and always close to his mother even visiting her in New York. Considering the fuss Kevin was to make later about his parentage, the compulsion to talk about his origins and the vicious attacks he made on his mother and Smallwood long after their deaths, he seems to have received the news calmly at the time. Kevin Andrews was a man who carefully reconstructed his own life and perhaps he was not as surprised as he later claimed. Either way, Roy Chapman Andrews, whom Kevin slyly boasted about to friends, the man who paid his school fees, was no longer his father. They never discussed the new situation together

On Saturday May 9 1954, Kevin and Nancy visited Cummings at 4 Patchin Place, New York, to announce their wedding and ask for his blessing. Kevin was dazzled by Cumming's celebrity and he and Nancy basked in the reflected glory of the renowned poet. Imagining Kevin to be on the verge of a brilliant career and being fond of the young man Cummings was delighted with the forthcoming marriage. Being jealous of anyone who came close to her lover Marion was less impressed.

Indecision dogged Kevin for much of his life. Internal turmoil caused deep depression, often leading him to threaten suicide. Even now he was not sure about Nancy; perhaps she was too powerful for him, perhaps he was just immature or still in love with Ioanna. But the marriage went ahead. A blur of furniture moving and letter writing preceded a very quiet wedding - so quiet that nobody in the family can say when it was. Kevin moved in with Nancy and the children while Yvette, once more, was living alone. The rapid changes affected Yvette's health. On May 16 she was near to collapse. Kevin took her out to dinner after which they sat in the park and talked. They had a lot to talk about.

In February 1955 Kevin and Nancy had a daughter. At Nancy's somewhat bizarre suggestion and in deference to Kevin's former lover, the baby was named Ioanna. By now the couple had decided to leave America and live in Greece. Kevin was to be a writer. They would live on Nancy's money. Wanting to see more of America before they left for Greece, Kevin went for a walk. Not just any walk but a marathon along the Appalachian Trail. He did it his own way carrying neither sleeping bag nor tent. Walking for weeks east and north through the mountains to New York he didn't even wear proper boots. .

Leaving America in June the family moved to a rented farmhouse in Switzerland near Chateau d'Oex. Yvette brought Smallwood to see the new granddaughter and to establish bonds between father and son. It is easy to imagine Kevin being nervous and excited but he never really took to Smallwood as a father and mocked his petty bourgeois background. Smallwood's ambition to write a book, *Horses I have known*, was easy to deride but Smallwood had had an interesting life. In and out of the armed forces for sixty years he served under six sovereigns. The outbreak of World War Two found him in the Royal Air Force at the headquarters of Fighter Command. He performed important operational duties during the Battle of Britain for which he was appointed an officer of the Order of the British Empire. Returning to the Far East in 1942 he held a number of staff and command appointments in India, Burma and China. He retired in 1945 with the rank of group captain before the Cold War saw him enrolling once again in 1947 in the Royal Observer Corps. Described as someone who

> extracted the maximum amount of humour and fun out of every situation no matter how unpromising,

he was also said to be

> self-effacing and totally devoid of self seeking.

Later he was awarded the CBE for, of all things, services to the Greyhound Racing Society.

Kevin could have been jealous of Smallwood. Brought up by his mother to be more of a consort than a son he may have resented the closeness between the older couple. Certainly his confidence was eroded by his so-called parents' wish to keep their long-term liaison discreet, supposedly to protect the Smallwood family from unnecessary gossip. Prevented from meeting his new half-family made him feel he was being denied a wider existence. Smallwood could not live up to his son's hopes and these two people, with different interests, backgrounds, upbringing and education, never hit it off. Identity, paternity and belonging became obsessions, which affected Kevin's writing and his relationship with his mother, wife and children. Almost from the beginning Kevin and Nancy were dragged into a thirty-year-old scandal, which weighed heavily on them. When I asked one of Kevin's close friends why his origins mattered so much she responded immediately:

> It was the deceit.

In *Expatriation to Excess: No Blame*, an essay published posthumously in *The Southeastern Review,* and referred to later in more detail, he explores a recurrent theme, displaying his usual self-loathing and self-pity and a hatred of his mother. Explaining why he did not belong in America Kevin says:

> My parents (ie, Yvette and RCA) said I did but they were lying in their teeth to save their skins... their contemporaries all lied too… the family, friends...

Unable even to acknowledge his mother's name, he says:

> To England she kept going back.. where a British cavalry officer (Smallwood) - of Empire building proclivities and no honourable intentions - had deposited me like a cuckoo's egg in the undeserving nest of her husband, a zoologist and explorer from Beloit, Wisconsin, by the name of Andrews.

All this from a man who had sired a daughter with another man's wife.

At the end of January 1956 Kevin's daughter Corinna came to Switzerland to stay with the Andrews family. Kevin promised her mother he would not reveal their true relationship but was so overcome with excitement on meeting Corinna he broke his promise and told her immediately:

> I am your father.

Of course, Corinna did not take him seriously. How could she? She had just left her father at home. In any case the oddity was quickly forgotten and she was soon preoccupied with meeting Elizabeth and Simon, Nancy and the baby Ioanna. Then came the walk and the fall, which Corinna remembered so poignantly. As he held her close to him she saw Kevin's anguish and recognised he had told the truth. Back at the house Kevin told Nancy what had happened. Wryly, Nancy told friends Kevin employed the same expression as E. E. Cummings when she found he was her father:

> *Ca y est.* We know who we are.

And for a while they did.

Corinna stayed three months with her new family before returning to her mother and her stepfather. Kevin told Corinna she could come back at any time but in truth did not know if this would be allowed. His fear was justified. Four years passed before he saw her again.

TWENTY

Hydra

Some species of raptor have a mating ritual so eloquent it could have been choreographed by Diaghilev. The birds eye one another for days, even weeks. One day they arrive in the same piece of sky hundreds of feet up at exactly the same moment. They hesitate, circle each other, dash and hold claws. With their wings extended, behaving like children whirling around in the playground, they plummet downwards letting go just before impact. Once, on Karpathos, I marvelled as two clinging Bonelli eagles spun down and separated so late that they touched the waves before letting go. Then they did the whole thing again. I watched for hours until the sky was dark and only their cries told me they were still playing this dangerous game. Kevin and Nancy resembled these eagles except they forgot to let go. They crashed. They held on to one another even though the marriage had failed and they were living in different countries.

Nancy Andrews was physically and psychologically frail, a woman who desperately strove to keep herself under control. Following her failed marriage to Roosevelt she suffered from depression for much of the time. She exerted massive pressure on the raw young man she then married but there was no way Kevin could save or comfort her, or redeem her wounded soul. He just did not have the empathy or patience to deal with such a demanding woman. After a mere two years of marriage Kevin began to feel the relationship was doomed.

With most married couples, initially at least, the marital bed offers an opportunity for succour and comfort. For the intermittently dysfunctional this opportunity does not exist. Minor disagreements are magnified rather than forgotten in tenderness or the act of love. But impotency was not Kevin's only problem. His mother, Yvette, could hardly bear Kevin as a baby. She sent him away to boarding schools and, at times, to America. Then, as she got older, she clung to him in her almost unbearable loneliness, probing, tormenting and manipulating. Neurotic mothers can severely damage their children and Kevin bore the scars for ever. Nor could he deal with the anger or frustration of his wife. He was not just inadequate, he had a phobia. Nancy was Yvette revisited for Kevin, a seemingly strong woman, older and from a good family. Nancy dominated his emotions, he escaped, was confused, returned and was confused, went away again, and on and on. Until it was too late.

Most of us learn how to love our children and to show affection from the way we were loved by our own parents. Kevin learned little that was positive from Yvette, learned nothing from RCA and was soon to despise Smallwood. Nancy did not discover till late in life that EEC was her father and his remoteness meant she learned little positive from him although when he died she seems to have suffered a genuine sense of loss. Even more remarkably Kevin too appeared to share this loss.

The Andrews' marriage was problematic from the beginning. Nancy's divorce left them both feeling guilty. The children from that marriage, Elizabeth and Simon, were at a vulnerable age and had to be cared for. And soon the new daughter, Ioanna, arrived. Things were not helped by Corinna's existence and Kevin's lingering feelings for her mother. Rarely can love have been spread so thinly so early in a marriage.

Then there was his illness and the side-effects of his medication. Even the *petits mals*

> bring death close several times a day.

In October 1956 Kevin, Nancy and the children travelled via Lombardy and Venice through the Adriatic on to Yugoslavia and

Montreux. Throughout Kevin tried to write his new book on Greece but spent more time filling notebooks about how he was going to write.

Still in October, the family arrived in Greece. This was a logical move for Kevin. He knew Athens, spoke the language and was well regarded as the author of *Castles of the Morea.* The rudimentary life and the Greek people separated him from England, from America, from the embarrassment of Smallwood and his mother, and from the painful memories of Roy Chapman Andrews. The new Greek book, soon to be titled *The Flight of Ikaros*, gave him something to do. For Nancy, an intelligent woman with literary pretensions, there were the children and there was Kevin. She loved him totally and was willing to follow him to what she regarded as one of the ends of the earth.

For a time the family lived in Ekali, a suburb of Athens. Then Simon was sent to a boarding school in America while Kevin, Nancy, Elizabeth and Ioanna moved to the quiet, seemingly idyllic island of Hydra. Kevin knew the island from his earlier stay in Greece. There were no roads and no cars. Then, as now, the houses of sea captains and merchants rose in tiers round the bustling horseshoe harbour. Above, mountains are sheer against the sky. Only fifty-five kilometres from Piraeus, it is served by a daily ferry, which, once a week, brought the doctor. Hydra was quiet but not isolated. It was also cheap.

Nancy was used to a metropolitan life, which Kevin could not support. Nancy had money, Kevin did not. They solved the conundrum by moving downmarket but it was not the answer. Nancy was resentful while Kevin was angry and frustrated at not being able to provide for his new family, furious he could not earn sufficient from his writing. Once, as Kevin stormed out, Nancy threw a hairbrush at him. Kevin must have been aware of what Nancy was going through but he made certain that he, Kevin Andrews, came first. He had a passion for Greece and he knew the life he wanted. Nancy compromised and made sacrifices; she became the victim, did the nappies, got the children ready, cooked the meals, cleaned the house. For her love was sacrifice.

Neither of them pulled their punches:

You should have been a man
Is that why you married me?

After rows Kevin walked the hills and the mountains, talked to the peasants, shopkeepers, farmers and fishermen while Nancy stayed at home to look after the children. Ioanna was at home all day and Elizabeth attended the village school. Elizabeth soon learnt the language and, with the help of the hospitable children of Hydra, made friends and fitted in with village life. Every afternoon she came home from school, up the little lane, through the gate and into the courtyard of their house, untroubled by the domestic turmoil.

Other non-Greeks on the island included Charmian Clift and her husband George Johnston, Australian journalists who had moved to Hydra in 1955 to write. A passionate but tragic couple, dogged by depression and alcohol, they nevertheless managed to complete several books, separately and together. On Hydra Charmian wrote *Mermaid Singing* and *Peel me a Lotus*. *Mermaid* is the better and describes the time the family spent on Kalymnos. It provides a good understanding of local people and emphasises the importance of child rearing and domestic life. *Peel me a Lotus* deals with their life on Hydra and is less successful, perhaps because the strain of living together was beginning to show, perhaps because of drinking problems or because Hydra is too close to Athens and its people are easier to portray as caricatures and Greek stereotypes. Whatever, it does not really ring true. Kevin and Nancy appear in *Peel me a Lotus* as Toby and Katherine, two Americans dreaming of islands, but they are not easily recognised. In *Closer to the Sun*, published in 1960, Johnston recounted the jealousies and liaisons of claustrophobic island life. When the couple returned to Australia George was discovered to have tuberculosis. Charmian committed suicide with barbiturates on July 8 1969. George died a year later.

The two couples embarked on a limited friendship. Because of his medication Kevin drank only rarely while Nancy did not drink at all. Clift and her husband were alcoholics. The four rarely met after dark. Instead they waited for the mail boat at the waterfront store owned by the brothers Nick and Toni Katsikas. Charmian and

George drank and gossipped, Nancy would leave early and Kevin followed.

Surprisingly neither Kevin nor Nancy read Clift's work. Kevin mocked the title *Peel me a Lotus* and was not impressed by Johnston, regarding him inadequate. Characteristically, he showed the couple no sympathy. He doubted their marriage was a success.

Nancy once met Charmian in the marketplace,

> radiating sweetness.

Inclined to probe behind a first impression, especially if it was a good one, Nancy added,

> I think she uses sweetness as a weapon.....

Kevin was fascinated by the tensions in the couple's life, the cliché about two people unable to live happily together or apart. Perhaps he was fascinated by Clift's passion compared with Nancy's cool command. Soon he started making notes about a novel initially called *The Jumblies,* based on two couples living on Hydra. Later, having abandoned it, Kevin explained,

> I do not have a novel in me.

Kevin's self-assessments were rarely balanced but he displayed surprising insight when he explained that all his characters were him in a different guise. Others told me that Kevin's problem was simple. He could not empathise - a serious defect for someone trying to be novelist.

Hydra is a pleasant place and a decade later became a hang-out for artists and hippies. But time spent there hardly benefited the Andrews family. Kevin said he was in despair of ever finding kindness, helpfulness, music, festivity, or anything unspoilt about the place. So they looked for another island paradise. Simon Karras, the musician and mentor of Domna Samiou and others, suggested Ikaria. Kevin's friend Louis MacNeice had been there and written poems about it. It sounded wild and romantic. Before trying this remote and difficult island, they took a brief and traumatic holiday in the Alpes Maritimes.

TWENTY-ONE

Brian Howard and Lura Chess

Kevin made friends with interesting people and wrote well about them. But he also befriended bullies, sadists, manipulators and empty people. In some cases the reasons are obvious: he liked Kostandis (see *The Flight of Ikaros*) because he envied him his physical prowess and male confidence. It's less easy to explain why he spent time with Lura Howard and her son, Brian Christian de Claiborne Howard.

Brian was born in March 1905 at Winkworth, Surrey, of wealthy American parents. His mother, Lura Chess, was a socially pretentious woman from Kentucky, his father, Tudie Howard, a friend of Whistler and an entrepreneur who drifted in and out of the English art scene. Brian was sent to prep schools and then to Eton. From the age of fifteen he was a published poet and had insinuated himself in circles where his irreverent, lightweight style was considered clever. An associate of Edith Sitwell, Evelyn Waugh, Harold Acton, Anthony Powell, David Cecil and Robert Powell, he achieved little and was described as a most extraordinary failure.

Brian went up to Christ Church, Oxford, in 1923 and joined the Hypocrites, a discussion group where clever people discussed clever things. Because he was gay, and homosexuality was considered by some to be a psychological illness, he was sent by his mother in 1927 to Dr Prinzhorn, a German psychiatrist in Frankfurt. Brian was not cured. As he grew older he gathered around him like-minded acquaintances including Tom Driberg, W. H. Auden and Christopher Isherwood. A latter-day Oscar Wilde but without the genius.

Brian drifted around Europe spending his mother's money and having affairs, some long lasting. He drank a lot. Readers of *Brideshead Revisited* might recognise the type. Surprisingly (or perhaps not, in view of subsequent revelations) Brian got a job in MI5, reporting on possible Nazi sympathisers, though whether he was capable of recognising one is far from clear. He was sacked a year later. He volunteered for the Royal Air Force and was accepted as a clerk in October 1942, managing to get himself posted to Bomber Command, High Wycombe, in the public relations department. Checked over for health problems at RAF Halton in June 1944 he was honourably discharged on December 1944 for being below Air Force physical standards, though fit for selected employment in civil life. He had often been in trouble, once losing his uniform in a public lavatory. By now he had met Sam, an Irishman born in Tralee and, at nineteen, in command of an air-sea rescue launch

After the war Brian continued to drift, mainly with Sam. He became alcoholic. He was expelled from France in 1950 as an undesirable person. In June 1952, while staying at the Villa La Mura, in the village of Asolo in Italy, he was mistaken for the missing spy and one-time friend Guy Burgess.

His health suffered and, during the 1950s, he became addicted to sedatives. He also had tuberculosis. In Tangier he cured his alcohol addiction by becoming dependent on drugs. After his father died in October 1954 Lura and Brian bought Le Verger, a house near Nice at Col de Bast, Vallon Obscur.

At least Yvette's regard for Lura seems obvious. Apart from providing her with accommodation and employment in the late thirties, Lura had achieved something in life. Her Chess Cosmetics was a major enterprise and even now her perfume glasses and jars are collectibles sold on eBay. Her glamour and name-dropping also made her good company. But, given his preoccupations, why would Kevin be bothered with such lightweights?

One reason may be curiosity. Like many young people Kevin was not only obsessed with sex, he was promiscuous. So was Brian. There is no firm evidence that Kevin had adult homosexual experiences but gayness certainly interested him and he often asked himself questions that most men shy away from. It could be Kevin used Brian to test his own sexuality.

Lura was an older, powerful woman for whom Kevin may have represented the heterosexual son she did not have. She was a strong influence over Kevin and his mother.

Whatever the reasons behind this social *ménage* the holiday spent at Lura's villa in summer 1957 proved unfortunately memorable. The weather was hot; there were forest fires, smoke and rumours of arson. Kevin, Nancy and Ioanna were accompanied by Simon and Elizabeth whose father, Willard Roosevelt, stayed nearby. In August an unwell Yvette, suffering from severe anxiety, arrived with her friend Pat Glenn. Concerns about money - debts, real and imaginary - seemed to plague Yvette and she wandered from room to room, tearing at her arms and muttering,

> I have a secret to tell. Will nobody listen to me? Will nobody listen?

Racked with guilt she drove Kevin crazy with self-recrimination, self-accusation and repentance. His instinct was to run away but he could not.

Nancy and Lura tried to convince him Yvette was going insane. Kevin prevaricated – he would not take responsibility for his mother. Amidst this turmoil the children played boisterously but wondered why nobody was caring for their grandmother. The pressure on Kevin exploded in a violent attack on his young daughter Ioanna. She had done something to upset him; he beat her viciously.

Perhaps this outburst was a catalyst for action as he finally took Yvette to a psychiatrist. She was given sedatives and stayed in the local hospital in Nice for a month before returning to England where she was treated for anxiety. Kevin and Nancy hardly visited her, though she did get a kind letter from Margot, Smallwood's wife. Later, a friend of the family, also a psychiatrist, who knew Lura, reportedly said Lura's dominance was enough to send anyone askew. After a while Yvette made a partial recovery but the exuberant self had gone. Her breakdown shattered Kevin and his own failure to act humiliated him. As a result he began to withdraw from her.

But why was 68-year-old Yvette so anxious? In her very brief journal for 1957 she mentions, a few days after Kevin's birthday, she was reading Perceval Landon's letters. Is it usual to read and reread letters from a lover, or maybe a friend, thirty years after his death on your son's birthday?

> January 25 - Reads PL's letters. January 26 - PL's letters. January 28 - Head my head sleep. January 31 - Don't feel very strong. February 6 - Really tired.

But she is so, so close to Smallwood:

> March 10 - Ask Pat (Glenn) re dinner with my dear love. He from Dagenham early 5.30. He tired off 10.30. March 8 - He not well. March 14 - He comes. He comes. Him home. March 17 - Dourley de Rous *(unexplained)* gives me life again

Yvette feels she has a secret she wants to tell. Clearly it is to do with the birth of Kevin. But what exactly? Kevin had been led to believe that the truth was out. But was it the whole truth or was there something else?

A year later, after a row, Yvette cursed Kevin:

> I hope Ioanna *(his daughter)* does not put you in a home.

What is interesting is that Kevin saw this episode as it affected him, not his mother. It was always thus. Kevin showed many faces to the outside world, and perhaps to himself. He was considerate, proud, arrogant, vain but, above all, he demanded attention. Later Kevin blamed Nancy for having forced him to check his mother into a mental clinic. Ironically, in one of those cycles typical of the Andrews saga, thirty years earlier Nancy's mother, Elaine, had signed the papers committing Scofield Thayer to a mental institution,

Until Yvette's breakdown the established relationships at the villa were maintained; the wealthy Lura dominated the dependent Yvette, with Kevin daunted by, and impressed by, the older, sexually experienced Brian. But soon after Yvette was taken to hospital Nancy was surprised to see Kevin come out of Brian's office. Shocked, she asked what he had been doing. Kevin said he had been going through Brian's briefcase reading his letters. He declared them sordid and decadent. From then on Kevin declared some kind of independence, breaking away from Lura's influence and whatever fear he had of Brian.

And Brian Howard himself? He and Sam moved to France to live in the villa at the beginning of January 1958. On January 11 Sam went for a bath. Workmen had removed an exhaust pipe and Sam was asphyxiated by fumes from the gas heater. He was 32. Four days later Brian Howard killed himself with sedatives. He was 52. After a double funeral they were buried together at the Caussade de Nice cemetery.

By then Kevin and his family were back in Greece.

TWENTY-TWO

Ikaria

Kevin was a young man looking for a Greece that existed outside the books of Lawrence Durrell or Henry Miller. Rather than depending on secondary sources he preferred to draw on the uninterrupted flow of wit from ancient times as he walked the Peloponnesus mountains and uplands, measuring and recording for his classical masterpiece *Castles of the Morea*. He cared a great deal about myths and stories, and despaired about the gradual disappearance of links with the old Greece. He sought refuge in isolated places in order to share the lives of ordinary Greeks, especially the pastoralists and peasants who still belonged to an older way of life.

Nancy, an east coast Scottish-American socialite, agreed to go to remote places because of her love for Kevin. Although her attitude towards the wild is unrecorded she was a romantic, saw herself as a writer and later published a number of poems.

Ikaria is wilder and less accessible than their first island home, Hydra, and lies between the better known Samos and Mykonos. Narrow, windswept, mountainous and covered in pine forests, the island was supposedly named after Ikaros who flew too close to the sun and drowned in the sea when the wax attaching the feathers to his wings melted. For many years it was a place of exile for radicals and revolutionaries; even today the island's politics is considered to be outside the mainstream. Successive governments sent their dissidents there; in the forties and fifties it accommodated Communist and cultural rebels together with democrats who resisted the right-wing governments. These exiles prosyletised the locals and converted many to their left-wing and democratic views. Outsiders were mistrusted. Into this social mix in autumn 1957 came the 34-year-old Kevin, his 38-year-old wife Nancy, Elizabeth and the baby Ioanna.

They arrived at night by the weekly ferry. Since there was no harbour they were rowed ashore in a small fishing boat to Armenisti, a fishing village of a dozen or so families. Light was provided by lanterns and donkeys carried the luggage. Kevin thought it was Shangri La but it was not. They stayed less than a year.

After a few days they moved to Raches (the Greek for backbone) a village on the island's spine. At the time no road connected Armenisti with Raches. Kevin hired a mule for the baggage and walked with his family on the narrow footpath through thick woods. Anthony Papalas, historian, author of ***Rebels and Radicals*** visited Raches a few years after the Andrews and said that apart from the Italian occupation of 1941-43, the village's most memorable event was the 1660 visit of Bishop Georgirenes.

The Andrews' primitive stone house still stands on a hill outside the village. A wall inside the rented house divided the landlady, Karoutsos, from the tenant family. The Andrews' half had one room where the fireplace and rudimentary cooking facilities were separated from the beds by a curtain. Westerners often dream of living in a Greek village but winters in Greece can be cold and wet and the neighbours very, very hard. Greek villages can also be riven with petty jealousies, fights and intrigue, mutual suspicion and, above all, family self-interest. Stubbornness and a memory of ancient wrongs are often the only unifying qualities.

The landlady, obsessively mean and suspicious, watched the Andrews all day to ensure they did not damage her property. She agreed to provide logs for the fire but, to prevent extravagance, she entered their side of the house every morning, washed the fireplace and threw water on the fire to stop the nighttime logs from smouldering. And to prevent the fire being lit again until the ashes had dried out. Initially the roof leaked and rain came in over the fireplace. Prompted by Nancy Kevin complained. Someone mounted the roof and the leak stopped. Another leak started over the bed. When Kevin pointed this out the landlady explained she would simply have the old tiles moved around to avoid wasting money on new ones, take it or leave it. Why they accepted this is difficult to say. Sometimes westerners are over-respectful of local customs and traditions and allow themselves to be bullied and oppressed. It happens in Wales, it happens in Greece. Being a liberal can be painful.

Kevin's Greek was nowhere near perfect since he still spoke with an American-Athenian accent. Nancy found it very difficult to communicate with the islanders and it was Elizabeth who had to mediate with the landlady when Kevin was away, or with Tsanteri the shopkeeper in Armenisti. In winter, cabbage was the only vegetable available and even that was sporadic.

While Ioanna stayed at home Elizabeth attended the local school. Despite being a foreigner she experienced no hostility from the local children and her memories are pleasant. Nancy and Elizabeth, and the three-year-old Ioanna, walked down every week to Armenisti to cash cheques paid out from Nancy's inheritance. There are no secrets on Greek islands; the fact that money arrived regularly from abroad raised suspicions among the locals who could not understand why foreigners would prefer such primitive circumstances when they could be living comfortably in Athens. To add to these suspicions Nancy and Kevin often spent more money on cheese and wine in one excursion than a local family spent on food in a month.

Kevin often escaped from his paradise, sometimes for several weeks, visiting Athens or, supposedly, seeking better accommodation on Ikaria. Understandably Nancy felt isolated and took out her loneliness and bitterness on him when he returned. As the atmosphere deteriorated Elizabeth became Nancy's confidante, learning more about family life than was good for her. Another added burden was that Kevin also began to confide in Elizabeth, finding her more congenial than her mother. Fights were frequent. The children grew up quickly even if the adults did not. As always Kevin went outdoors to clear his mind and to escape the oppressive atmosphere. Sometimes he took Ioanna with him but these could be unpleasant excursions. Kevin sought to push himself to the limit and enjoyed physical suffering. Forcing Ioanna to do the same exceeded Spartan training and verged on abuse. Encountering an obstacle – a boulder, a stream, a patch of mud – too difficult for a young girl, Kevin, rather than offering help, goaded her on. If she failed, more often than not he abandoned her, returning to the house alone and in a tantrum.

In Greece January 6, *ta Fota,* the Light, is a day of celebration, a magic day. Each island, often each village, has its own customs but the basic ceremony consists of taking the cross out of the church and down to the sea to bless the waters. Sometimes children are dipped in the sea, sometimes they jump in, sometimes there are swimming races. Early in the New Year 1958 Ioanna had a cold and on January 6 Kevin, once again, was away. A silent band of women appeared at the door of the Andrews house wanting to throw Ioanna into the sea.

> *Ta nera einai aigasmena*
> The water is blessed. Give her to us, we will throw her into the sea and she will be made better.

They meant no harm by this local tradition but a petrified Nancy clung on to her youngest daughter as Elizabeth sought to translate what was going on.

Another event could have had a more sinister ending. Kevin and Nancy were having a fight at Armenisti. Ioanna wandered off to play by the sea. In Greece the mentally ill are rarely locked up or hidden away, they are cared for by the community. One such, a demented widow dressed in black with long straggling black hair, appeared by Ioanna's side.

> Come with me into the deep sea.

She took Ioanna's hand and walked into the waves. Soon she was waist deep and Ioanna, now floating, was being dragged out to sea. When Kevin and Nancy saw what was happening they stopped their fight and rushed down the beach to save their daughter. The widow ran off, leaving behind a trail of sea water.

Along one side of the Andrews' house was a lean-to shed, their study. Nancy used to sit there by lamplight, trying to write, mesmerised as fleas hopped over the pages. She and Kevin had agreed to take it in turns looking after Ioanna while the other wrote in the shed. They then exchanged their work for criticism. Maybe they had been impressed by the ability of Charmian Clift and George

Johnston to write successful novels together but nothing better illustrates Nancy's powerful hold over Kevin. Remarkably, Nancy considered herself the more gifted writer; she was after all a published poet and the daughter of E. E. Cummings. Kevin wrote very slowly and regarded each comma as vitally important. Daily he submitted what he had written to Nancy who added and crossed out bits, rewrote chapters and then handed it back.

In writing *The Flight of Ikaros* he made many concessions to maintain peace. He later claimed the first edition was inhibited by the politics of the time, notably Greece's series of right-wing governments and America's hysterical McCarthyism. This is difficult to sustain. As Kevin matured he convinced himself the original version was not his own work. More than twenty-five years later he rewrote the book resulting in the present literary and artistic triumph.

Kevin mixed with the local peasants, fishermen and shepherds. He played his *flogera* and enjoyed what he thought were intimate friendships. When Domna Samiou, the singer and musicologist, passed through Ikaria Kevin accompanied her in an impromptu concert at the edge of a ravine in the remote village of Aghios Polikarpos. Decades later villagers still remember her emotion and wonderful performance. Domna, unmarried and childless, felt close to Kevin and loved the children. She described Elizabeth as

> the most golden child of the world.

Kevin became absorbed in Raches and never missed a *panigyri* (village festival). Anthony Papalas interviewed local people about him in the nineties and they described him treking over a mountain peak during a rare snowstorm to attend a *vaptismos* (baptism) in a remote village. He loved local food and referred to the local dried mushrooms as *ambrosia*, food of the Gods. He often dressed like an Ikarian shepherd in a heavy sheepskin coat and, when he took the boat to and from Piraeus, he stayed on the deck playing the *flogera*, slyly drawing attention to himself in his understated, but deliberate, fashion. Greeks and tourists alike gathered around and children asked:

> *Pexe allo ena, barba.*
> Play another one uncle.

Dressing up as a local was an affectation, marking him out from the norm. Or perhaps he just felt happier in someone else's skin.

Kevin always revelled in the company of handsome, physical men. Despite his looks and his athleticism he felt inadequate with those who led physical lives and, foolishly, was driven to compete with them. He revered the *palikaria* with whom he associated. However in deliberately underplaying his class, intellect and education - attributes Greeks hold in high esteem - he raised suspicions among the more doubtful islanders. His closest friend on the island was Vangeli Tsanteris, the baker in Raches, the only survivor of fifteen *andartes* who had gone to Samos to fight the Germans in World War Two. Built like a heavyweight boxer and undoubtedly brave, he was also a quarrelsome bully, seeking to use his studied body language to overwhelm people. A sucker for physical prowess Kevin revelled in his company and the two spent many hours talking, composing songs and playing music. Greek villagers can be closed and difficult, hard and vindictive to one another but they are surprisingly open to foreigners. The Greek word for stranger, *xenos,* is also the Greek word for guest. If you are open-minded, seemingly incongruous friendships can be formed. Kevin felt he was very close to Vangeli and tried to impress him with his physical ability – not always successfully. On one occasion, noticing Vangeli walking alone along a sunken lane, Kevin attempted to surprise him by vaulting over a stone wall from an adjoining field. Unfortunately he caught his foot and fell headlong, cracking his head on the cobbles and amusing Vangeli. Such buffoonery didn't prevent Vangeli from providing Kevin with the friendship he craved. But for Nancy there was nobody.

Throughout his time on the island Kevin continued to suffer from fits and hysteria. His basic instincts, augmented by the side-effects of his powerful medication, prevented him from acting spontaneously or making up his mind. He had to think beforehand, weigh up alternatives. Fear of action drove him to anger, despair and, once again, talk of slashing his wrists.

Kevin loved the rugged conditions but Nancy, who bore the majority of the child rearing and the domestic work, was unhappy especially in winter when she was stuck in the house for long periods. Villagers still comment on her surly expression. The Andrews tried to cope with the poor accommodation, the cold, the rain and Kevin's unpredictable bipolar affliction, but by the spring of 1958 Nancy had had enough. Even Kevin recognised that while he enjoyed living on Ikaria more than anywhere else Nancy needed shops and books, good food and sophisticated company. In 1958 they decided to return to Athens. Nancy rarely got her own way but from then on Kevin became a city-dweller.

Kevin who wrote so well about Greek peasants and fishermen could be naive when dealing with them and hurt by their behaviour. He often took normal exchanges of supply and demand as generosity. Conversely he failed to understand that sudden acts of meanness were not intentionally wounding but were deliberate demonstrations of the limits of kinship or friendship. It was natural that Ikarians would suspect a man who spoke Greek with a foreign accent, dressed like a shepherd, had no obvious work, received regular cheques and was knowledgeable about the civil war. However, he was shattered when he learnt belatedly that some local people believed him to be a spy or even a *chafies* (police informer).

Thirty years later, talking to Marc Dubin about his time in Ikaria, Kevin said somewhat bitterly:

> Never be a pioneer. Never, ever be a pioneer.

TWENTY-THREE

Athens

By the spring of 1958, Kevin's second book on Greece had been accepted for publication but still needed a title. He floated several among his friends: *The Light is Alive* - too poetic, *A Journey into Greece* - attractive but not very exciting, *A Voyage from the Sun* - refers only to departure, before settling on *The Flight of Ikaros*. This appealed to his sense of history, linking an ancient myth to a modern civil war, and perhaps the journey of a naïve young man who fell to the sea while trying to follow his father. The appearance of the first edition began to cement his reputation and enabled him to take himself more seriously as a writer. *Castles of the Morea*, well reviewed, was not a big earner. *Ikaros*, also well reviewed, sold 8000 or so but wasn't a gold mine, leaving him disgusted that he had never managed to earn a living from his writing. This first edition of *The Flight of Ikaros* reveals little about the author except for one startling statement in the foreword when alluding to his own background:

> I do not belong to it.

There is no elaboration, however he does reveal his feelings for Greece and its people. The book is a

> partial reflection of an autobiography in the mirror of an alien landscape and the lives of those in it who by all accounts should have been alien as well. Precisely because they were not

> it is to them, with their ferocity and warmth of heart, their delicacy and impatience and also because none of them will read it... that this book is dedicated, with my thanks.

In June of 1958 the Andrews left Greece, went to London and for a while, under pressure from Nancy, considered settling in England. Having sought help from a London neurologist Kevin was told he had an anxiety neurosis. He now firmly believed that the number of epileptic attacks diminished when he was absent from Yvette and that his seizures were a reaction to a life-sucking mother. Later Nancy got the blame.

Yvette, 68 years old and increasingly a rather sad woman, had decided to move from the USA to England to be close to Chips Smallwood.

Rather than responding compassionately and gratefully to the fact that these two old people were finding comfort in being close, Kevin was affronted by Smallwood whom he blamed for not publicly recognising him as his son.

When Kevin was young his mother rejected him, later he felt smothered, even revolted, by her affection. Now, while he appreciated her independence and strength of character, he was riled by the way she fussed over Smallwood. Perhaps Kevin did not like being replaced.

Certainly he and, possibly, Smallwood were unaware that another name from the Peking days had re-entered Yvette's thoughts. In 1958, more than fifty years after the death of Perceval Landon, she was visited by his nephew Lt Col L H Landon. Unfortunately there is no record of their conversation.

Kevin could not settle in England and three months were enough. Suffocated by the country, and blaming his divided and uncertain inheritance, he had to live in Greece. He never asked what would be best for his wife and children and it is unlikely that Nancy pressed him. She sacrificed, he got his way. The family moved back to Athens in the autumn of 1958, living at 41 Loukianou, a little house half-way up Mount Lycabettus. Because it was on a steep hill the bottom floor had less space than the top. The views were wonderful although the best was from the toilet.

Even though he had a study downstairs Kevin lacked the peace he demanded in such a crowded household. When things were going well he worked obsessively at a large wooden table. When things were going badly he sat immobilised, sometimes week after week while the children tiptoed above him. Moodiness followed by bad temper were often a prelude to lengthy walks on nearby hills. Seeking a break from his wife and children he sometimes went further afield, disappearing for days on end into the Greek hinterland.

Soon he was reunited with the family of Nikiphoros the feverish young man he had adored and envied after they met in hospital and who - as he said so eloquently in *The Flight of Ikaros* - had more life than anyone he knew. Six years had passed since Nikiphoros's death. The reunion with the family was on the name day of Nikophoros's younger brother, Taxiarchi, and Kevin was honoured to be invited. However he did not fool himself. He knew his privileged background and comfortable life would always set him aside from the humble and steadfast Greeks he so admired. He no longer felt American but didn't yet feel Greek. He lived in Athens but had no sense of location.

Kevin was away when his mother died. Nancy sent a cable but he was far from telephone and telegraph and three days elapsed before he knew. He was stunned. The mother he had loved and grown to hate, the diminutive and beautiful woman who had filled his life was dead and he was alone. When he returned, a controlled and calm Nancy explained what had happened but could not comfort him.

Yvette had been holidaying in Spain with her cousin, Patricia Emmett, and another couple. They were trying to catch up with their friends when the car, driven by Patricia, left the road and hit a tree killing her and Yvette It was April 12 1959.

The Greeks say the umbilical chord is not cut at birth but when the mother dies. Kevin was about to feel the truth of this saying. There would be no more phone calls, no more visits, no more worries about Yvette's sanity, no more suppers together, no more explanations to make, questions to answer. A letter from Yvette, written and posted in Paris, arrived after her death. Then there was silence.

Kevin's brother George knew that Yvette wished to be cremated. This was not allowed in Catholic Spain so George arranged for her body to be transported to the USA. Her ashes were taken to the Dale cemetery in Ossining, New York, where they were placed next to the grave of George Borup the brother she adored. Her son George's journal says:

> so ended the eventful life of this altogether remarkable woman, star crossed, often troubled, very loving, misunderstood, beautiful and brave. Later in life she was alone and lonely, but surrounded by friends

However Kevin - the writer - never managed to record his thoughts on the death of his mother.

Pat Glenn, friend of both Kevin and Yvette during the New York days and now living in London, arranged a memorial service at Chelsea Old Church in London on June 9 1959. Nancy and Kevin made the journey. He was almost comatose but there was no funeral for him to attend, no graveside to visit and perhaps no closure.

From now on Kevin became increasingly obsessed with his roots, a subject which consumed his thoughts and his feelings, friendships and conversations. Few people have been so affected by their confused origins as Kevin Andrews. Maybe his mother died too soon after telling him about Smallwood, perhaps there had not been enough time to ask questions, to digest answers and above all to forgive.

Back in Athens Kevin and Nancy resumed their busy social life. Academics and intellectuals called in and invited them out. They went to embassy parties, British Council concerts and plays. Kevin had his music, his Greek friends and those he called the Old Hats, outsiders, mostly English, who he believed treated Greece as their own beer garden. These included such distinguished names as Xan Fielding and Paddy Leigh Fermor. Elitist and right-wing, they had known Greece for years, spoke the language fluently and, in Kevin's view, mistook the politeness of the people for devotion to the Raj. The survivors can still be found today though many have returned to the USA or to the UK. They tend to tell the same story: Kevin the amusing man - always up for a meal, Kevin the storyteller, Kevin who thought himself more Greek than the Greeks. But Kevin's love of Greece *was* different; his aim was to understand the lives of nomads, peasants and shepherds. He was critical of his first book *Castles of the Morea,* believing that it failed because his approach to history had been too mystical. But he liked *The Flight of Ikaros*. It did not exceed its bounds and he had been able to record, if intermittently, the physical and emotional reality of Greece. It succeeded because it was simple. Kevin sent copies to his father-in-law E. E. Cummings who expressed deep admiration for *Ikaros*. Kevin wrote regularly to Cummings, also keeping him abreast of progress on the novel. By January 1960 he was working on the second draft and Cummings was delighted. Nancy sent her father copies of her collection of poems, *Three Kings*. Again he was delighted but offered no critical comment to either.

Soon Nancy was pregnant again. Alexis was born in the spring of 1960 and Nancy, never robust, went into hospital in London in July, leaving Kevin in Athens to look after the children with the help of a nanny. When Nancy returned to Greece, Simon (aged 16) and Elizabeth (14) came to stay, the only time all four children were together. A photograph of them taken by Kevin carries the weight of history and an aura of sadness. This was not a lucky family.

During eleven years of marriage neither Nancy nor her previous husband Willard raised their voices; they were not used to expressing overt emotion. Nancy used to think it was good to hide emotion. Not now, however. Shouting, she decided, relieved tension and she and Kevin had noisy, even violent, fights. Kevin's temper was uncontrollable and he had a penchant for hurling things. Once he threw a full coffee-pot out of the dining room window, narrowly missing the Greek nanny who was walking the six-month-old Alexis in her arms. Coffee splashed all over them. After such explosions Kevin would return to normal, especially if there were visitors. For much of the time he was warm, loving, and funny, keeping the children amused with stories, games and jokes. But he found it difficult to understand a child's moral horizon. Echoing his own upbringing he judged them by his adult standards and treated them harshly. Nancy not only condoned such behaviour she encouraged it. I think Ioanna needs a spanking, she would say, and Kevin would grab the screaming child by the wrist, drag her across the floor as she tried to hold on to the furniture, and administer the beating. Nancy would stand by, watching, as Ioanna was hurled into her room, the shutters closed, and the door slammed shut and locked. There she would be left without dinner until the next morning. When the family were on holiday in Limni, Euboeia, Kevin threw Ioanna, aged five, out of the house because she had woken six-month-old Alexis early in the morning to play with him.

Get out of this house and never come back, he shouted. Ioanna was left to wander alone round the fields, almost falling down an uncovered cistern, before being accosted by a lone shepherd. Terrified of the dark, she finally made her way home and sat on the doorstep, crying, until the maid opened the door and asked her father if she might be let in. Friends rarely glimpsed this side of the man – he saved it for home.

At the end of October 1960 E. E. Cummings and his long-time lover, Marion Morehouse, visited Athens. The poet was worried about the health of his daughter and wanted to meet his new grandchildren. The couple stayed at the Hotel Grande Bretagne in the centre not far from the Andrews' home. Cummings and Nancy never had an expressive relationship while Marion was obsessively jealous about her lover. The Andrews didn't have a phone and, lacking a formal letter of invitation, Cummings and Marion refused to visit the house. Eventually Marion wrote a terse note to Nancy who trooped off to the Grande Bretagne with Kevin. Marion was there by herself, shouting about the plumbing, the cold, the hotel, the Greeks and the family. Kevin, always wary of angry women, took off with Nancy to the market where he bought a small electric fire for his in-laws. When they returned, Marion refused to open the door properly, snatched the heater without listening to Kevin's instructions and slammed the door in his face. The fire was plugged in incorrectly and blew the fuse. Nancy still had not seen her father. She wrote him a note. He responded. They came to lunch at the Andrews' although Marion was furious about the informality of having a

family lunch with grandchildren present.

A few days later all of them climbed Mount Hymettus to look at a Byzantine monastery. Kevin the expert took the opportunity to impress his father-in-law with his knowledge of Greek history.

Marion and Cummings left for Paris in mid-November. Nancy never saw her father again.

TWENTY-FOUR

The mutual friend

One great stroke of luck in writing this book was being introduced to Pat Glenn in 2006. I think we became friends; I hope so. For the sake of the narrative I have combined several interviews.

Pat is grey haired and wears glasses. She sits bright as a button, laughing and giggling, clutching her phone. She is 81 but her memory is as clear as ice. She likes to talk and this is good. For this is Pat Glenn, friend of Kevin Andrews, his mother Yvette and her lover Smallwood, a fountain of knowledge on most of the major characters in this book. We are in South Kensington, a pleasant room in a grand house where Pat has lived for 53 years. She says,

> Kevin used to sleep on that settee when he came to stay. Chips and Yvette met here too. It was a haven for them.

She has a lot to say but first she wants to ensure that nothing should be used to hurt anybody. That's easy - nothing she says could be used to hurt anybody. A kind, generous woman.

Can we start from the beginning? I say, thinking of the 1930s or 40s

Suddenly we are back to 1700 in New York when The Reverend Cutting is marrying Ann Livingston Heyward, someone called Dorothy DuBose is involved, as is a signature on the Declaration of Independence. Decades fly past and briefly we reach the civil war. Then, off again. Surely I must know that DuBose Heyward wrote

Porgy and Bess, not just the book but the libretto and nearly half the arias. And there's Pat's cousin, Charles Suydam Cutting, who lived with the Dalai Lama and wrote about it in *The Fire Ox and other Years* in 1940.

> It's around here somewhere, let me get it for you.

Somehow the book is never found.

> When did you first know Yvette?
> Always.

I am confused, but soon we are on common ground. Pat's mother was Constance Cutting the supposed interior designer who visited Yvette in Peking. She helped decorate the Manchu palace Yvette loved so much. Pat's parents, Constance and Heyward Cutting, took a world tour for their honeymoon, calling in at Peking to meet their east coast friends, Yvette and Roy Chapman Andrews. As a child Constance met the six-year-old Yvette for the first time at a train station outside New York, kicking off her shoes and, surprise, surprise, showing off. The two became lifelong friends.

Hayward even had a contract with the American Museum of Natural History to collect animals. Dead ones. They knew Smallwood, for Peking was a small place. In the autumn they returned to New York and in December Pat's brother was born.

Pat never knew her father. He was killed in an car accident in Locust Valley in 1926 while his wife and three young children were in France with his mother. Constance remained close friends with Yvette, and Pat inherited that friendship, even adopting Yvette with the title:

> My illegitimate mother.

Later, Kevin said, things changed and Pat became Yvette's mother.

Pat Glenn never met Roy Chapman Andrews but Yvette described him for her.

> He was very sexy, sexually demanding, rapacious.

I think Yvette probably was too, I offer. Well yes, Pat responds, that's what they had in common. But it was too much for Yvette. So they parted.

I question Pat about Kevin's parentage. I know RCA was in Peking about the time Kevin was conceived and I think Perceval Landon was there too. Pat says,

> It definitely wasn't RCA, it was Smallwood.

I say,

> But she was really in love with Landon.

I know, says Pat laughing. Years later she asked Yvette: What did you think you were doing? Yvette's matter-of-fact innocence is almost audible in Pat's voice as she mimics her friend:

> It's perfectly possible to be in love with two people at the same time, you know.

Pat says that although Perceval Landon was the love of her life, and she considered herself engaged to him, Yvette believed only Smallwood could be the father of her second son.

We talk about Smallwood and my prejudices are smashed aside. He was a super guy. They were together until she died.

> I had to tell him she'd died. I couldn't explain over the phone because of his wife. Come round and see me. Something terrible has happened. He came here, sat in that settee and I told him.

Another picture emerges. Not The Bounder, not a fly-by-night taking advantage of a beautiful woman after the break-up of her marriage to his friend. A new Chips Smallwood: a man in his seventies, crumpled on a settee, the love of his life dead, a passion of nearly forty years at an end, a secret no longer worth keeping. He is devastated.

Smallwood and Yvette were together all those years from 1923. In Peking, Oxford, New York and London they had dates, assignations, stolen time. When they couldn't meet they wrote to each other. Smallwood converted to Catholicism when he married and could not divorce. He wanted to protect his wife, Margot, a decent woman, and Yvette tried to do so too. A *ménage à trois* with all three behaving helpfully, sensitively. Smallwood and Yvette became mature people in love.

By the time Yvette died Smallwood had acknowledged Kevin as his son. They had met and talked. Smallwood even visited Nancy and Kevin in Switzerland. The photographs show a white-haired man with his grandchildren. Kevin wanted to tell everyone he had a new father but Smallwood begged him not to:

> Please do not disturb my family.

Kevin took this very badly. Another rejection.

Was Yvette a Catholic? Oh no. We were into mystic religion. Does Gurdjieff mean anything to you? We were in a group that included Patricia Emmett, Yvette's cousin.

In the late thirties Yvette lived at Tudor Cottage, on the large estate of Lura Howard near Witley, Surrey. In 1939 she moved to New York to escape the coming war. Strolling through Manhattan she bumped into Constance:

> Thank God you are here.

And soon she was living with the Cuttings.

By 1942 Kevin, then at Harvard, was a close friend of Lucien Kinsolving, later to become a distinguished diplomat and Arabist. Kevin and Lucien drank, sometimes in bouts, and Yvette worried about Kevin's drinking. Another of Kevin's good friends was Robbie Cabot and the two enlisted together in the US Army.

Nominally in censorship during the war, Yvette was a spy of sorts. As she read German POW letters, her knowledge of German and her friendship with senior members of German society meant she understood what needed to be cut. Also she was able to keep an eye on what messages were being transmitted to whom.

Later Yvette and Pat shared a flat at 149 E 75 street. Pat had a bedroom and sitting room at the front and Yvette a little bed-sitter at the back. Yvette, always a smoker, kept taking Pat's matches. Pat left a box tied down with cotton on the table. She laughs as she tells me how Yvette grabbed the box, turned, and matches were scattered over the floor.

Working in sales at Steuben Glass Yvette tried to sell an (English accent) vase to a customer who wanted to look at another (American accent) vase.

When does a varze become a vaize? asked the customer. When it costs more than $100, said Yvette. And Pat laughs again.

When Chips and Margot were trying to make a living in the USA Margot turned up unannounced at the shared New York flat. Pat, thinking fast, asked her to wait in the sitting room and went to the toilet via Yvette's bedroom, snatching Smallwood's photograph from Yvette's desk and hiding it in the lingerie drawer. Later Yvette arrived and the three of them had a civilised conversation about the old days in Peking.

Pat liked Kevin. She told me he was kind, had a sense of humour, and played tricks and games. She laughs again as she recalls how, in 1946, on a sunny day near Christmas, she was sitting in the window seat of her flat, recuperating as best she could after several weeks in hospital. There was a commotion outside; in the street Kevin was marching up and down the sidewalk playing the bagpipes. He had come to cheer her up.

Pat saw Kevin as a nervy, handsome, charming young man but also unhappy and volatile. A difficult man, but always laughing. He was interested in sex and talked to his mother about it. Pat says,

> Kevin was a marvellous friend to me, but a late developer. He took a long time to grow up.

As the conversation jumps about Pat reveals something startling. Contrary to what I had been told, RCA knew he was not Kevin's father early on. Hélène (Nana), the Swiss nurse, told him. And, in one of the mysteries and coincidences surrounding Kevin Andrews, a friend of Yvette's – Peter Norton? We cannot be sure. - was on a train in France, perhaps in 1931, and overheard a man and a woman talking English. The friend recognised RCA's voice and guessed the woman was Nana. Incredibly, Nana was telling RCA he was not Kevin's father. When this was relayed to Yvette she felt betrayed by Nana as, of course, RCA felt betrayed by Yvette.

When Kevin joined the army, Yvette was worried yet also proud, keeping an album of cuttings about his unit. George enlisted as a pilot in the USAF. A nice man, she was proud of him too. But kept no album. Yvette worked hard in New York but was not well off. She worshipped Kevin, she dreamed of Smallwood and she kept her sense of humour.

Pat and Yvette travelled to Europe together, meeting friends and relatives. Once they went as far as Athens, visiting Kevin and his family. Sisi, by now Queen Consort of Greece, was busy with a state visit and could not see them at first, although the three of them got together when things quietened down. It was Pat who laughingly told me that the Andrews' house on Lycabettus had a toilet with the best view of the Athens skyline. Although illness restricted Pat's mobility, Kevin insisted they walk to the Parthenon; he helped her up the hill and carried her inside. And then there was that terrible time when Yvette had a breakdown in Lura's villa near Nice.

From 1958 Yvette lived in a little flat on the Kings Road, Chelsea, then an artistic rather than a fashionable area. She had Smallwood and friends, went to the theatre and the ballet, and sometimes Kevin came to stay. She and Kevin had a good relationship, perhaps over-close but not cloying.

Yvette's death was a complete shock. She was on holiday in Spain with her cousin, Patricia Emmett. Friends accompanying them had gone ahead and were waiting in a restaurant. Told about an accident they went back up the road and saw the car in a ditch. There was just one tree and the car had hit it at speed. Patricia in the driving seat had multiple injuries. Yvette was thrown clear but died of internal bleeding. The London police told Pat the next morning. The Kings Road flat had been sealed but Pat talked her way in and, still the loyal friend, removed diaries and pictures that might link Yvette to Smallwood.

Smallwood was at Yvette's memorial service, Nancy and Kevin too, he suffering terribly from *petit mal*, one attack succeeding another, sometimes at fifteen-minutes intervals. He neither visited the doctor nor took medication. Nancy and Pat eventually persuaded him to go to a specialist. These may not be fits, he was told, just nervous seizures, but they have to be stopped or your brain could suffer permanent damage Kevin took his medication and the seizures stopped

Pat says he had major seizures in Greece under the Junta. He behaved erratically. A difficult man, but he loved his children.

I asked Pat about Nancy. She was used to money. She hated her mother's beauty and wanted to look plain. Quiet, little Miss Prim. When she and Kevin started to fight she took the children away. Even so she could not give her children goodnight kisses. Her mother was cold to her when she was a child and she found it difficult to show affection

I get up to go. Pat was looking forward to Glyndebourne and going to the country to see a horse or two. Do you like horses? I asked.

Yes. When I was young I rode all the time.

The illness Pat suffered in 1946 was polio though she did not once mention it to me. Her health has deteriorated and she is now confined to a wheelchair. A wonderful woman.

TWENTY-FIVE

Domna's story

Domna Samiou is the grande dame of Greek music and, since the fifties, she and her teacher, Simon Karras, have fought to protect it against western pop culture. The Balkans is a kaleidoscope of musical influences and Greece is its fountain. Once each region, each island and even each village had its own style and influences; Domna and people like her have worked hard to preserve these traditions. Greece owes a lot to her campaigning spirit and her fierce pride. Her energy has often led her into conflict with the state and its institutions. In March 2003, at the Hall of Music in Thessaloniki, she performed traditional carnival songs. These are particularly bawdy and when they were subsequently broadcast on the state-run TV station ET3 right-wing politicians made a formal complaint. Facing a jail sentence Domna's response was typical:

> Let them come and arrest me.

I wrote to Domna Samiou and was surprised to hear her voice on my mobile phone. She speaks no English and my Greek is not of the best but we managed.

In the Samiou front room I find myself looking at a small, grey-haired woman trying to remember dates and occasions. She is approaching eighty, has had a hard and difficult life but is eager to talk. Shelves and glass cases are loaded with awards, trophies and musical instruments - a lute, a *lyra*, books on music, CDs, statuettes and gold plaques. The instruments are used, the books are read, the music is alive; this is a home not a museum. And it seems she met Kevin when he first came to Greece in the forties.

She says a group used to gather twice a week in central Athens in a two-storey building with a wooden staircase.

We had a big room, there was a blackboard with chalk. We were there to sing and to dance. I was a student of Karras, I was there to dance, but we sang in the choir too. Songs from the old times, songs from Byzantium, not just the well-known ones, but from Constantinople, the Black Sea, everywhere. One day we were introduced to a new person, Kevin, an American, but not like other foreigners. He seemed Greek. He sang in the choir. He toured with us. We went to other places. We performed at the ceremonies: October 28, May 29, the anniversary of the 1453 war against the Turks. Poor Greece: so many struggles, so many anniversaries. We celebrated our victories when the Germans were here and at the time of the colonels. It was important for us. For Greece.

She knew him for thirty years and then they drifted apart; she does not remember why.

Kevin was a big man, Domna continues, blue eyes, fair hair. He was tall, maybe four years older than I was, *me alli parousia* (with a certain presence). Kevin played the *gaida,* a kind of bagpipes.

The *gaida* differs from the *tsambouna* bagpipes they play on Karpathos. He played the *flogera* and made his own versions of this shepherd's flute. Domna adds,

Kevin was a very… shy… man.

She makes a theatrical gesture of a true performer. She mimes a man standing with his collar up, shows him taking out the flute from a pocket inside his jacket and playing with the instrument concealed inside his coat. A brilliant performance.

He was *semnos anthropos, evgenikos* (a modest man, courteous), *palikari* special praise in Greece.

He suffered from his illness. When an attack came he did not fall down but stood there, holding onto something, and we knew he was in another world. When it passed he sat down and held his head in his hand, totally exhausted.

Domna and Kevin were very close. He sometimes referred to her as a little peasant girl but not to her face. I ask if she met Nancy.

> Oh yes we met Nancy but she was different.

Domna makes a cuddling motion with her arms.

Kevin loved everyone, she says, and you see the man putting his arms around his friends and colleagues.

> But Nancy was cold to us. Distant. Jealous.

I wait but she does not want to say more. Our conversation drifts on but there is a language barrier. I begin to say my farewells. I thank her, collect my things, stand up and she shows me to the door. Then a strange thing happens. She says,

> Stop there, under the light. Turn that way.

I turn and she touches my chin. Intimately. She is turning an interview into a drama.

> You are like him between here and there.

She touches my nose.

> But his nose was bigger and his hair started here.

She touches my forehead.

> Has nobody said this before?
> Nobody.
> Well you are.

It is raining out in the street. I am pleased to be told I look like Kevin. And strangely moved.

TWENTY-SIX

Karpathos

Karpathos is a long, narrow Greek island between Crete and Rhodes. It is wild and mountainous, with plenty of pine cover, and is defined by deep ravines and steep cliffs tumbling into an often violent sea. Diafani is a small, sheltered village towards the north on the east coast. Olymbos, an older, larger village is an hour or more away by foot. Culturally, economically and socially the two villages are indistinguishable. Olymbos and Diafani people are to be found in Iran, Malaysia, Africa, Europe and, of course, the USA where they gather in New Jersey and above all Baltimore. Wherever they go they maintain their traditions, their customs, music and poetry; wherever they are they refer to Olymbos simply as *to chorio* (the village).

These days there is a road, partially paved, up to Olymbos, Spoa and the developed south of the island. Telephones and the internet provide external links. Diafani now even has a shop and, for several months of the year, there are tourists. For the past ten years Diafani has had a harbour which shelters fishing boats from the *sirocco* in the winter and provides a landing place for the weekly ferries. It's a pleasant place in the summer but winter is another story. Many villagers go to Rhodes, Athens or the USA to work or for holidays.

It was different fifty years ago. Many of the houses, now standing empty, were homes to large families and the schools were full.

There were no bars and restaurants, only the *cafeneion,* managed by Irene in her bossy, no-nonsense style, much as her daughter Anna runs the place today. In 1961 when Kevin Andrews arrived, Diafani was truly isolated and perhaps that was why he came. There were no roads in the north; you walked or you went by boat. If you walked and had a load you used a donkey. If it was a long journey or the load was heavy you took a mule. Apart from the odd wheelbarrow there were no wheels in the north. There never had been. The donkey paths and footpaths did not encourage such new fangled inventions. Donkey tracks ran from Diafani to Avlona and on to Tristomo and Vragounda; another went south from Olymbos to Spoa and from there you could walk on to Pigadia. Some tracks were surfaced with stone by the Minoans, others were added more recently, some survive today. The north of the island is still covered by footpaths radiating out from Olymbos.

Karpathos weather is unpredictable. There was no safe harbour on the east coast then and the boats were small. In bad weather you sometimes had to choose a beach, ride through the surf, leap out with your companions and haul your *barca* out of the pursuing waves. You then walked home to Olymbos. You followed a footpath and every beach in the north has one. The boats in those days were made from pine and they were, and are, beautiful objects. Several still exist, nearly 100 years old. Powered by oar and sail they are well used and well looked after. In the old days village men were immensely strong and could row all day. Outboard motors only arrived in the fifties. The most reliable was the Seagull, a British make dating from World War Two. Several Seagulls still lie around the village, unused and discarded.

For decades the only link with the outside world was by *caique.* Even after I arrived, the *Panormitis,* a small passenger ferry, was met out at sea by fishing boats. Depending on the wind she stayed perhaps a kilometre offshore while passengers, goats and goods were loaded and unloaded. The men in the little boats shouted greetings or swore at the ferry's captain when he allowed his ship to turn into the wind and exposed them to the rough seas. The *Panormitis* arrived every Friday 14.15 sharp, connecting Diafani for a few minutes with the outside world. Then, with a cow's hoot, saluted the village and left for Pigadia and Kassos, returning later that day, on her way back to Rhodes. Now there is a harbour and something has gone from village life.

The people haven't changed. They can be hardworking, hospitable, stubborn yet open to ideas, although there are also those who believe in the fates, who curse and are cursed by the evil eye, are suspicious of strangers and are remote from the twenty-first century. Kevin came to Greece to meet such people. He first arrived in Diafani in April 1961 on the 130-ton *caique,* the *Agios Yorgios,* that plied regularly between Rhodes and Karpathos.

Older people remember him with affection. He is referred to as *palikari.* Having loved the place and the people he is regarded as one of them. On arrival he was adopted by the Balaskas family, hardworking people, suspicious, but smart and generous. They found lodgings for him and made certain he had plenty to eat.

Soon after there was a big *fassaria* (fuss). A woman was sick. She had just come from Saria, the wilder island to the north, and was in agony. There was a doctor in Olymbos but he refused to come down to Diafani so they carried her up the mountain to him. He said it was worms, others thought a miscarriage. They talked about renting a *caique* to transfer her to Rhodes but they hadn't enough money. In the morning she was carried to the regular Tuesday *caique* for Pigadia and there at the harbourside she died – probably of appendicitis. They returned her body on the same *caique.* Kevin was shocked and excited by these events. Diafani was isolated, another paradise.

The villagers found him a place to rent in the *Vounara* (Big Mountain) area, near the old school behind my present house. The views are spectacular. Each day he walked the paths, climbed the mountains, edged along the cliff tops. When he came across farmers and shepherds they asked him to pause, share some cheese and olives, drink the good water. He sat with them, as I have done, with a sense of privilege. Sometimes when he returned to the village he found – as I do - half a fresh loaf, some salt fish, some honey left near his door by his neighbours. He cooked by himself and then walked down to the *cafeneion* to catch the news of the day. When he arrived at Olymbos for the first time he was stunned by the panorama of the village; he told the locals it had fallen from the sky,

> encircled with chapels on every rock and spur, to avert the entry of the evil spirit.

Diafani and Olymbos are immersed in traditions and festivals, some of them ancient, even pre-Christian, some of them unique. When invited to these celebrations Kevin gravitated towards musicians of which there are plenty in *to chorio*. He impressed them with his ability to play the *flogera* which is not indigenous to the Dodecanese. Not knowing he had already mastered the *gaida*, and even the Scottish bagpipes, villagers were astonished when he learned the *tsambouna* in only an hour.

In Olymbos music is not regarded as performance but as ceremony. You do not play just for fun but as part of a wedding, baptism or birthday party. Music is integrated with the tapestry of the village, woven into the language, the *mantinades* verses, the women's clothes, the local food, geography and family names. A great musician is not just technically proficient, he must also have the spirit and empathy to create *kefi* (good feeling). Such a *meraklese* (one who can change the mood) at the right moment will lead the ensemble through feelings of despair and sadness, fun and happiness, joy and ecstasy. One of Kevin's friends, Ilias Minatsis, was a shepherd, a renowned *meraklese* and *tsambouna* player. He died a few years ago but I am friendly with his son, like his father a primitive man, wild from birth, a law unto himself. Kevin wrote a *mantinada* for Ilias. It describes walking up a steep 1000 m mountain, near Olymbos, to the *panigyri* of Profitis Elias.

> *Stin Agelia ebriska se pousi kai fortuna*
> *Den elpiza Elias mou na'akouw tyn tsambouna.*
> (On St Elias I went up through clouds and storms
> I did not expect Illias mine to hear the horns).

Often Kevin walked up the valley from Diafani to Olymbos Then, as now, there were more *cafeneion* in the higher village and more of an opportunity to find a party or someone to talk to. Illness restrained Kevin's alcohol intake to a glass or two of *retsina, ouzo or raki*. There were no hotels in Olymbos so he slept overnight in a cell in a building used as an *exoria* (place of exile) for the state's opponents. Later it became a prison and now it is *To Anemos*, a quiet and comfortable boutique hotel. In the morning Kevin walked down to Diafani again or perhaps northwards to Avlona, then Tristomo, Steno and back along the cliff tops to Vananda and Diafani. Exhilarating views, a wild sea, eagles, buzzards, sea birds and, in the summer months, Eleanora falcons, exciting raptors that migrate from Madagascar to breed on the steep cliffs of Karpathos and Saria.

On the first visit to Karpathos Kevin was driven by a wish to escape from his wife after yet another violent argument.

> Why don't you take me then, since you like it so much?
> I would if you were twenty years younger.

He was content to be alone, even telling villagers that he and his wife were separated. This would have been news to Nancy who waited for him with the children in Athens. For a while he recognised he was better suited to write about the decline of a rural community than the manners of intellectual élites. So he stopped struggling with his novel and wrote about real people in their spectacular landscape. His prose, unpublished, is evocative and sparse. Karpathos is,

> the last place in the world where human figures are still beautiful. Like trees in a landscape....

He returned to Athens for a few days in May when he and Nancy resumed circling one another, probing, questioning, answering the wrong questions, ignoring the difficult answers.

Soon he was back in Diafani, sitting in the seat where I sometimes sit at night outside the *cafeneion* looking northwards at

> the grey, warm, luminous shore echoing to a low rhythm.

At the festival of St John, still held in Vrougounda, he was moved by the procession of women winding down the mountainside, carrying provisions on their heads for the three-day event. He heard the *mantinades* of the young men, the flight of the *lyra*, the rhythms of the *lauto* (stringed instrument similar to a guitar) and the primitive wail of the *tsambouna*. He watched people dancing in circles, slowly at first, (the *kato horo*), followed by the gradual evolution of pace and mood into the much faster *pano horo*. Then as now the dances were performed outside on the *alona* (threshing floors), the only flat spaces in a rocky landscape. Before Minoan times these spaces gave rise to the Greek custom of dancing in circles.

Kevin left his paradise in October for Athens, once again to struggle with the ever confused novel, aptly named *The Jumblies*. He was pleased to see his children. Alexis, now 20 months, and Ioanna who amused him by asking: Why, when you get to the end of a book, is it written: The end? He explained that this marked the end of the book. Using a child's logic she explained, you know that there isn't any more left, the next page is empty.

Kevin Andrews loved north Karpathos, embraced the people and became *fisiognomia* (celebrity). He wore local clothes, sang the songs, partied with the men and helped the old ladies. Above all he loved to sit and look at the sea and, when it was decided that a coming storm could no longer be ignored, he helped the men lift the anchors and haul the heavy fishing boats up the beach away from the surf. Bending his back, chanting the songs, pulling the boats, he felt alive and free. He felt he belonged.

Kevin returned to Karpathos several times and tried to get Nancy to join him. He phoned her from Diafani's single telephone exchange in the front room of a private house, arguing and cajoling her while half the village listened. Once she decided to come and although Kevin was short of money he got one of the many carpenters to make three beds for his family. But the gods decreed otherwise. Nancy once got as far as Rhodes with her daughter Elizabeth, only to encounter bad weather which prevented the *caique* from sailing. The storms lasted for days, Nancy grew impatient and she and Elizabeth returned to Athens. Not wanting to waste his money Kevin decided to take the beds to Athens, but the sea was still rough and the *caique's* itinerary irregular. In those days the villagers watched to see it appear round the headland then dashed with their cases, goats, grannies, fish and onions out to the mole . Kevin is said to have made this journey three or four times, carrying his heavy beds down the steep hill only to carry them back up again when the *caique* failed to stop. Finally he sat damp and disconsolate in the *cafeneion* to be asked by a small boy:

> Where's your *flogera* now?

I know the small boy, now a middle-aged man. He told me Kevin did not laugh at the question but he did receive a cuff from his father.

Although people loved this strange man, their very nature made some suspicious. They could not find it within themselves to trust an American who arrived from nowhere and seemed to know everything. Forty-five years after his arrival I asked a friend of mine if he knew Kevin Andrews. He thought for a while then echoed the people of Ikaria,

> Oh, yes. Kevin the spy.

He never explained who Kevin was spying for.

TWENTY-SEVEN

Respect the sea

The only link between Diafani and mainland Greece in the sixties was the 60-ton *Sebasti*. Enlightened tourists might call such a boat a *caique* but I am assured the proper name is *karaboskaro.* Black-and-white or sepia photographs of such craft adorn the walls of *cafeneia* and tourist bars in the islands. A photograph of Pigadia harbour, in the south of Karpathos, taken before World War Two, shows forty such vessels They transported cargo all over the Eastern Aegean, even to Turkey, Egypt and the Lebanon. Equipped with one mast and two sails (*floko* - forward, *pani* - main sail - aft) they had powerful diesel engines. I have a model of one before me now, crudely carved from a solid lump of wood, gaudily painted by an old man from Olymbos, aimed at tourists. They carried freight and livestock and brought news and gossip from the outside world. *Sebasti* took sheep and goats to Piraeus and, on return, fetched cement for the building boom that was starting .

One voyage, still talked about in Diafani, illustrates the relationship between the local people and Kevin Andrews. I have interviewed the three survivors, Nikos Meleissis, Nikos Orfanos and Vasillis Protopapas. Also present were the captain, Vasillis Sofolis, Manolis Kritikos and Kevin's close friend Ilias Minatsis. Nikos Orfanos was twelve at the time; the others were in their thirties, on their way to work in Athens, Germany or, in one case, Canada.

Sebasti was not licensed to carry passengers but friends of the captain were allowed. On May 4 1961 the north wind, *meltemi,* blew strongly, about seven or eight Beaufort, but Vasillis Sofolis was eager to go. I never met Vasillis but I know his family: good people who understand the sea. It was Ilias Minatsis who invited Kevin along for the trip. So six men and a boy set off in the 70 ft boat, chugging up the coast, sails furled, engine straining against the oncoming waves. The first destination was the small Dodecanese island, Astipalia. At Karpathos' furthest northern point *Sebasti* turned west through the narrow straights of Steno, separating Saria and Karpathos. Until then Kevin stood on deck facing forward, balancing with difficulty as the boat bounced about, his back on the mast, jotting impressions of the sounds, the sights, the light, the birds and the people.

> The peacock sea. The radiation of light in fans white, green, glittering purple....
>
> light sliding over water, water sliding, bouncing up the rocks; sinking pouring back into the foam.

The weather was very bad and the men called Kevin in to the little cabin to take shelter. He heard,

> The soft put-put-put-put of the kerosene lantern swinging on its hook;
>
> the wind across the hatch....
>
> the giggle and slap of waves along the prow.

It was dangerous to be on deck but the boat was sturdy, the captain knew what he was doing and there were experienced men to help. The technique, then as now, was to butt into the sea, heading into the wind or, if possible, slightly off-wind. Turn beam on and there's a risk of getting wet or even capsizing. At that wind strength from the north the waves are up to three metres with white furies from the tips. By now the captain knew he could not make Astipalia and decided to run for Astakida, rocky islands some thirty kilometres or so west of Karpathos. It took five hours; four hours heading north-north-west into the wind and, after turning south following a lull, another hour at speed with the wind astern.

Suddenly Nikos Orfanos, who had been fiddling with the engine to stop it smoking, appeared from below. Kevin was amazed.

> *Apo pou erthes?*
> Where did you come from?

Nikos explained and Kevin shared some chocolates with the *pitsiriki* (street boy), now a prominent local entrepreneur.

The three small Astakida islands provided shelter from the wind. *Sebasti* was secured with anchors and ropes. The men were safe, they had water and a little food. Kevin heard,

> The growl of the anchor chain....
>
> the creak of the stays...
>
> the booming foam there on the rocks.

The weather was still bad the next day. Some of the men busied themselves: catching crabs, baiting hooks, fishing for *scarros* the much prized local fish. Others collected salt to preserve the catch and Nikos Meleisses built a pit with stones and gravel as a fireplace for cooking. Kevin went off on his own.

I have been in similar situations. The people around are competent, they have generations of experience, you like them and you want to impress them, to be recognised as an equal. Sometimes you do something stupid. Kevin did something stupid. He went for a swim. This might have been excusable had he stayed within the shelter of the three islands. But he swam in the open sea. As he made his way back a wave smashed him on the rocks. Then another wave, then another - four or five times. Kevin was a strong swimmer but a blow to his head and he could have drowned. The men were unaware of this until they saw Kevin, slowly walking towards them, dazed and dripping blood. The first thing Greeks do in these situations is blame the victim. They shouted at Kevin then, realising he was badly hurt, went to his aid. Nothing was broken but his back was badly lacerated and stones were embedded beneath the skin. With Kevin lying face down on a sail Vasillis Protopapas picked the stones from his battered body, cleaned him up, stopped the flow of blood and applied a heavy dose of iodine. This hurt and made Kevin cry with pain. The relationship with these men he was trying to impress was not strong enough for the intimacy of tears. He was ashamed. Village people are relentless, they are angry, they want to know why you were so stupid. They show no sympathy at the time even though they feel it. Later they made their peace, explaining they were angry because they were worried. He was good and brave but, they insist, he must learn to respect the sea.

There was time for all this. They were four days in Astakida before the waves and the wind subsided. They fished, split the fish, rubbed them with salt and dried them in the sun. They cooked and talked. Kevin was silent for most of the time, sleeping, taking notes, playing the *flogera,* until once again they set off for Astipalia, calling in for fuel since the north wind had taken its toll on consumption.

Kevin went ashore and did his best to show he belonged to this group of hard men born to the sea. He bought them a large *stamna,* a clay pot of wine, which they took back to the boat and drank. Kevin did not drink much, one glass to their three or four, they tell me. When they reached Piraeus, Kevin went home to Mount Lycabettus. He said little to his family about the wounds but he revelled in the attention. The villagers slept on board *Sebasti*, helping out while they arranged their lodgings, found work, or bought plane or train tickets. After three days Kevin returned. He invited them to a party. They drank wine and ouzo and ate *mezedes*, the nibbles Greeks love so much.

The men of the village liked Kevin. But, they insisted, you must respect the sea.

TWENTY-EIGHT

Woman in a rage

Back in Athens, still living at 41 Likianou, Nancy and Kevin continued to raise the children, deal with summer visitors, socialise with a narrow section of society consisting of American and British expats, and fray one another's nerves.

Kevin's spent many hours on the ground floor in his private domain. This consisted of two rooms and a kitchen with weathered blue doors and windows, bare plank floors, orange-rose wash walls and a white ceiling. Furniture included bookcases, tables, a bed for afternoon naps and a rocking chair. One wall surprisingly carried a huge bullfighting poster:

Tres Grandes Espetaculos Taurinos

Outside was a lush garden, with orange, lemon and pomegranate trees, a grapevine, oleanders, geraniums and roses. And, unusually for Athens, a lawn. All this was achieved with the help of Andreas, the American School gardener. Access to Kevin's rooms and the garden was via a blue gate set in a whitewashed wall.

Kevin had no direct contact with Corinna for several years following her stay in Switzerland. He flooded her with letters which brought no response; Christmas presents also disappeared into the void. Corinna alternated between boarding school in Germany and home in Athens but Kevin was only able to garner clues about her wellbeing from friends and relatives. He did not see her again until she settled with her family near Mount Lycabettus when she started secretly to visit the Andrews. Nancy tried to be kind and receptive but sometimes showed her feelings. Perhaps to provoke her, Kevin liked to pretend they were all one happy family. On one occasion he brought in Corinna, unannounced, for lunch. Nancy laid the extra place but a visitor told me she was noticeably cold and withdrawn.

In September 1962, to escape the summer heat, the family stayed at Porto Raphi, a small coastal resort forty kilometres from Athens. Judith Binder, a spirited but little-known archaeologist, was staying in Kevin's den at the house on Mount Lycabettus, watering the garden and keeping the place clean. A young girl arrived with a telegram for Nancy. Judith took it to Porto Raphi where the Andrews learned that E.E. Cummings had died in America on September 3 from a cerebral haemorrhage. Nancy had become very close to her father and letters between Cummings and the Andrews show a light touch and a deal of affection. Both Kevin and Nancy were moved by Cummings' death They were genuinely fond of the man.

The reappearance of Corinna and the death of Cummings triggered Kevin's tendency to discuss personal problems with all and sundry: questions of identity, difficulties he and Nancy had with her parents, the belief that Smallwood had let him down. He could not write, he said, because

> I do not know who I am.

But, rather than writing about Greece, he wasted time on his novel. He floundered, blaming his mother, his wife and his home life and ended up with little to show for the hours spent. One perceptive observer asked:

> In his writing where is a hero or heroine who seizes hold of our imaginations?

then pointed to the heart of the matter:

> Whom did Kevin truly care for, who mattered more than himself to him?

And the answer is simple: Kevin could only observe and write about Greece and the Greeks.

The obsession with identity grew over the best part of three decades eventually filling his whole horizon. For a while in the early sixties close friends thought Kevin to be unbalanced, given his lack of productivity and his self-obsessions. He had been interested in Christianity as a schoolboy and on subsequent brief occasions. Now he revisited it again, focusing his attention on the Lord's Prayer, analysing its meanings and nuances over and over. Ioanna was required to include it in her prayers every night while kneeling on the hard wooden floor. Kevin loved the ritual of Christianity and, at Christmas and Easter, regaled the children with readings from the Bible in both English and in Greek. During Lent the children were forbidden ice cream or the use of swings in children's playgrounds. Kevin predictably concentrated on the opening words of the Lord's Prayer, Our Father (*Pateras Mon).* He argued with friends that the possessive pronoun was irrelevant and *Pateras* carried all the required meaning - especially true for him since he believed he had been denied his birthright.

Kevin had many friends among the Greeks and expatriates in Athens: artists, adventurers, scholars, academics. When he needed to he left home and was sometimes away in the mountains for weeks. It was not so easy for Nancy. Although her Greek was grammatically flawless she spoke it flatly, with no feeling for the language, and had few friends. On top of this I was told she had to put up with

> being inspected by friends of Kevin who had no interest in Nancy as an individual, with her own history and personality but only to see if she belonged in their culture.

As a result:

> She kept quiet about her own life. Kevin's coterie had no idea who she was nor had the slightest sympathy for her plight. They did not recognize her isolation nor respond to her sensitivity

Of course she had children to look after. Not that this provided sufficient solace. By now she recognised that life in Greece was not the glamourous adventure Kevin had painted. She spent hours in a darkened room, weeping and crying. Elizabeth and Ioanna did their best to comfort her until Elizabeth, the elder, eventually left for an American boarding school and to be close to her father, Willard.

Both Kevin and Nancy were too consumed by their thoughts and feelings to protect the children from their mood swings and the ensuing arguments. Their relationship offered extremes but rarely peace. Somehow they found the courage to admit their problems and sought help from a London psychoanalyst, Dr. E Graham Howe, one of the most important men in his field in mid-twentieth century Britain. Howe was friendly with Krishnamurti the philosopher and exerted considerable influence on both R. D. Laing and Alan Watts. Kevin and Nancy visited him in London and Kevin saw him regularly over several months. Kevin had many problems but the one Howe seems to have helped him identify was Woman in a Rage. Kevin always had problems with women older than himself and could not deal with their anger or disapproval – he had a phobia. Psychotherapists these days would immediately identify his mother as the cause. Back in 1928, when Yvette arrived in England from Peking and discovered Smallwood would not, or could not, leave his wife her loneliness, frustration and despair caused her to lose control. Her bouts of rage made a damaging impression on her young son. Without anyone else to protect him Kevin was frozen with fear by these outburst. I can sympathise. My mother had difficulties and left me with a deep and debilitating fear of loss which dominated my life for nearly half a century.

It must be emphasised a phobia is not just a fear or a neurosis. It is an uncontrollable state, so powerful it can cause an adult to panic, freeze or run away.

Like all therapists Howe had sayings and catch-phrases which Kevin remembered years later. Regarding his obsession with fear he quoted Howe:

> You can't be too afraid. Those who aren't, are not to be envied.

And:

> You don't have to bear it; just know it is unbearable.

This new knowledge could not, however, save the Andrews' relationship and maybe it allowed Nancy to increase her power over Kevin. There was also the epilepsy medication which continued to impair his sexual performance and add to his feelings of inadequacy. Moments of happiness were snatched when Kevin's sense of fun re-emerged and they functioned briefly as a couple. But it was hard going. A friend told me it was sometimes excruciating for Nancy to watch

> Kevin putting on a boisterous song-and-dance act, ingratiating himself with outsiders.... very different from the arbitrary tyrant inside his home.... sometimes he was a real person, sometimes consciously acting a part, other times unconsciously.

When an old friend from the mountains visited Kevin left him in the garden with his children so they could become acquainted. Casually and cruelly, in a way often typical of Greek peasants, this *palikari* showed the children how to pull the wings off butterflies. Pleased with their new found skill they rushed to tell their mother. Nancy went berserk and a terrible row ensued.

Although he sought other relationships to bolster his self-esteem fear prevented him from escaping his wife. During this period the family employed a series of *au pairs* from England. One, a striking, capable but contained girl, went up to her room one afternoon and found the master of the house waiting in bed for her. She told him to get out.

> With anyone else I would have left, but Baba was different.

The family's travails were public knowledge within Athens but there were those who were genuinely fond of the couple and provided support. One was Kevin's old friend Robbie Cabot. In the summer of 1963 he received news of a crisis at the Andrews. He believed Kevin felt trapped. They met after an exchange of letters and telegrams and Cabot at least managed to solve an immediate problem by giving Kevin enough money to

> bail me out for a year.

While walking round Paddington on a visit to London in autumn 1963 Kevin noticed a pub name - The Old Rising Sun - and thought it might do as the title of his novel. *The Jumblies*, a temporary title for nearly a decade, was no more.

On October 17 he attended the memorial service for his old friend Louis MacNeice held at All Souls, Langham Place. The address, given by Auden, contained sentiments that could have been directed at Kevin.

> When it can be said of a poet that, without in any way sacrificing his artistic integrity to Mammon, he sponged on no one, he cheated no one, he provided for his family, and he paid his bills, these facts, I consider, deserved to be recorded

During the same visit Kevin contacted Smallwood and they met in Westminster Abbey where his father was an honorary steward. The eighty-year-old Smallwood did not recognise Kevin immediately and was confused when he approached. Uncertainly, he said:

> Smallwood's the name.

To which Kevin supposedly replied:

> Basically mine is too.

They exchanged news but nothing profound. They never saw one another again. Smallwood died on January 4 1968 but Kevin only found out eighteen months later.

In March 1965 Kevin and Nancy suffered a hammer blow when Simon, her son by Willard, was killed in a road accident in America. He was nineteen. It is impossible to comfort a mother who has lost a son. Kevin did his best but Nancy was dragged down to the point where the rows became silences

Children can be clear-sighted and resilient beyond their years. Ioanna was not happy at home and in 1965, aged ten, started at a progressive co-educational school in Switzerland.

Somehow Kevin managed to produce another book. In a Phoenix House series about the cities of the world Kevin contributed *Athens*. Published in 1967 it was no tourist guide, rather a broadside against the chancers and speculators who, together with corrupt local and national politicians, were pulling down Athens' old villas and mansions and replacing them with concrete. It did not make much of an impact. History intervened.

On April 21 1967 the colonels seized power in Greece. Kevin was seeing Dr Howe in London and Nancy was alone in Athens with Alexis. As soon as she could she joined her husband. The Junta invaded every aspect of Greek life, banning miniskirts, bikinis and pop music. Trade unionists, leftists, democrats and liberals were persecuted, imprisoned, tortured and killed. Nancy did not want to raise her children in an atmosphere of oppression and fear and, having no deep love for Greece, saw no reason why she should suffer. Kevin however loved Greece and had involved himself discreetly in its politics since the late forties. Now the underdog needed help.

In summer 1967 boys at Alexis' school in Athens were told to have their heads shaved. To avoid this ignominy Alexis too was sent to school in Switzerland. Although the nest was now empty the parents still maintained the cycle of separation and reconciliation. When Nancy went to London for medical treatment Kevin claimed, once again, he was a deserted husband. On her return Nancy made it clear she was not going to live

in a dictator-warped Greece.

and he had to make a choice. He chose Greece and she left. While selling the furniture and finding a new place to live, he suffered a severe epileptic attack and ended up in hospital. Nancy flew out from England, they were reconciled, argued, separated, went on holiday together, had a few months' happiness, had major problems, separated, tried again. So it went.

The following year Ioanna was at a summer camp in Czechoslovakia. Kevin and Nancy were spending the summer with Alexis in a rented house on the island of Aegina, not far from Athens. Two days before the Czech camp ended, Ioanna received a letter from Kevin boasting he had successfully thrown Nancy out of the house. To understand why a man would brag about such a thing to his daughter it is necessary to understand his phobia. Kevin had sought to break away from Nancy for years. He could not; he was too frightened. Now he was free, even euphoric. It felt like a triumph.

Ioanna was devastated and tore up the letter. After summer camp she travelled to Prague, supposedly for a week's sightseeing. Arriving on the night of the Soviet invasion, she spent a week camping with her classmates in the grounds of the US embassy while the city burned. Finally she left on the only train allowed out of the country, reaching her mother and Alexis in Zurich. The children returned to school in the Bernese Oberland while Nancy went to London and lived in a flat once owned by the mother of

Oscar Wilde. Kevin visited her there, perhaps seeking reconciliation. She accused him of some transgression. Hurt by this Kevin put his hand on her arm and asked: you don't believe that do you? Nancy was hysterical, thought she was being threatened and called the police. Kevin later gave a wildly hilarious description of how he vainly attempted to explain his peaceful intentions as the policemen hauled him off. Narrowly escaping being charged with assault, Kevin had not the faintest idea that Nancy had been close to the end of her tether.

In 1969, Nancy persuaded Kevin to holiday with her in County Cork, Ireland. They stayed in a village near their old friend Hedley MacNiece, widow of Louis, who owned a gourmet fish restaurant in Kinsale. After two weeks, rows and hysteria set in and Kevin stormed back to Greece. In Athens he started selling off their possessions once again.

By now Kevin lived in a little house in Mets. With the help of Andreas he not only moved his belongings but plants and even trees. Together they performed the minor miracle of keeping the trees alive in summer by soaking them for days in gallons of water. To this day Andreas is still proud of his work.

Kevin's Andrews' version of events, which he stuck to until his death, was that Nancy had left him and taken the children away, forbidding him from seeing them again. He broadcast this version in 1974 by self-publishing the extended poem, *First Will and Testament* (see Chapter 32). But his version is false. The children in England telephoned him and begged him to visit them. On occasion he did so but avoided his wife whenever possible.

Nancy never gave up on Kevin. She knew he would not renounce Greece but continued to hope he would consider living part of the time elsewhere. On several occasions she tried to interest him in finding a place together. England, Scotland, Ireland, Wales, Italy and Switzerland were considered. Off they went house-hunting with the children until he had to make a choice. Then the phobia kicked in. Kevin panicked, exploded in anger and left his family behind. He was chronically unable to make up his mind and all attempts at reconciliation ended in fights, tears and insults, leading to suitcases and rucksacks being packed and the door slammed as Kevin set out once again for Athens.

Nancy lived for decades in temporary accommodation, paying rent by the month, believing she and Kevin would get back together. As late as 1988 she sent Kevin a newspaper article about a 78-year-old couple, separated for many years, who accidentally met up in Spain, fell in love again and lived happily ever after. She hoped Kevin might be inspired. He wasn't.

Psychotherapists and marriage counsellors sometimes show their clients a triangle with three characters, one at each corner. They ask them to choose the role they have been playing: persecutor, rescuer or victim? Kevin and Nancy swapped roles taking turns at being persecutor and victim. But they could not communicate with one another and there was nobody to rescue them. They never divorced.

TWENTY-NINE

Greece in the dark

To understand Kevin Andrews' life from the late sixties it is necessary to step back a little and explore post-war Greek history. Having touched on the civil war in Chapter 16 it is vital to remember that civil wars do not end easily. Even today, after sixty years, the historic truth is rarely made public about those terrible years, although everyone knows which side their parents or grandparents were on.

The twentieth century dictatorships in Europe were not confined to Germany and Italy in World War Two, they continued in Portugal and Spain until the seventies, maintained, of course, by the self-righteously democratic America. Well into the eighties Italy teetered on dictatorship. Universal suffrage is comparatively recent in Europe and it was not until 1989 that the last Swiss canton conceded women the right to vote. Greece is often said to be the cradle of democracy but in ancient times slaves and women didn't share contemporary equality. Modern Greece did not experience unfettered parliamentary freedom until the late seventies.

A major figure in post-war Greek politics was George Papandreou, a demagogue of the centre though undoubtedly a social democrat. Papandreou used his strength among the working classes of Athens to fight the right-wing in Greece for decades. In 1965 his son, Andreas, more to the left, was under investigation for involvement in what was known as the Aspida Affair. This led King

Constantine II to reject George Papandreou as minister for defence. Greece was a cauldron of feuding factions and Papandreou's supporters took to the streets, protesting at what they called a royal *coup d'état*. For eighteen months, and during several changes of government, there were massive street demonstrations and strikes, though very little violence. The slogan of Papandreou's supporters became *Ena Ena Tessara* (*114*), a reference to a vague clause in the 1952 constitution that entrusted its maintenance to the Greek people. Elections were due on May 28 1967 but senior army officers, fearful that the left would win, made plans with the King to intervene. Greek politics has always been conspiratorial and often farcical. Unknown to these army leaders a different group of junior officers had also planned their own intervention. Using a Nato (ie, US) plan known as Prometheus 2, they struck at 2 am on April 21. Their cause was mixed and included resentment of the metropolitan élite, low status, fear of the left, fear of job losses, fear of the twentieth century. They held nationalistic and right-wing views and strongly believed that Greece's religious and traditional values should be preserved against the decadent secular values of the west. Above all, the Colonels feared young people and wanted to control them. The Greek war of the generations in the sixties and seventies was a real war, with real guns and bullets. It was mainly the young who were killed and their elders did the shooting. But it was not deaths alone that cowed the population. They were subjugated by the real or imagined presence of the secret police and the fear of kidnap, disappearance and psychological and physical torture.

The leading triumvirate of the new dictatorship were Colonels George Papadopoulos and Nickolas Makarezos and Brigadier Stylianos Pattakos. Papadopoulos was declared prime minister and his associated officers were known, then and now, as the Colonels or the Junta. Martial law was established and civil liberties suspended. Feeble attempts at a counter-coup by the King and right-wing loyalists failed, leading to purges of royalist sympathisers within the armed force and elsewhere. The Junta took firm control, King Constantine went into exile and General Zoitakis became regent. Prime minister Papadopoulos, clearly an energetic man, also assumed the offices of minister of foreign affairs, minister of defence, minister to the prime minister, minister of education and minister of government policy. Throughout this period America propped up the régime and was the major supplier of military equipment. Greece is strategically located between Europe, the Middle East and North Africa, with Israel just over the horizon. In June 1967 the Six Days War occurred and throughout this period the Cold War was at its height. Because America wanted to establish and expand its bases in Greece it supported the Junta. So did Nato and initially the EEC.

In April 1968 Kevin was invited to the *mnimosino,* or memorial service, of his old friend and *koumbaros* Andonis who had died twelve months before. These ceremonies are sombre, grief-ridden affairs. The family feel the spirit of the deceased is still with them and, while the women cook and gossip, intimate conversations are sometimes held with the deceased. Kevin travelled alone to Megara by bus and by foot. He could not fail to notice the depopulation of the Megara and began to realise the Greece of his dreams was passing. The resin gatherers and forest shepherds had emigrated to Athens and to America, and their parents were alone and isolated or dead. The twentieth century was imposing itself on the old ways, the ballads were gone and there was no longer music in the mountains. Not in the Megara anyway

Alone in Athens Kevin felt sorry for himself but from now on there were subtle changes in his behaviour. Perhaps he was helped by being away from Nancy or maybe the presence of the Junta; whatever the reason he was paying more attention to the outside world.

The publication of his book on Athens rekindled an affection for the old city and he developed a greater interest in world affairs, particularly the American involvement in Greece. Much of the world seemed to be in turmoil. The Vietnam war was slaughtering Vietnamese, brutalising the American army and tearing America apart. Martin Luther King had been assassinated and demonstrators were beaten up at the Chicago Democratic convention. Problems were also developing behind the Iron Curtain. Kevin's alert mind made the connection between world events and the political situation in Greece, and for some time he'd been concerned about the impact of the Cold War on the future of Cyprus. In September 1968 a national referendum was held on a new constitution to replace that of 1952. By now the media were controlled by the Junta and the country was under martial law. Voting booths were occupied by soldiers and, to nobody's surprise, the referendum was carried by more than 90 per cent. This supposedly legitimised the Junta's rule. Kevin was in Olymbos on Karpathos during the referendum. Voting was compulsory and, as is still the practice, the government paid for transport to the home village. People came to Olymbos from Rhodes, Piraeus, Thessaloniki and all over Greece. The national situation was grave but the people of *to chorio,* briefly united with their families, decided to celebrate. They danced and sang for four days until the ferry came to take them away.

Bolstered by victory in the referendum the Colonels' régime became more brutal as the security services (*Asphaleia*) and military police (*ESA*) efficiently broke up attempts to organise resistance. Communists, democrats and trade unionists were imprisoned, tortured, sent into internal exile and murdered. Prison camps were opened on the Greek islands. It took courage to make a public stand and those who did protest, including Andreas Papandreou, Melina Mercouri and Mikis Theodorakis, were expelled from the country. In exile they organised an effective propaganda campaign against the Colonels, principally using cultural, academic and artistic links. Music became a focal point for resistance, especially among the young. This was not pop music as westerners would understand it but a new form, buried in folk and traditional roots. Domna Samiou and others resisted the Junta in music and song but open public protest was difficult and crowds were only allowed at funerals. As a foreigner Kevin was under threat of expulsion if he transgressed the strict laws governing the country and he kept a low profile.

Internal resistance to the Junta – discreet, passive, low key, but brave - came mainly from anonymous opponents: students, trade unionists, democrats and socialists. Alexander Panagoulis, a mathematician and army officer, took another route. On the morning of August 13 1968 Papadopoulos, escorted by his personal security guards on motorcycles, was travelling by car from his seaside retreat in Lagosini to Athens Panagoulis attempted to assassinate the dictator by planting a bomb. The attempt failed and Panagoulis was imprisoned, savagely tortured and sentenced to death. In 1969 he escaped, was betrayed, caught again and imprisoned again. He faced continuous torture yet, despite being under sentence of death for five years, maintained his defiance. Following international protests the death sentence was commuted to life imprisonment. Panagoulis became a hero and, when parliamentary democracy was restored, was elected an MP for a centrist party. He then made a series of allegations against mainstream politicians who, he said, had openly or secretly collaborated with the Junta. On May 1 1976, a few days before he was due to publish secret files on *ESA*, Panagoulis aged 36 was killed in a car crash in Athens. Few people believe his death was an accident. The files never materialised. Panagoulis had all the attributes that Kevin most admired, particularly bravery and the ability to act.. He viewed him as the bravest man in modern Greek history.

Most people are not equipped to behave in this way, but Greeks know how to resist tyranny, and even dictators find it difficult to control funerals. When George Papandreou died, in November 1968, his *cortège* provided an opportunity for ordinary people to take to the streets. The turnout was enormous: songs of resistance were sung, slogans chanted and news exchanged. These acts of defiance did wonders for the Greeks, it proved they had power. They also stirred Kevin

From June 68 Kevin began to compile *Athens Alive*, darkly subtitled *The practical tourist's companion to the fall of man,* a collection of excerpts from Ovid to the modern age which was not published until 1979. *Athens Alive* suffers severely from self-censorship and carefully avoids the modern era that gave rise to the Junta. Perhaps recognising this Kevin's preface mentions that the book should be regarded as a companion to another volume which appeared later and brought the story up to date. In fact Kevin did write anti-Junta articles, sometimes obliquely, sometimes under a pseudonym and mostly for the foreign press. They are fine polemical works enhanced by genuine and serious scholarship. The rule of the Junta focused his attention on the Greek people and his commitment to them. As he became politicised by the repression he became more and more alienated from right-wing English and American writers who pontificated on Greek affairs. Kevin recognised the continuing thread between World War Two resistance, the civil war, the Cold War and opposition to the Junta. Critical of foreign intervention in Greek affairs he described C. M.

Woodehouse, a giant of modern Greek history and a hero from World War Two, as one who

> ...condescends to award laurels despite infinite and slightly withering disenchantment.

It was natural that Kevin would feel upstaged by Patrick Leigh Fermor, another hero from the World War Two, but the animosity between them was political as well as personal. Fermor was an old fashioned, well connected conservative, so it's not surprising Kevin thought his politics conveniently agreed with British foreign policy. He was sceptical of the Fermors' relationship with the Greeks they supposedly lived among, given their new house was built on a private peninsula, presumably to keep villagers out.

In September 1971 another great figure passed away. George Seferis, a Nobel prize winner, was the nation's most distinguished pre-war poet whose work often reflected a deep tragic sense of the Greek people. A few months before his death Seferis publicly denounced the Junta and became a focal point of the resistance. Kevin wrote movingly of the thousands of young people who marched to the cemetery with his coffin, creating one of the largest mass demonstrations ever against the dictatorship. The resistance was growing. Kevin and others like him became more open about their affiliations and their opposition to the Colonels. Kevin's more political friends began to refer to him as an anti-fascist. He was proud of the label.

In January 1973, several students were put on trial for forming a political party and distributing leaflets criticising the Junta. After students at the *Polytechnion* (Polytechnic University of Athens) began boycotting lessons the Junta passed a law saying students missing classes would be drafted. As a result eighty-eight unfortunate young men were forced into the armed forces where they suffered deprivation and torture. But the student body was not intimidated and, on February 21 1973, Polytechnic law students went on strike, barricading themselves inside the building and demanding this repressive law be repealed. The police entered the law school and many students were beaten up. Learning from similar protests in the UK, France, Germany and the USA, though risking far more, the young people continued to reinforce their movement by basing resistance on legitimate day-to-day demands.

Against all the odds, the Law Faculty of Athens Polytechnic was occupied once again in March. In May an unsuccessful mutiny in the navy was led by Tzannis Tzanetakis - the first major sign of discontent in the armed forces. The Junta was losing control.

In response a parliamentary republic was hurriedly introduced with a president elected for an eight-year term. Papadopoulos was the only candidate for this elected dictatorship and was formally sworn in on August 19 1973. In early November a memorial service for George Papandreou was followed by violent clashes with the police. Some days later students occupied the Athens Polytechnic once again, along with university buildings in Salonica and Patras. Political feeling had changed, hope was in the air and the demonstrations were attracting sympathy from the public. Polytechnic students set up a clandestine radio station which, in the jargon of the day, called for a worker-student alliance to overthrow the dictatorship. Papadopoulos sent in troops and tanks; many students and others were killed, several hundred wounded and almost a thousand arrested. The ruthless use of force in the centre of Athens caused widespread national and international revulsion. Led by the Scandinavians Europe applied pressure. Papdopoulos responded by imposing martial law.

Under the Colonels' rule Kevin Andrews became alive; resistance to their suppression forced him to look outwards, made him feel important. Writing articles, attending meetings and going on demonstrations may not seem much but under a dictatorship these are not trivial gestures, particularly if you carry a foreign passport and could be exiled from the land where you have chosen to live. Kevin had grown up feeling an outsider, not belonging. Now, with Nancy and the children gone, free to do as he pleased, he engaged with the resistance. He was radicalised, had comrades - he belonged.

But it wasn't just the struggle that enlivened him. For some reason he loved the secrecy and subterfuge. He was exhilarated by stealthy getaways, the cryptic relaying of messages and being pursued - both in real life or in his imagination. He was forced

> to keep written comments anonymous or shrouded, and devise language for correspondence and every word over the telephone.

Perhaps he fantasised about or exaggerated the subterfuge but it must be remembered his grandfather had been expelled from France for spying, his mother had worked for the US intelligence in World War Two, and Roy Chapman Andrews was a paid-up spook, writing letters in invisible ink.

Kevin was opposed to the repression and had been making his protests felt in a subdued way since the 1950s; now he threw himself into the struggle. Possibly his medical condition played a role. Epileptics tend not to suffer attacks when forced to concentrate, or when in danger. In the sea or in the mountains Kevin pushed himself and those with him to the limits. Possibly the danger in his own home and in the city made him feel better. For the first time in his adult life he may have realised his emotional problems, no matter how exaggerated, were minor compared to what was going on around him. The threat – day and night - to the people he knew best served to forge a stronger link with them and made him concentrate attention on the external world.

In a few years his life was transformed as he wrote articles, smuggled them out of the country, secretly listened to the BBC and passed on news in muffled telephone conversations.

> Under these nightmarish conditions you learned who were your friends.....

Kevin did not come from a left-wing tradition and never saw the struggle against the Colonels in terms of class. Essentially he was a poor little rich boy with nannies, opportunities, fine schooling, pretty woman, travel and hidden pain. He had no access, nor much of an interest in, trade unions or political parties. Kevin saw the struggle in Greece as one of national liberation with people fighting for democratic rights. And the oppressor? Simple. It was America.

Greece in the dark... 1967 – 1974, published by Adolf M. Hakkert in 1980, the companion to *Athens Alive,* is a collection of Kevin's writing from the period; every stop and every dash in the title is chosen and located purposefully and precisely. Five hundred copies were printed at his own expense after the fall of the Junta and he badgered his friends to buy them with little success. Most of the fifteen articles, some pseudonymous for security, were originally smuggled out of the country by friends and passing acquaintances. They were at risk and so was he.

Writing under pressure and even fear, he demonstrates a clarity of understanding and expression that was not to reappear until the final edition of *The Flight of Ikaros* in 1984. He shows himself to be a fine journalist and polemicist with work accepted, *inter alia,* by *The New York Review of Books, The Times* (of London), *The Massachusetts Review, The Boston University Journal* as well as the local English language papers published in Greece: *The Athenian* and *Athens News*. The subjects cover the referendum, pollution, culture under dictatorship, the death of Seferis, the massacre at the Polytechnic (plus a poem on the same subject), freedom of expression, rivalry between ancient Athens and Corinth, medieval Greece, Cyprus, the return of resistance heroes, the potential for war with Turkey, the prison camps, the murder of Panagoulis, and again Cyprus. Not only is the range remarkable, he turns the pieces into a coherent whole despite being written over nearly ten years. In doing so he makes sense of the Greek labyrinth even though he had had no training in modern history nor as a journalist. Having buried himself in the warp and weft of Greek social and political life since his arrival in the country in 1947 he manages to place personalities and events, from ancient times to the Cold War, in the same historical context. He precisely identifies the damage caused to the Greek psyche by the dictatorship:

> There is no word to translate *philotimo* because it comprises every form of pride, vanity, self-respect and sense of honour from the finest to the most ridiculous, from the most puffed-out and narcissistic to the most generous and forgiving.... This is what was taken away from them (the Greeks) on the night of April 21st 1967.

Writing about the death of Panagoulis, Kevin links it to the death of a young student on the same day:

> Athens, Mayday 1976, and two more dead in the struggle against tyranny. One obscure, the other famous. Panagoulis (was) a Liberal, but an extremist in everything, even in the totality of his moderation. As long as Panagoulis was alive - alive, free, and in a responsible position - the thought of him gave one an illogical sense of safety.

Now, more than thirty years after, the references to Cyprus are worth reading today: the betrayals and the meddling that brought about the slaughter of 5000 islanders, created 200,000 refugees and partitioned this small independent state.

Perhaps the finest article is in the form of a letter to *The New York Review of Books*. Kevin took umbrage at a review of two books on Lord Byron by David Jackson who supposedly spent most of the year in Greece. A keynote sentence in the review includes:

> Beware of bearing gifts to the Greeks,

in which Jackson refers to a can of red paint thrown at a statue of Harry Truman some two years before. Jackson seems to think Truman was one of the many saviours of Greece in its past 155 years and implies Greece should be grateful for this beneficence. Kevin takes Jackson to task, using scholarly but determined prose to shred Jackson's argument, pointing out that the Truman plan was not philanthropic but was seen by the Americans themselves as a holding action against the Soviet Union. Also that the reconstruction of roads, railroads and bridges was necessary to prosecute their side of the civil war against the left.

Jackson apparently claimed that Truman can hardly be blamed for Nato, the CIA, the recent dictatorship and the betrayal of Cyprus, so Kevin asks,

> does he really not believe that these things are precisely the consequence of Truman's Cold War policy? Does Jackson really have to be told where Nato plans are formulated?

But this is a review of two books about Byron and Kevin takes Jackson apart line by line for his ignorance and bias against the Greeks. In a masterclass of scholarship and erudition Kevin is both knowledgeable:

> Jackson has difficulty with the Greek language, so doesn't understand that a street named after another historic figure, Hastings, would read too much like the Greek for *shit on her* to be universally acceptable on a street sign.

and direct:

> Mr Jackson's next bunch of assertions is the opposite of fact.

> Mr Jackson has some bizarre things to tell us about the Greek War of Independence.
>
> Mr Jackson is apparently blind to......
>
> (Mr Jackson's aside) should not be taken for anything more important than the usual noises made by any ignoramus embarrassed by a piece of truth.

Greece in the Dark is a formidable collection of essays that locates the sixties and seventies in the flow of Greek history. The best of its kind.

Forced to concentrate on other people's wishes and demands, Kevin did not prevaricate. He had something tangible to fight for, a group of people it was legitimate to hate and, above all, the opportunity to associate publicly with the land and the people he loved. Kevin did more than write; sometimes he was in the thick of the action.

THIRTY

The Athens Polytechnic

Despite the best efforts of journalists, academics and politicians, historic memory only resonates within small sections of society: a group of comrades, colleagues or friends, a select age group or a single political affiliation. The events at the Athens Polytechnic in 1973 have real meaning for only a handful of British people who were then about twenty years old, possibly members of trade unions and/or involved in left-wing political parties. To most Americans the reference means nothing. However, despite years of censorship, all Greeks know what happened during those days in November 1973. Certainly Kevin recognised their significance. In his journalism he portrayed them as a battle between young and old. His article *1973. Blood* describes the young taking desperate and brave actions which only provoke hatred and savagery among their elders.

> Hate beyond the logic of revenge, jealousy surpassing the Tables of the Law or the policy of governments.... the nation's armoured might called out on the streets of its own capital, killing off its children, as many as possible as fast as possible.

These may sound overblown but Kevin had the right to employ such sentiments. He was there, saw what happened and suffered for his witness. He did not belong to any political party or group, was not involved with those physically resisting the Junta and, when he set out from his Mets house on Wednesday November 14 1973, was unaware of what the students were planning at the Polytechnic. He intended to see a movie.

On a Number 3 trolley from Omonia Square, passing down Patissia Boulevard, he saw thousands of young people around the Polytechnic buildings chanting slogans. He got off and made his way to the demonstration. He was not worried for himself but he doubted he had the right to be there. He felt he was an outsider, albeit an observer.

The atmosphere was exciting, full of promise, controlled. No police were to be seen but the students were organised, discipline was maintained, the traffic was directed, placards waved, slogans chanted: *Down with the Junta. Americans out-114. 114-freedom. Education. Bread. Down with Papadopoulos*

Soon Kevin could not resist getting involved, copying *114* on pages of textbooks and plastering them on cars and buses. But there were dangers. Amid the ecstasy of freedom and resistance Kevin was warned,

> They (plain clothes police) have noticed you. Better to go.

So he went… to the cinema. No *andarte*, no freedom fighter, no *palikari*.

The next morning he was back. The crowds were bigger, the slogans more explicit: *Torture chambers. Prison cells. General strike now*.

More and more young people were gathering and, by evening, tens of thousands massed round the Polytechnic. Kevin did not wait, he went to another cinema and saw a historic film from the time of Venizelos. It involved Royalist officers, manipulated by the major powers, bringing about the defeat of Greece in Asia Minor and leading to the disastrous and bloody exchange of populations. The twenties and seventies were linked. The audience understood.

By Friday November 16 it was clear something was about to happen. The autonomous and disciplined action of the students had brought in hundreds of thousands of demonstrators. Using megaphones they controlled the crowds, forbade provocative actions, posters and slogans, broadcast details of meetings and resolutions to the surrounding area over their radio, issued press releases and equipped and opened a medical centre. Opposition groups consisting of peasants, workers, students and trade unionists, waved banners and shouted slogans. A people united. The Junta had to react.

Kevin went home in the afternoon to sleep . He had epilepsy; he had to take care. But by 8 pm he was back. Tear gas had been released by the police but the students did not retaliate. They lit fires to disperse the gas, held wet handkerchiefs to their faces and applied vaseline to red eyes. Soon there was sporadic gunfire followed by appeals for doctors and then priests. Doctors came, then an ambulance. Kevin saw no priests. By now he was being driven around by Willard Manus, journalist and writer from America, a long time resident of Rhodes. They fetched food, water and medical supplies from areas still free from police barricades. Gradually the police closed in and the two Americans abandoned their car.

When the Polytechnic gates were closed the crowd outside was separated from the brave ones inside. Police snipers opened fire from the Acropole Palace Hotel. Kevin was under fire for the first time for nearly thirty years. Some people were shot, some killed

Kevin and Willard phoned foreign journalists from a sympathiser's flat, urging them to report to the world what was happening. The army sent in tanks, dozens of tanks. Kevin ran into the road to see. Troops arrived. Kevin tried to escape but was trapped, then punched, kicked and clubbed. He screamed he had epilepsy and they shouldn't hit him on the head but to no avail. When he regained consciousness he was covered with blood, his eyesight blurred, and both his identity card and his money were gone. A taxi with an open door was available but a slow drive ended with a smirk from the taxi driver, another line of police and another beating.

Friends asked afterwards why he didn't tell them he was American. He had forgotten. A seminal moment or a theatrical embellishment? No matter. Kevin no longer felt a foreigner.

Trying to find his way home he was beaten again and left in the road. A group of Cypriot students found him, put him in a car, took him to a doctor who cut the hair round the gash in his head, washed the wound and bound it with dark plasters that would be less conspicuous. Then a nightmare journey through a city under siege and curfew, dodging tanks, the army, armed police and the *Asphaleia* At 4.30 in the morning they came across a telephone kiosk that was working and Kevin got through to a foreign, probably British, correspondent who told the story to the outside world. Later he was treated for cuts, bumps and a damaged hand at the home of a friend who had resisted the German occupation (perhaps Vana Hadzimichalis), after which he collapsed into a bed. Without the

> hard emotionless concentration on survival... he sobbed his way to sleep.

By now the tanks had broken down the gates of the Polytechnic and students had been beaten and shot. There was blood on the streets, broken glass, cartridge cases. The crowds had gone. The resistance had been defeated; for the time being the men with the guns had won.

The next day Kevin's hand was grotesquely swollen and needed x-raying. He imagined the hospitals were full of spies. He made phone calls, found a name, and the x-ray revealed a diagonal fracture across the hand. He was offered no treatment, he might be spotted, it was too dangerous.

> When you get home, take a piece of cardboard and bend it round your wrist and tie it up with a string. It should be all right till Monday.

Careful not to draw attention to himself he walked home across the deserted city, went in, closed the door and collapsed.

Few of the expatriates in Greece actively resisted the Junta. For a while Kevin achieved some kudos among his coterie though there are some, even today, who doubt his story. Others believed he was a marked man and some urged him to carry on the struggle abroad. More relaxed was the young Cypriot Kevin met in the local police station when renewing his residence permit a few weeks later. By remarkable coincidence this man was one of those who assisted Kevin the night he was beaten up. He insisted on talking about it in front of the police before a panicky Kevin managed to shut him up.

Kevin did get away from Athens. He stayed at Kardamyli with Paddy Leigh Fermor. Close to hysteria Kevin became furious with Fermor whose feigned ignorance played into the hands of the Junta. Fermor asked,

> What are these people like? Why don't the two sides get together round a table and talk? Is it like the Roundheads and Cavaliers all over again?

Kevin turned on the man, asking why, with all his influence, he had done nothing. He had always been jealous of Fermor's commercial success and the relationship had been difficult. Now it was impossible.

On the larger stage it was time for the international community to intervene. Students, trades unionists and social democrats throughout Europe passed resolutions and occupied buildings. Parliaments were convened. Greece was awake, the Junta was shaky. Murdering youth in the name of democracy was clearly going too far.

Under pressure the Junta set up an enquiry and asked people to come forward with the names of the dead. Nobody did. Kevin went to a soirée at the British Council where this was raised by someone who believed the Government version of events and rejected the idea of fatalities. Kevin exploded:

> How can you not understand? If you went to the Junta they would know you were with the opposition. They would lock you up.

The events at the Polytechnic discredited the military rulers, Under the weight of the Cyprus misadventure and the face-off with Turkey the Junta collapsed in July 1974 and some freedoms were restored. Greece began clawing its way towards twentieth century parliamentary democracy.

Each year, on November 17, Greek schools and universities are closed. The Athens Polytechnic is also closed on the November 15. Students and politicians lay wreaths on a monument within the Polytechnic inscribed with the names of Polytechnic students killed during Greek resistance to the Germans in the 1940s. The commemoration day ends with a demonstration that starts on the Polytechnic campus and ends - as Kevin would surely approve - at the United States embassy .

THIRTY-ONE

Save my papers

Throughout the early seventies Kevin lived alone in Athens, writing, agitating, travelling to old haunts and visiting old acquaintances.

He missed Alexis and Ioanna but, frozen by inertia, incapable of resolving his marital situation or of confronting Nancy, he rarely saw them. During autumn 1971 he suffered a number of major epileptic attacks and was in hospital for several weeks in October and November after a particularly bad *grand mal* which led to more than forty convulsions in a day. He stayed with his old friend Simon Karras while recuperating under heavy sedation. About this time he began to suffer from dysphasia, an intermittent inability to speak sense. Words and sentences formulated in his mind came out as nonsense in attacks which could last several hours. Nothing could be more debilitating for a writer. Kevin was embarrassed and scared by this new condition. Forbidden emotional involvement, he was told it was dangerous to live alone but continued to do so. Despite visits from friends and trips to the theatre, parties and receptions he was desperately lonely. Four empty walls, he told his friends.

Although close to several women he had no regular lover. His forays were half-hearted, more a cry for attention than an expression of lust. In November 1972 he made a prolonged visit to London to see the children and to talk about the future with Nancy but the attempt solved nothing. He wanted to live in Greece where he felt safe, he wanted to be Greek. They squabbled.

In February 1973 Kevin met his half-brother, John Smallwood, in a pub in Earls Court Road, London. For the first time they acknowledged their relationship, but it was too late. They never became friends.

After he returned to Athens life continued in its ramshackle way. He gardened, made jewellery, tried offhandedly to seduce various female friends, wrote poetry and articles about the Junta. Kevin was regarded as a celebrity by the Athens expatriates. But then he differed from them. While they tended to speak to each other he mixed with Greeks and could interpret aspects of the Greek character they found inaccessible. Some considered him difficult. He was obsessed by Nancy, publicly abusing her and claiming she was turning the children against him and vetting their letters. Friends of the couple found such animosity boring, distasteful and embarrassing. They drifted away. However, when speaking Greek, its seems he was a subtly different character - more optimistic, less prone to outburst and less inclined to reveal his feelings about Nancy.

He continued to live in Mets at 69 Trivonianou, a house facing the Mirtia taverna which he called the Cookhouse and which he refused to patronise because it was used by a notorious torturer for the Junta. Instead he ate at Platia Varnava in a refugee-era shack known as Vellis. The menu was short and unvarying - soup, *keftedhes,* sardines and dish of the day.

Throughout the Junta's rule Kevin was rarely in a position to offer direct resistance but he was convinced that American meddling in Greek affairs had led directly to the repression. The exaggerated memory of his treatment by Roy Chapman Andrews added to the shame and disgust he felt for his American passport. Impressed by the way Greeks from all strata of society had behaved under tyranny, he decided on a major step – he would become a Greek citizen.

Ioanna and Alexis stayed with Kevin in September 1974 , and Nancy joined them after several days, the first time the couple had occupied the same house since their attempted reconciliation five years before. Nancy was concerned about Kevin's decision to take Greek nationality since this had serious implications for Alexis.

Sons of Greek citizens were then, as now, liable for service in the armed forces. Delicate conversations with Kevin were not easy. He and Nancy disagreed most of the time and, in the subsequent heightened tension, he would panic and fly into a temper. Frequently an epileptic attack followed. Nancy's coolness and self-control further infuriated Kevin. The tension on this occasion was already high. He had given her a copy of his long and bitter poem, *First Will and Testament*, (see next chapter) in which he claimed she had forbidden him to see his children.

Nancy was deeply hurt by *First Will* and an argument broke out as the family sat in the yard around a clay oven, preparing to cook steaks over a charcoal fire. As Kevin lit the fire a cat got in the way and he slapped it on the nose. A child shouted, accusations were followed by counter-accusations. Kevin stared wildly at the fire, threatening to throw hot coals over Nancy.

Suddenly he ran into the house, took a knife from the kitchen and tried – unsuccessfully - to cut his wrists. Hoping that lack of an audience might reduce the drama, Nancy shouted to the children to sit in the bedroom and close the door. But nothing could stem what followed. In the bathroom Kevin unwrapped a Wilkinson razor blade and calmly slashed first his left wrist then his right. In his study he opened drawers and threw paper everywhere. He retrieved his identity card, supposedly to ease police identification of his body. Stuffing a sheaf of documents under his arm he ran out of the house and up the hill shouting,

> My papers, I must save my papers.

These papers were articles, press cuttings and essays he had written about life under the Junta and, perhaps more important, his application for citizenship.

Following a trail of blood and manuscript pages a terrified Ioanna ran after her father under the astonished stares and pointed fingers of passers by.

> My papers, save my papers.

He ran through the streets of Mets to the house of Manolis Philipakis, his friend from Olymbos who now lived nearby. Finding the house empty, Kevin took a piece of cardboard and wrote in letters of blood in Greek,

Save my papers,

leaving it propped up on the stairs to be discovered by Manolis later that day. Kevin then disappeared.

Close to panic, Ioanna returned to the house on Trivonianou. When Manolis called to find out what had happened he found Ioanna and her brother washing their father's blood off the walls and floors Mid-morning the next day Kevin returned with bandaged arms. At first he did not speak. Later he told Manolis that he had started running in order to speed up the emptying of his veins; however, his blood coagulated too quickly. Realising he would not die however fast he ran, he took a trolley bus and looked for a hospital. In those days Athenians believed that hashish was so strongly addictive that, if none were available, addicts would perforce try to kill themselves. Understandably this wild man, with blood running from his wrists on to his clothes and feet, scared the passengers who left the trolley with cries of ***hashisti*** (hashish addict). At the hospital Kevin was surprised and disappointed to be received without sympathy. The duty doctor brusquely bound up his wounds and sent him away without comfort.

There was little sympathy at home either. Their father's gruesome gesture had alienated and shocked the children. Over the next two weeks Kevin, who deliberately refused to clean the congealed blood from his sandals, threatened a repeat performance on several occasions until Ioanna, expressing her acute distress and that of Alexis, told him to go ahead and do it. Anything was preferable to the impending threat.

Friends and acquaintances of Kevin Andrews find it difficult to accept that someone they knew as vivacious, amusing, attractive and intelligent was also outlandish and self-centred. By now arguments with Nancy fuelled his phobia and he had to have his own way. He felt she was trying to stop him from shedding his American skin and he couldn't stand being denied. Conflict and danger released him from the need for self-control, made him feel alive. Getting into scrapes, arguments and difficulties were part of his way of life. When he was on the edge he felt free.

Kevin expressed no shame for what he had done. Writing to his brother George he described slitting his wrists without remorse. He regularly flirted - almost coyly - with the idea of killing himself, as if suicide or its threat were sexually charged, something to be proud of. Occasionally he started a conversation,

> Nice day for a suicide.

Then there was that childhood memory of his mother holding him as she contemplated suicide from Battersea bridge in London. On a later occasion, very much in torment, she had scratched at her wrists and repeated,

> Why won't somebody listen to me? Why won't they hear what I say?

That day in Mets all Kevin's demons attacked at the same time: his mother, the Colonels, his wife, Smallwood, Roy Chapman Andrews, his sickness, his origins, his insecurity and his dreadful indecision. There are questions about whether his death fifteen years later was accidental or suicide but in Mets he clearly tried to kill himself.

After time some normality returned. The family managed to talk about the future. Italy was discussed as a kind of halfway house between England and Greece. Nancy would settle there, the children would go to school and Kevin would come to stay.

It was all a dream. The children went back to boarding school and Nancy returned to London. Kevin stayed in Athens.

THIRTY-TWO

First Will and Testament

For a few years after he and Nancy separated (1969), Kevin had worthwhile things to do: supporting the resistance, writing articles, agitating against the Colonels. Even so he was still in turmoil, still trying to understand and explain. He had grown to resent his dead mother for deceiving him about his father. He had never respected Smallwood and now it was too late. Smallwood too was dead.

But Kevin was a writer; of his writing it is his poetry that deserves closest scrutiny. A poem offers no hiding place; its compressed nature must convey the truth or it is nothing. During 1972 and 1973 he wrote an autobiographical poem, *First Will and Testament*, published in 1974 the year of his fiftieth birthday. The title could well have been in influenced by *Last Will and Testament* by Louis MacNiece and W. H. Auden and it probably sums up his life at that point. However, as in nearly everything he did, some background knowledge does help. The poem is addressed to his children, Corinna, Ioanna and Alexis. He describes his birth:

> Life begins in winter...
> That winter must have been a bad one.

In no time at all he launches a broadside at Chips Smallwood who left a suit behind in Yvette's wardrobe in her cottage in England, presumably so that he could stay the night and leave for work looking smart.

> ....the Emperor -
> half-Irish
> with a delish
> (they called it in the Thirties) sense of humour,
> who bequeathed an actual suit
> of clothes to a discarded
> inconveniently pissed-
> off mistress as a keepsake
> for their promising though a bit retarded
> offspring, on condition she not make
> a scene or spill
> the beans:---a kindly man who missed
> the point,

From what is known about the loving relationship between Smallwood and Yvette it is Kevin who missed the point. Kevin continues

> And so his secret unanointed son
> must carry on
> and go about
> without
> the suit of clothes that didn't fit
> in any case and left *him* (it
> so happens) naked rather
> than the Emperor his father

The bitterness of the bastard boy, is there. His wish to defend his mother, dead for fifteen years, rings true although the suggestion that he believes himself to be slightly retarded does not.

He is more honest if a little harsh in describing himself:

> Otherwise he didn't do too badly: - looks, books, and the
> once
> convenient smarm produced by that
> expensive education also
> available to the unjustifiably less affluent
> in scholarships (that weren't so much a sign of brilliance
> as of indecent

poverty), now out of date. Plus even a little experience
  of War

Kevin Andrews at fifty with three fine children, two good books and a record of resistance against oppression, is full of self-doubt.

I travel light, he said.
  He travelled lighter than he knew, however.

In sprinkly twenties
after the stammering teens were over,
he learned that he could trade on charm,
glittering shallows, reefs of smarm, and youth,
....
  And then he found
  (if only by their sound)
  that words meant
  what they said exactly, and his wife went
  off, taking the children with her.
        And the clock stopped.

Then a passage that reveals deep bitterness and profound self-pity:

Years went by
when it was forbidden that his children
come to see him

It sounds heart-rending but it isn't true. The children may not have been able to go to Athens but Kevin could have gone to Switzerland, where they were at school, and did in fact go to England during the holidays. Kevin was not denied access to his children and, if he didn't see them as often as he might the blame lay with him rather than elsewhere. Nancy could have sent them to Greece to stay with their father but his erratic behaviour made him an unreliable guardian. Also, Athens was dangerous under the Junta, a place they might be allowed to visit when older and more able to care for themselves. This is not to deny that Kevin was lonely or missed his children. Of course he did:

shudder of hope!--the ringing phone burst on
his eardrum as the voices of his children
calling his name once tore him limb by limb
into a world of love and terror made

especially for them; where to wake up
at nighttime in an empty room was death,

Kevin confirms Athens' dangers:

The times were difficult. It wasn't safe
to send incriminating messages
by post:

The secrecy, the spies, the plain clothes police are described before he returns to loneliness again:

What is there in solitude but furniture?
One's
own furniture.
                And if I have another twenty years of life
                will I still have this furniture?

We know now he did not have another score of years. He taunts us about his capacity for self-destruction, writing archly:

The principle of suicide
is inborn:

and later combines the pain of writing with mortality:

Not to be able
to find words
for things:
the end of life.

Returning to his parents he imagines socking his mother on the jaw and longs to hear from a father:

Get on with you, beloved son in whom I am well pleased....

Corinna was his first-born whom he abandoned, he says, but to whom he still wrote letters. He concedes that Nancy, who already had two children when he married her, had ample

willingness to love

before crushing us with cruelty:

And the early nail goes
                        easily into a coffin.

Kevin involves us in life's minutiae: a phone installed, problems at the Swiss school which pleases him and for which he blames Nancy. That same Nancy pleads in her sweet voice

> Could we not meet half way?
> I have so much to say

He gives the game away completely: this time he might get through. It never seems to have crossed his mind she might be having difficulties getting through to him. Off they go to Rome. To try once more, to no avail. There appears to be nothing good in his life until

> ....the one
> magic strangling redemption
>   life-giving - my son!

Remember this is a summing up of a fifty-year-old's life and it is addressed to his children; Corinna in her twenties, Ioanna her late teens and Alexis fourteen. Nothing demonstrates more clearly his failure to understand family life or his inability to empathise with children. He does not tell us: life-giving - my children. Only: life-giving - my son. How are the three children expected to respond to that?

But he is also lyrical, taking us into the mountains of Greece, described by him as the little locked and salty continent. He warns:

> .... Up there when
> the mist
> comes down, you're lost.

Inevitably Kevin, who thrived on the edge, exhorts:

> Up the long low ridges
> through the orchards, forests,
> past the final cedar
> after earth
> sheds night

Before returning to Nancy:

> But you're not there.
> You'll never come.
>   Not that it matters.
> NO!

> Let not the children join us any longer.
> No longer may they join in the deceit
> that we have practised systematically
> against each other.

Finally he reaches the point of the Will in a dialogue with Nancy:

> Then why subject yourself?
> There is no substitute for place, my children.
> Oh dear! then that means place has stronger
> ties for you than
> people - me, your children...

It's true. He will not compromise, living six months here and six there. Perhaps he is trapped in Greece. He will abandon his children.

> I'm fifty now, a door has shut.
> .... DO NOT FORGIVE -
> not me while there is still time nor
> when it's too late

And, brutally,

> I leave you
> nothing.
> The love I gave I took away;
> I couldn't hold.
> .....
> Alone the dust is
> capable
> of pardon.
> Let your hearts be hardened
> to the deceitful mercies
> of impenetrable
> Justice.

Would anyone - child or adult – wish their father to write such a poem? So why did he write it? Why expose his children to the pain of reading the lines and between the lines, looking for a sign of love or hint at affection? Except for the reference to Alexis he does not deem it worthwhile to state his love for his children in any clear and meaningful way. This from a man who wanted to hear from his father that he was a:

> beloved son in whom I am well pleased..

First Will and Testament is full of beautiful words and carefully constructed insights into the heart and mind of Kevin Andrews. Unfortunately it is one-sided and delusional, an exercise in self-excuse. It does not represent the truth nor is it noble. What he bequeaths to his children is not love, merely self-justification and massive self-pity.

THIRTY-THREE

Kalimera patrida
(Good morning homeland)

Most of us have some idea who we are: parents, nationality, class, race. In Greece you are defined by the village, in the USA by the state. Much of this bedrock was unavailable to Kevin Andrews. He was not even certain about his birthplace: his army recruitment document said China, or Mongolia, or Sinkian or... Until 1954 he thought he knew who his father was and that he was American. But he was wrong.

Explaining his origins in *Expatriation to Excess: No Blame* (see Chapter 37) he talks of RCA

> I was not his son… I left America because I did not in fact belong there… already I had been four years in Greece and there known independence for the first time ever... I wrenched myself away (from Greece) with the greatest effort and the worst of will..... After Greece, America in the early fifties was a form of exile....

During his first visit to Greece, 1947 - 1951, Kevin had grown to love the people. Baffled by the national proclivity for murderous behaviour he had stood aside during the civil war, naively denying the Communists were involved in atrocities and claiming they were only reacting to right-wing oppression. Under the Junta he was more secure and took sides. He knew where he belonged. By

1974 he accepted that the earlier Greece had gone for ever. Peasants had left their homes for the city and a wage economy. Wild and remote places had been damaged by roads and hotels catering for mass tourism.

> I had come to Greece in time to experience these intimate, ancient conditions... people who had never seen a foreigner, or learned to read, or travelled to a town, or else who had migrated to the slums of Athens in the 1930s out of a necessity beyond my comprehension, but whose hearts were in the mountains still, and their hospitality commensurate. To forget all this was to break faith.

But it was danger that forged his will to be a Greek citizen:

> Danger provided free and universal education with a compulsory curriculum… In any case the conditions that had affected multitudes provided for me the ultimate spike... after the tyranny fell... when the new government granted me the citizenship I asked for.

Few people take the step that Kevin took. Normally they fight hard for the American passport that Kevin chose to reject.

Kevin described the big event in Greek magazines and published the original, with a translation, in *Greece in the Dark*. His joy is palpable, he says. This is the most important day he has ever lived through.

> When I first set foot in this country... a voice inside me said may I never leave this place!

Becoming a Greek was more than a desire, it was a vital need. Kevin says, opaquely, the need was something to do with his father.

> I grew up without a father (the little I know about him is that he was not American); that I was always looking for a fatherland was an inevitable consequence.

The first part of this sentence is clearly muddled. To disentangle it we must remember that while RCA was mainly absent during Kevin's youth he was American. Smallwood, on the other hand, wasn't American, was present as Kevin grew up and was probably his real father!

Kevin had no illusions:

> Greece is the country of countries where someone born a foreigner will remain foreign to the end of his days.

At fifty Kevin had spent nearly half of his life in Greece. His quest to become a citizen took months of bureaucratic wrangling and required the support of a senior lawyer. In October 1974 he handed in his application at the Ministry of the Interior. After a long, long wait, the letter arrived:

> ...pursuant upon the decision of the Ministry you are required to present yourself for the oath taking.

He had to wait until the office opened again, needed to take a five drachma government stamp, his passport and his birth certificate. He rose before dawn.

> Our Father, give us this day a fatherland....

He cleaned his house, put on a tie, cleaned his shoes, delivered the laundry and wasted as much time as possible before presenting himself at the Ministry:

> Excuse me, I've come to take an oath

His voice seemed to come from elsewhere. He presented his papers, the five-drachma stamp, his American passport and his birth certificate. As always with Kevin there were complications. The certificate issued in 1927 – three years after he was born! – contained medieval language that defied translation:

> And further depondent saith nont.

Nevertheless with the help of his US Army discharge papers and his marriage certificate he was able to prove he had been born. He placed his hand on the Bible and repeated the oath:

> I swear
> to preserve faith
> in the fatherland
> obedience to the Constitution
> and to the laws of the State
> and conscientiously to fulfil
> the duties of a Hellene

Kalimera patrida
(Good morning homeland)
Now you are Greek. Congratulations

Less than an hour has passed. It was 11.55 on February 26, 1975. Release from the past with a clean skin, a new life. All the ordinary things took on a different hue - descending in the lift, crossing Omonia square, taking the Number 12 trolley. He phoned friends and acquaintances, telling them:

I am Greek.

Later, writing in Greek about his feelings, he cannot hide his insecurity even on this momentous day

> Today, I have become a Greek.... Today I have become your fellow-countryman and I feel like a long chat before the end of what has been, I think, the most important day of my life... I am still talking to you because I don't want this day to end... Farewell, from your fellow-countryman, whether you want me or not.

Nevertheless he was now Greek and, for a while was released from his tormenting demons. But only for a while.

He visited the American embassy to explain he was no longer American. They told him:

It isn't allowed, you are still American.

Kevin threw a tantrum, tore up his American passport, hurled it into a wastepaper basket and stormed out. Whether he liked it or not, he continued to be American for the time being. Shedding his past was not that easy. He had not achieved the fresh start he desired. His new passport was simply a state document not a guarantee of happiness.

THIRTY-FOUR

Magouche's story

Robert Cabot told me Magouche Fielding was a friend of Kevin Andrews and she would talk to me. Oh, and that she had been married to Arshile Gorky, the surrealist painter, whose works hang in the Museum of Modern Art in New York and Tate Modern. Gorky committed suicide in 1948.

Magouche's life touched on major events of the twentieth century. She married Xan Fielding, the British special agent, hero of the Cretan resistance, who also fought on the Greek mainland and with the SOE in France where he was awarded the *Croix de Guerre*. Fielding was captured by the SS along with Francis Cammaerts, whom I knew when he was president of my trade union. I mentioned this to Magouche when I phoned and she revealed Cammaerts was Xan's great hero. Perhaps that is why she agreed to see me. She also asked my age and, foolishly, I asked if she was flirting. No, I just want to place your generation.

I was so nervous I went to the wrong house where I knocked loudly on the door. Fortunately nobody answered. Having noticed my mistake I crossed the road, found the right house, and rang the bell.

Magouche is tall, slim, rather severe looking, immaculately dressed, in command of herself, of me and, no doubt, of any situation that might crop up. Kevin said her Russian name meant Powerful She; this proved quite appropriate. I was escorted into what in earlier times would be called a drawing room and offered whisky. I settled for white wine and was assessed as she expertly rolled up a skinny cigarette. No doubt she could have rolled a joint with similar ease.

I tried to steer the conversation logically but my efforts came to nothing against her wish to tell her story the way she wanted. The first tack threw me:

> It was Corinna's mother he loved. I don't know why he didn't stay with her.
>
> Well she was twenty years older and...
>
> So was Colette and she managed.

I had the distinct feeling Magouche had met Colette but did not pursue the matter. Instead I asked her about *The Flight of Ikaros:*

> How could such a young man write such a good book? He was on fire. When he came to Greece it was like he was drunk on the place.

You could imagine this young man, intellectually equipped to study, research and write *Castles of the Morea*, bursting to explore the Greece that would live so vividly in *The Flight of Ikaros.*

She continued, Paddy (she is a friend of Leigh Fermor) said,

> It was the best book. He should know, he wrote books on Greece.

We meandered a little. She was off to stay with Paddy the following week. He had asked for a pen and she had spent all day in Oxford Street looking for exactly the right type. Kevin used to make the same demands. She was tired and yesterday was her eighty-fifth birthday. It turned out Paddy had not stopped short of wanting a pen – he also fancied an Olivetti portable typewriter. He wasn't going to get one and the word bugger arose:

> Maybe he needs one of those typewriters with large letters (his sight isn't all that good). Perhaps I should ring the Blind.

I would have loved to talk about Paddy but dragged her back to when she first met Kevin. In the sixties or seventies?

No, for sure the sixties (when Kevin was about forty). We lived in Chapel Street, Belgravia, and Kevin used to stay with our friends the Nortons (Sir Clifford and Lady Peter Norton) who lived on the other side of the street. They had friends staying, so he stayed with us. A little bed in the basement. He looked like he had just got off a bus. Suitcases in his hands. Nobody told me about the epilepsy and that was the first thing that happened. Kevin told me to put a pillow between his teeth.

He came several times to stay. He was a great friend of Robbie's. He was in love with Robbie Cabot.

What were her first impressions? He had amazing, piercing, blue eyes. He was charming, strange, unexpected, jumpy. He did not try to impress. He was civilised, went from happy to sad in ten minutes.

Did he talk about his father? Oh yes. He was staying with us when he went off to see, what was his name, the army fellow? Yes, Smallwood, Captain Smallwood. He went off to see them one Christmas Day. Walked in uninvited on the family Christmas. Walked in and said, Father. Told the family having their Christmas day: I am your brother, I am your son. I don't think he was particularly welcome.

I have not been able to verify this detail.

The Nortons were friends of Kevin's. Peter Norton was his godmother. It was she who told him - when he was a young man - RCA is not your father. They were walking down Park Avenue, New York, at the time. How marvellous, said Kevin, leaping up and down, I am a bastard, a bastard.

Another contradiction! Another twist! This could be important. Perhaps he did know before Yvette told him over Christmas 1953

He hated RCA. Didn't like him at all. Maybe he was jealous of all the things he had done. RCA paid for his education, sent him to Harvard, but Kevin savaged him. Kevin was twisted. He could not be normal. He seemed to think everyone was sick and twisted.

Kevin stayed with Xan and Magouche on several occasions. Once Magouche drove Kevin from London to Athens.

As Magouche ponders I find myself imagining it was a Bentley or a Lagonda; but probably not. Magouche resumes: We drove for several days. We stopped for a drink in bars on the way. Kevin would stand at the bar and have a small fit, stand there shaking. I could see people looking at us.

Magouche does not pull her punches. She slapped me down when she detected my leftish perspective on the Greek civil war, telling me sternly that Paddy and Xan were not about to hand Greece over to the Communists.

Well quite.

Kevin was rude to Xan. He rowed with him and with Paddy. Why? He was jealous of them. They were more Greek than he was. In fact several people got fed up with Kevin's claim to be Greek

Vanna Hadzimikalis was a near neighbour of Kevin's in Mets. She told Kevin, whatever you get in papers you are not Greek. You are American.

I imagine this hurt. I have never occupied the position Kevin found himself in so it would not matter to me but I remember a story from Diafani. Two men are talking:

> *Pioi einai oi anthropi aftoi*
> Who are those people over there?
>
> *Den enai anthroupoi enai tourists.*
> They are not people they are tourists.

Magouche agreed Kevin was hurt by Vanna's comments: But he was an egotist. He had no intuition of other people. He could not empathise. He could not understand PLF's generosity. He wounded Paddy and Xan. Kevin did not do much in the time of the dictatorship. Others did much more. Paddy could not do much, he did a bit, but the Mani, where Paddy lives, was basically royalist. But Kevin did not do much. He was with the boys in the cafés.

I asked about Kevin's death. Had she met Elizabeth Herring? (on holiday with Kevin when he died).

No, but Vanna did. Herring was terribly pushy. I read the Herring book – *Farewell to Ikaros* - in manuscript form. It is all in terribly bad taste. Herring sent it to Paddy for comment. He told her not to publish it. They were all terribly upset.

Kevin needed someone to tell him how wonderful he was. Perhaps Herring was that woman. Poor Kevin. Poor, poor Kevin.

I did not ask about Herring's account of Kevin's death but Magouche volunteered: He made her a gift. He never took off his bracelet when he went swimming. He made her a gift. It seemed Magouche thought it was suicide.

Did Kevin talk about suicide to you? Oh yes. Often. Did he use it as a sexual thing? I can commit suicide, I am a real man? No, not that, but certainly a ploy.

Then Magouche was revealed: I fell in love with my first husband at a young age. I was 18. He hung himself when I was 28. I know about suicide.

I feel about five years old.

Magouche first went to Greece in 1962. Her marriage to Xan and his friendship with Paddy opened many doors for her.

She talked about Kevin's marriage with Nancy: He took her off to that island. (Ikaria) She could not speak Greek. Kevin always had problems getting on with women. Nancy could not understand him at all. They could not get on and he could not leave her. Kevin was promiscuous. He was unfaithful from the beginning. He was ambivalent about sexuality, male and female. All this was mixed with guilt and charged with emotion and doubt. Nancy was a bastard child as well. But he wanted a mother and he wanted to fuck his mother. It was all Oedipal.

I pointed out that in researching this book I have come across famous names and often their behaviour was not the norm. Oh yes, we were in those circles. All of us knew famous people. And many of them had bastards. Some of them were bastards.

Magouche did not go to the funeral: We could not. We had not spoken to him for two or three years before he died. He was so rude to Xan. He had a big row with Paddy. He threatened to kill him.

By now Magouche was tired. Two hours had gone by. I wanted to continue but I was tired too. Her portrait of Kevin is of a confused and bitter man, an erratic man. Not Homeric, not Tolstoyan. A pygmy among the people she was close to, but she liked him.

I asked about her children: I have children. They are scattered over the world. My daughter was just here. She was married to that Amis fellow, Martin, the writer.

I put away my pen and my notebook. I asked if anyone was working on her biography:

No thank you, I am in other people's.

THIRTY-FIVE

The outsider

As a result of the beating Kevin took at the hands of the Junta the meniscus in his left knee was ruptured. Increasingly this gave him trouble and he complained to family and friends about the pain, the cost of the operation and his lack of money. Eventually a group clubbed together and, in the spring of 1975, he had a successful operation and was able to climb mountains again. Other legacies from the beating included occasional amnesia and - to the disadvantage of those around him - frequent loss of temper.

Nevertheless some normality had returned to Greece and to his life. With Nancy out of the way he developed as a freelance writer, analysing both Greek history and the modern state. Of all his contemporaries only he emphasised the inherent and long-term stability of the Greek people who, for over two thousand years, had seen themselves as one nation at the centre of the world. Others - Russia, Turkey, Britain and especially the USA – had seen Greece as an awkward young country getting in the way of their ambitions.

Kevin became increasingly interested in the Greek experience of World War Two, the subsequent civil war and the debacle of Cyprus. He visited Cyprus and wrote many articles about that island, so cruelly divided and occupied by the Turkish invasion. In 1978 he spent six weeks there, helping to make a film for Greek television. This was a fruitful period. He earned money from translation, he was proof-reading *Greece in the Dark* (published 1980),

Athens Alive was published at the end of 1979 and *Byzantine Blues*, a satirical poetic frolic lampooning Greek politics, followed soon after.

Kevin still had emotional problems and found it difficult to maintain a close relationship with Ioanna and Alexis. He thought they were astonishingly gifted and was proud of them. He was, however, suspicious of what he described to his brother George as the weird and ghoulish atmosphere they were growing up in, thinking they were being brainwashed. His health was not good either. Epilepsy required him to take a two-hour siesta each afternoon together with a dozen sedatives a day.

On July 1978 Corinna was married but Kevin was not invited to the wedding. He installed himself some way from the church watching the proceedings from a hillside. That evening the Cyprus film was broadcast on television and there was a party. After the party Corinna rang Kevin and he finally saw bride and groom. At the time he seemed not too put out but the situation gnawed at him and grew in importance. A decade later he still complained – even to relative strangers - about the slight he had suffered.

Some enjoy being an outsider but for Kevin location was supreme and he was saddened by his perceived role as an intruder. As a self-described misfit and a maverick, he regarded his childhood as a series of insertions into households, schools, groups and countries where he did not belong. England, America and his mother's high stratum of society were all alien. He was an embarrassment, an inconvenience. Even his time in the army was seen as an imposition, despite his honourable service and the friends he made. Once he had been at home in peasant and élite societies, now he felt an intruder in both.

He concluded bitterly he had not even been welcome in Ikaria. His insecurity even led him to believe he had intruded on Greece by becoming Greek. Not being able to give his daughter away in marriage brought these things home to him. He could not resolve his children's and friends' affection and the welcome he received almost everywhere with his feelings of loneliness, rejection and of not belonging. When he was down he was bitter and angry towards those closest to him; when he was up, his euphoria made him charming, amusing and gregarious.

Kevin was distraught that Greece's arrival into the twentieth century helped destroy local and village communities and vulgarised national life. Even so he never hid from the truth. He knew the old days were going and despaired at those who portrayed Greece in anything other than its true light. At a British Council meeting he was outraged by *The Sunday Times* film critic, Dilys Powell, who gave

> the most excruciating, gushy and essentially fraudulent warble I have ever heard (about Greece).

By the end of the seventies the once presentable Kevin Andrews, now a grandfather thanks to Corinna, was losing his hair and putting on weight. He had problems with his teeth, eyes and ears, and his marathon swims and long walks were now infrequent. Epilepsy exhausted him, while dysphasia made life difficult, especially when teaching college or university students. Battling with his weight and his diet, jumping on to weighing machines like any teenage girl, he resisted his loss of looks and was vulnerable to younger women who stoked his vanity.

In spring 1980 he visited Alexis and Ioanna, in London and got to know his young grandson, Ram, born to Ioanna a few weeks earlier. There was another brief contact with his half-brother, John Smallwood, before he returned to Athens. Ioanna followed and, joy of joys, moved herself and Ram in with her father. For a while Kevin had a home with a family and one, sometimes two, grandchildren to baby-sit. He insisted the children and grandchildren call him *baba* or *papou*; to be called Kevin was disrespectful. When Ioanna, holding six-month-old Ram, accidentally referred to him as Kevin while speaking to someone on the phone, she had to duck as her father threw a full *briki* of Turkish coffee straight from the gas ring. It hit the wall behind her and, echoing a similar outburst twenty years previously, splashed mother and child with scalding liquid.

Despite such irresponsibility he was a dedicated grandfather and dealt competently and gently with his grandchildren. Ram had a black father and Kevin struggled with this. Notwithstanding his new nationality he was at heart still an upper-class East Coast American, trapped in the bubble of a xenophobic and monocultural Greece a country that even in the twenty-first century finds it difficult to recognise that black Europeans exist. His knowledge of young people was limited and he over-reacted towards drugs, believing, along with the Greek tabloids, that marijuana leads inexorably to serious addiction, probably violence and even murder. Kevin was rarely at peace with his children, never seeing them as young people needing to be led and nurtured. Later his extreme and hysterical views, coupled with childish jealousy, caused arguments with Alexis and fractured his relationship with Ioanna.

Kevin still had difficulties making his mind up. Either through psychological or neurological dysfunction, his life was shadowed by fear that encouraged inaction, especially when trying to deal with those closest to him. The only weapon that helped him was *The I Ching*, a book beloved by hippies and new agers which he gravely consulted on a regular basis.

THIRTY-SIX

Ikaros reborn

In *The Flight of Ikaros* Kevin Andrews and his friend, Nikiphoros, are both in hospital. Nikiphoros asks:

> What sort of a person would you like to be, Andriko?

Kevin's answer was typically convoluted as he struggled to translate and simplify abstractions like subjectivity and consciousness. As it was, Nikiphoros was ahead of him:

> I think I understand you. You really wish you could act without thinking.

That surely is Kevin Andrews. He was never confident he was doing the right thing, found it difficult to make up his mind and, after equivocation, often threw a tantrum or slunk away in humiliation. Writing the first version of *Ikaros* was painful but, as he grew older, he became more confident, capable of delivering more words per day. As he matured politically and improved as a writer he recognised limitations in the first edition due to the self-censorship he practised during the McCarthy years. Contemporary left-wing reviewers were struck by the way he leant over backwards to be impartial. A quarter of a century later he accepted the criticism.

On June 13 1980, *The Times Literary Supplement* printed a review by Patrick Leigh Fermor of *Athens Alive*. Overall it was favourable, and might have been expected to add a few hundred sales to this worthy and scholarly book. However, in leading up to the critique, Leigh Fermor declared himself a friend of Kevin Andrews and referred to all his published work.

> The writings of Kevin Andrews stand completely on their own and they are neglected at peril by anyone concerned with contemporary Greece.

Castles of the Morea is described as a classic of scholarship and he felt it was high time *The Flight of Ikaros* was reprinted. The review included a romantic description of Kevin which created a lasting impression of the man:

> wandering in the mountains, sleeping on brushwood... with his shepherd friends in caves and on high mountains...... cloaked and shaggy.... a blue eyed scholar gypsy.

Paddy Leigh Fermor was considered a major figure of post-war British writing, well connected and a war hero. Kevin Andrews was about to become a commercial author.

The first edition of *The Flight of Ikaros* was a literary success but sold less than 8000 copies – not negligible but not enough to live on. Fermor's review led Kevin to tinker with the book again and to look for a new publisher. John Chapple, an American publisher in Athens, contracted to bring out a new edition but, unable to find the time or the money, released Kevin from the agreement. Advised by Fermor he sent Penguin copies of all his books and in May 1983 received a letter from the commissioning editor, Geraldine Cooke. She had enjoyed reading *Ikaros* and wanted to publish a new edition. Kevin was overjoyed but had suffered a *grand mal* attack two days before and was still dazed and in pain from a subsequent fall. He took time to understand and appreciate what might happen. Unfamiliar with success, he was apprehensive and suspicious. He didn't know if he could cope.

Then Geraldine telephoned and he gave an emphatic yes. They discussed the jacket. She told him it had to be a photograph to fit in with a travel series Penguin were planning, and asked if he had anything suitable. Kevin agreed to look through his files. He began to rewrite *The Flight of Ikaros,* strengthening and rearranging the text, adding, subtracting, often rewriting whole sections. He cut himself off from friends and family, refused to baby-sit and took the phone off the hook. Working ten to twenty hours a day he re-wrote 100,000 words in eight weeks and considered the new version swift, resonant and penetrating. During this period the evil of epilepsy left him alone and he suffered very few attacks. Having probably enjoyed the healthiest and happiest months ever since the original diagnosis, nearly forty years before, he now experienced neurological links working in his favour. As always he worried. There was no pressure from Geraldine and Penguin didn't censor authors. But Kevin imagined he was being too outspoken for a reading public mainly living in Thatcher's right-wing Britain.

He wanted the book to sell and he'd always wanted to be published by Penguin. Success was very close and he believed he had to compromise. He diluted the polemic but he added a strapline to the title: *Travels in Greece during a Civil War*. On July 7 he took nearly 300 typed pages to the central post office in Athens and sent them to London. After 25 years he was satisfied.

Perhaps fearful of meeting Nancy he did not want to travel to England to sign a contract. Instead he and Geraldine met in Zackinthos, an island she visited regularly. She stayed in the house of the Greek author Solomos and Kevin occupied a small room there. They agreed the standard contract for those times, a £750 advance against royalties of 7.5% home and 6% foreign sales. Geraldine remembers his bright blue eyes and his beard

> almost as if he were in disguise.

She offers a vignette. The mother of her landlady, a refugee from Smyrna, was ill. Kevin wanted to cheer her up and stood below her window playing folk songs from her homeland on the *flogera*

Later, he offered to take Geraldine walking with him in the mountains. She accepted but the walk never happened. Perhaps she was fortunate given Kevin's growing proclivity for mishaps. Kevin returned to Athens and a few days later took bus and taxi to Kineta to walk in the country of his *koumbaros* and to

> look in the face of God

At the old sheepfold and hut, after a torrential rainfall, he met a member of the *koumbaros'* family, recently returned to goat herding and resin tapping. He told Kevin the terrible news that his godson was addicted to drugs. Even these people were being destroyed by the twentieth century.

By the new year 1984, Kevin and Geraldine had agreed a layout for the cover of *Ikaros.* It was based on an oil painting of a photograph he had taken in 1950. Kostandis, holding a rifle, is standing with his back to the camera and seems to threaten anyone who dares open the book. Clearly this would not be an ordinary travel book.

When the proposed layout arrived Kevin was disappointed and said so. While the gunman looked authentic the rock on which he was standing looked artificial. But he did not prevaricate too long. In early March a large envelope containing the proofs arrived at 69 Trivonianou. This was one of the greatest moments of his life. He worried that they had printed the wrong text or gone back on their agreed alterations but no, it was as he wanted. He read it through and was overjoyed. He felt justice had been done. The new version took him back to that time, those places and those people. After twenty-five years he was satisfied..

Publication was scheduled for October 25 and at the beginning of the month another parcel - advance copies of the new edition. On the front was Patrick Leigh Fermor's reaction taken from the *TLS review*:

> One of the great and lasting books about Greece.

On the back, the definitive judgement of Louis MacNeice:

> If you want the truth about Greece, here it is.

Later Kevin told friends that holding the two copies in his hand he had a mild seizure. Sounding strangely like an abused child, he said of his wife,

> She cannot hurt me now.

This was his book and a better one than the first edition which, he now explained, Nancy had practically dictated.

THIRTY-SEVEN

The Flight of Ikaros

Perhaps this is the time to step back from Kevin Andrews' life and examine more closely his masterpiece and compare in some detail the first and final editions.

From the time he arrived in Athens in 1947 until he left four years later Kevin sought the wild places of Greece and their inhabitants. Travelling mostly by foot he took copious notes, recording over 200,000 words in little black notebooks. From these notes over many years he wrote and rewrote *The Flight of Ikaros*. The first edition (1959 Weidenfeld and Nicolson) carries the strapline, *A Journey into Greece.* By the last edition (1984 Penguin), at Kevin's insistence, this has become *Travels in Greece during a Civil War,* indicating a change of emphasis and providing an insight into the development of Kevin Andrews as a writer and as a man.

Despite having

> revised the text throughout

for the final edition, and divesting

> the narrative of some clattering adornments

much of the original remans - and so it should. Using deliberate prose he gives us

> an outsider's abrupt and startling experience of a country during a civil war

Very little of this precocious and gifted young man is directly revealed in either edition. *The Flight of Ikaros* is not a biography nor a travel book; like much of Bruce Chatwin's work it offers more literary then historic truth. Kevin's obsession with his origins is barely hinted at in the earlier edition, just a puzzling reference in the foreword:

> I state one noticeable fact about my own (background): I do not belong to it.

By 1984 his sense of betrayal by his mother and Smallwood had grown and the preface contains that full full-blown tirade:

> A multi-racial ancestry, a shrouded origin in an outlandish birthplace, a divided heritage, and a mistaken belief in my natural right to a quiet surname and an American passport.

Both editions avoid these obsessions and the overwhelming emphasis is on wild landscapes and oppressed and dignified people torn apart by civil war.

Kevin trumpeted that Nancy had too much influence on the early edition and there are changes in style. In 1959 he opens with the startling line

> Daylight burned red on the eyelids - in my nostrils the smell of tar, hot from the deck-boards throbbing under my head.

vividly establishing time and place: early morning in post-war Greece on the deck of a *caique,* or small steamship. For the Penguin edition he adopts a more experimental, more courageous formulation:

> Daylight burned red on the eyelids - tar-smell hot in the nostrils from deckboards throbbing under my cheekbone.

And now the reader is nailed to that deck. Soon after the author is on an unnamed island with the family of Mrs Condor (Kondorini) who, in the 1959 edition, is

> darting scowls of fury at her daughters.

By 1984 the scowls are gone but her antipathy has hardened into condemning

> the evil of children.

The revised prose is more confident, more incisive; perhaps the hand of Nancy really has been lifted.

> ...while the afternoon changed from from white to blue and then from gold to violet (1959)

becomes the more memorable

> while the long noon deepened from blue and gold to violet and an assault of stars (1984)

Kevin is at his best describing landscape, the demands it makes on its inhabitants and everyday moments. Early on he gives us the heat:

> The eyes ached at noonday in the fields where the freighted vines cracked underfoot and their leaves hung withered, and the black grapes lay rich and hot over the parched clods, unpicked.

He sleeps in the afternoon

> when all life withdrew into small corners.

By 1984 he had learned enough about dialogue and demotic language to include more of it, albeit without the he said/she said exchanges novices resort to. This more direct style suits his subject matter and and the reader fills in the gaps. His island idyll is interrupted by a telegram:

> For me?
>
> Who else? There is no other foreigner.
>
> Saying what?
>
> Go back.

And he has to return to Athens.

Kevin remained politically cautious but makes his sympathies clear. On the ferry to Piraeus he meets political prisoners:

> Good people. Democratic people. Exiles -prisoners...

In 1959 the prisoners remained mainly silent; now, they are allowed to spell out what happened on that terrible day, December 3, 1944, when fighting broke out in Constitution Square in Athens:

> the collaborationist-police fired into our crowd: in one minute twenty-eight dead, hundreds more wounded

Kevin expands his views, condemming the interference by Stalin and Churchill. The latter had previously considered the EAM Liberation Front and the ELAS Popular Liberation Army as

> gallant guerillas

but, when it suited the British government, condemned them as

> miserable Greek banditti... masquerading as the saviours of their country.

A significant addition to the later edition is an early chapter, The Half-Way House, describing Kevin's arrival and early dislike for the American School:

> How either of us stuck each other I don't know... I had been warned… I clashed head-on... and quickly developed a talent for making myself scarce whenever potsherds or foundation-stones were on the unsmiling agenda.

Kevin was a dreamer, but soon found out

> archaeology was the glue you mended pots with... and the duller the better.

He does not hide his distaste for the staff:

> Another of our teachers was a tireless, lean factotum…

Mercifully for Kevin he is eventually released and sets off on the fieldwork which led to *Castles of the Morea*:

> across the empty air... a rampart of vast, radiant, sinuous massifs and plunging gorges dark with fir forests, all sweeping up towards the 7000-foot-high ridge of Taygetos: a single soaring wall of rock, striated and smooth and lemon-yellow in the afternoon...

Soon he is on his way to Mistra where he meets the men and women of the villages and mountains he so admired. There is Kleomeni, the hospitable restaurateur, and the sinister Kostandi, evil and thuggish, whose attributes Kevin confused with manliness. Rather than the respectful *Anglos* the rural people call him *Englezos;* older people of Karpathos refer to me the same way, always with a chuckle. The 24-year-old Kevin naively believed in the beneficence of American aid and argued with the men of the hinterland. They were puzzled by his interest in the ruins scattered over the wild places and believed him to be a spy.

Back to Athens again and by 1984 (though not 1959) Kevin reveals he felt curiously at home in Greece. He was diagnosed with epilepsy in 1948 and describes with great delicacy the two months spent in an Athens hospital where he became friends with the doomed joker Nikiphoros. The two versions are much the same, though short and ugly Nikiphoros becomes short and plain. One sad rewrite:

> I am afraid of certain things in my character - hesitation, indecision; all around me I see people overcoming just those things. Most of all I am afraid of never becoming involved in life; yet here I am close to it

evolves after a quarter of a century into the despairing:

> All my life long I've been terrified - terrified of my own hesitation, fright, indecision,

exposing in one curt sentence the core of the man.

Released from hospital Kevin walks through Athens

> to Lykabettos with its white Aegean church and trickle of blue-shadows in the rocks - bright, watery, translucent.

By April 1949 Kevin merely quotes from his diaries as he explores the Mani, an unconvincing device which even with additional commentary seems artificial:

> Loneliness is the spectre of night-time in a foreign city.

Pure tosh and, if it really was in his diary, should have stayed there.

With relief Kevin turns to Andonis who wants him to be his *koumbaros*. The high mountains of the Megara are evoked:

> herdsmen milking, womens' voices, barking dogs

He lies on the ground in the evening and receives

> the imprint of the stars on my eyes before I fell asleep.

When he opens them again to

> a sickle moon hung in the sapphire sky of four o'clock in the morning.

Being *koumbaros* is an honour but also a duty more likely to be granted if you are perceived to have money. Kevin was a naive American and they thought he had money, so, when Andonis' son was baptised, Kevin duly paid for the ceremony. However it is clear he loved these people and the emotion was reciprocated. Perhaps the distance of language and culture ensured empathy and insight:

> In Greece friends often become strangers before a departure

Something I have noticed in Diafani where a close friend often picks a fight with me before I go away in the winter.

Kevin loved the mountains. Again on the Taygetos he has breakfast:

> while the shadow of the earth's eastern rim slid down the ridge above us.

Later, before leaving for America, there is the terrifying description of getting lost on Mount Olympos. He is descending a sheer cliff at dusk under a heavy bank of cloud:

> A few feet off was the top of a fir tree. I stood up and jumped.
>
> Branches whipped, cracked, poked in the eye and the tree-top swayed out into space. But it didn't break off.

He repeats the process down 2000 feet (3000 feet in 1959) of ledges and cliffs for four hours in the dark!

Back up the mountain again, at dawn, as the cloud cleared,

> there stood out one by one the Lesser Mytikas and the Skala and Skolio, to the North Stephani and Prophiti-Ilias. The mist drew back over the sea, soft and azure 9850 feet below, and the sun came out from behind the clouds and an intimate sky smiled down...

Kevin Andrews took himself to the edge and took the reader with him.

Returning to America he visits old friends from Greece in the kitchen of a restaurant in Washington; proud men of the mountains, shepherds and resin collectors reduced to waiting tables and washing dishes. Spare short sentences describe their pain and his longing. Later a letter arrives from Greece alerting Kevin to the death of Nikiphoros. It ends:

> I stop my letter here because the memory of that time is more
> than I can bear. With boundless esteem. Kallirhoi

There is a little bundle of notes from Nikiphoros, misspelt and incoherent except in its random dignity. The final sentence ends in the middle of the page and there is no signature. That night Kevin sat in candlelight trying to catch an echo of Nikiphoros' voice, or

> of all the other voices, cries and silences familiar once across
> an ebb-tide running out into the dark

But he cannot. Only

> night noises of the city came in through the window.

A sombre ending simply told. Nikiphoros is dead and Kevin feels the pain of exile from the people he loves and the country that one day he could call his own.

THIRTY-EIGHT

On the edge

The last few years of Kevin Andrews' life are more or less an open book. A minor member of Athenian society, especially among the small group of expatriates committed to what they called Real Greece, he continued to share his thoughts and feelings about the poisonous wife, the kidnapped children and other familiar excesses. Twenty years later, stories of his mishaps, his loves and his frequent outbursts of temper continue to emerge.

He lived frugally though this may have been his choice. Considering himself to be a writer he had not applied for a regular job since 1951. He liked young people and from time to time taught Greek history for a few hours – a task he took very seriously. In the past he had been offered work as a translator but had always been choosy. Now he took everything, even working on marketing material for Papas Oil. Recognising he had crossed a line he explained

> my communist friends do not approve

In May 1984 his brother George, with his wife Mary Nancy, arrived in Athens. The brothers had kept in touch by post but had not met for over thirty years so George was only vaguely aware of Kevin's problems. Now, perhaps for the first time, he began to appreciate his brother's epilepsy. During a lecture on the history of Athens Kevin was giving to a group of students, George recognised the strange look on Kevin's face as he stopped in mid-sentence.

George took his place and read from the notes until he heard Kevin say he was OK and the lectern could be handed back. A simple act of fraternal love, missing from Kevin's life since the forties.

When George and Mary Nancy hired a car to tour the sights their superbly qualified escort even went to the length of buying a Blue Guide. They stayed in simple hotels but even this was too indulgent for the ascetic Kevin who chose to sleep outside in his sleeping bag. In the evening Kevin introduced them to the vagaries of rural Greek cooking while they drank *kitro* (a lemon liqueur) and gossiped. Taking afternoon siestas in olive groves to accommodate Kevin's illness, they drove to Old Corinth, then Argos and over the Arcadian Highlands, through Mystras to the highlands where Kevin and Yvette had walked in 1948 as the army burnt the guerrillas out of Mount Parnon. Naturally Kevin couldn't resist pointing out the buildings he had surveyed when researching *Castles of the Morea*. They returned to Athens on May 30 and George and Mary Nancy left the following day. Kevin had never known happy family life and must have been devastated by the sudden silence of his empty house. Sadly, despite writing and telephoning regularly, the two brothers never met again.

On August 16 Alexis came to Athens with his girlfriend, the first of several visits. Alexis had tried his best to stay close to his errant father but it was a painful and thankless task - tension always existed between Kevin and his children. They tried to be honest but Kevin was aware that Alexis believed he had grown up without a father and that Ioanna had missed Kevin in her formative years. Relationships were not helped by Kevin's obsessive mistrust of their mother Nancy.

Kevin nevertheless thought a lot of Alexis, regarding him as great-hearted, witty and wonderful to look at. For the remainder of his life he either went walking alone or with his son; nobody else was welcome. Walking with Kevin could be an ordeal. He was no longer as fit as he had been, suffered from amnesia when tired, and frequently lost his temper. His Athenian friends thought it amusing and talked about Kevin's scrapes, but mountains are dangerous and Kevin took risks. Once he and Alexis got lost and took shelter for the night by breaking into a Greek Alpine Club refuge. There was an unpleasant scene the following morning as father and son were confronted by angry club members wanting to know why these foreigners had damaged their property. On another occasion, while walking with Alexis and his girlfriend, Kevin lost his water bottle, suffered an attack, got separated from the others, came down the mountain alone, and returned to Athens, complaining to everyone that he had been abandoned by his children.

Ioanna fared no better. On one of his visits Kevin was overtaken by an uncontrollable rage and stormed out of Ioanna's house. He appeared later in the courtyard with his arms full of things she had given him over the years - a carpet, coffee pot, some sweaters - dumping them on the steps, shouting,

> I don't need these things, I never did,

slamming the door before he could hear her response.

Never one to accept responsibility for his actions Kevin blamed his daughter and

> the shady but potent legacy of Elaine Orr… working its way into the third generation.

He explained away his anger as a kind of hysteria brought about by his epilepsy.

Notwithstanding these outbursts the number of epileptic episodes was diminishing. During his sixties he might go for several days without a *petit mal* , and the dysphasia attacks fell to a handful. These improvements to his health may have been due to better medication, better self-understanding, greater maturity or a combination of these factors. For him, the improvements dated back to Nancy's departure.

A danger in the mountains Kevin could also be a liability when swimming. Andia Frantzi, who taught with Kevin during the 1970s on a Greece-USA exchange programme, recalls a visit to the western coast of Kalymnos. Kevin swam alone towards the horizon; hours passed and she was scared enough to summon local fishermen to search for him. Virtually given up for dead, he suddenly appeared out of the water at sundown, grinning broadly and clearly pleased with himself. He neither explained his behaviour nor apologised for the fuss he had caused. Andia was not surprised when she heard how he died.

Holidaying in Karpathos in 1976 he swam far out to sea with Ioanna. The wind was Force Seven and the waves a metre high.

Without once looking back he told his daughter to follow, oblivious to her screams. Ioanna feared leaving her father in case he drowned, or she did, or both. The ordeal lasted over an hour and left her with a profound fear of the sea. Kevin did not even acknowledge her distress.

Something similar happened - eerily foreshadowing the way he lost his life - during the August 1984 visit by Alexis and his girlfriend. The three of them went to a beach near to Athens where Kevin, having neglected to take his tablets, struck out to sea alone. Writing to George he describes:

> a misguided attempt to reach an island that looked deceptively close from the shore, but that still seemed to be a long way away after two energetic and wave buffeted hours. It was finally wiser to turn back.

The traumatised young couple spent hours searching for him. When he was finally spotted they ran into the sea to help him ashore. He was unaware of their concern.

> After four hours non-stop swimming I never felt more limber in my life. God watches out for idiots.

In June 1986 one source of irritation was removed. The US embassy telephoned to say his certificate of loss of (American) nationality had come through from Washington. An hour later Kevin was there, dressed in his best black trousers, carrying his birth certificate, finally leaving with a (US) State Department certificate saying Kevin Andrews had been naturalised as a citizen of Greece and therefore expatriated himself from being a citizen of the USA. Kevin loved the word expatriation and embarked on a self-indulgent autobiographical essay on this theme. He rewrote it several times but during his lifetime it was always rejected, often after violent rows with the editor of one obscure journal or another. It was not published until after his death.

The essay, *Expatriation to Excess: No Blame,* surely the least elegant of his titles, lashes out at his mother, his father(s) the USA, Winston Churchill, several modern English historians and many others except - just for once - long-suffering Nancy. Not that there was any hint of softening on his side. Despite her regular letters and phone calls, trying to discuss the children and continuing to hope for reconciliation, her efforts were futile. He no longer feared her and once he shouted down the phone,

> Get a divorce.

Proud of this new independence, he shared the details of this outburst with even casual aquaintances.

Marc Dubin, a renowned walker, sent Kevin a copy of his new book, *Greece on Foot,* in August 1986. The fact that it contained appreciative words about ***The Flight of Ikaros*** and ***Greece in the Dark*** didn't prevent Kevin from pointing out

> innumerable misprints, spelling mistakes, misplacing of accents, and errors of fact, not all minor.

However, inspired by the younger man's enthusiasm Kevin was tempted by the wild again and set off in the autumn for Northern Pindos, an area he had not visited before. He spent five happy weeks walking the Vrikos gorge, and the mountains of Gamila, Smolikas, and Grammos, wild and dangerous places resembling the Greece Kevin had known forty years before. Venturing into such places alone was risky but he preferred

> hiking alone to the noisy excursions with (members of) alpine clubs.

Often losing his way, misplacing several walking sticks and even, disastrously, his rucksack, he survived to return again to the

> depression of city life,

which he considered had,

> his ankles hobbled.

In the 1980s Kevin had several unconsummated relationships with younger expatriate women. Each caused a flurry of activity. He had his hair cut, cleaned the house and went on a crash diet. Earlier he had purloined a pair of his son's Diesel jeans. To ensure they fitted he starved himself and walked long distances until he felt he had the body of a teenager. His image of women was old-fashioned and he was a long way from being a feminist. When things were going badly with one girlfriend he slammed down the phone in front of a visitor, shouting,

Bitches, they are all bitches.

In early 1987 Letta Duye Christopoulou, a beautiful mother of two, separated from her husband, entered Kevin's life. They met at a party and began a gentle, lasting and loving relationship . They wrote, telephoned and met regularly, and even spent the occasional night together. Soon Kevin believed that breakfasting with Letta was one of the most civilised rituals of his life. Similarly with shared cinema trips, meals she cooked, nights at the local taverna in Mets and time spent listening to Dowland. But he held back, convinced his failure to offer physical love precluded the emotional intimacy he desired. He trusted Letta, nevertheless, and even suggested she translate into Greek his most precious creation, *The Flight of Ikaros*. As a test he suggested a specific page and with, characteristic pedantry, explained every nuance, echo and cadence. The effort exhausted them both, so they went for a walk in the hills. Later he saw the two pages of translation and decided they were not good enough. Despite this, the relationship survived. Letta faced many options and had seriously considered moving to France. Both knew she would stay in Greece to be with him. They met nearly every day except when he had suffered an attack and did not want to see anybody. When they were together he thought her straightforward, fearless and uncluttered; he was haunted by her beautiful black eyes and took simple pleasure in the marvellous shape of her nose.

In September Kevin returned to the Northern Pindos for another three weeks and ended up in a remote summer village. He was thrilled to be offered a job looking after the livestock of a peasant who wisely moved his family down to the Thessaly plains each winter. Given that a peasant's livestock is his wealth it's difficult to judge how serious this offer was. Kevin, ever the romantic, claimed he wanted to take up the job but had to return to Athens. However it is hard to imagine a city-dwelling man of his age and with his illness attempting to survive the winter snow and rain alone in a near deserted uplands Greek village.

As he got older Kevin grew closer politically to Marion Sarafis, a writer about modern Greece and wife of General Sarafis the wartime resistance leader. He was also much exercised by *The Hidden War*, a British TV film that used the words of ordinary people to tell the story of the civil war and its aftermath. He assisted in the copying and distribution of this film which was banned in Greece and even suppressed in the UK. He also worked closely with Amy Mims, translator of Katzanzakis, Ritsos, and others, on the Cyprus tragedy, agitating, studying and writing numerous essays.

His political views can best be judged from a reading list he recommended to Marc Dubin:

- Lawrence Wittner, *American Intervention in Greec*e, 1943-1949.
- Heinze Richter, *British Intervention in Greece, from Varkiza to Civil War (trans. Marion Sarafis),* which Kevin felt dealt meticulously with the immediate aftermath of the civil war.
- Gen Stefanos Sarafis, *ELAS, Greek Resistance Arm*y – the introduction to the revised translation, by Marion Sarafis, Kevin considered the best concise history of latterday Greece.

These tell more than *Eleni*, said Kevin, referring to Nicolas Cage's harrowing and tragic best-seller.

Visitors to Kevin in Mets recall a small, dark, slightly musty house which was, however, inexpensive to rent and maintain. He had two bedrooms and the garden where he tended his prized fruit trees. Never tidy, he occasionally spent a day cleaning one room, then leaving it to fester for six months before tackling it again. Each year the battle against moths was renewed. Clothes and blankets at risk were washed and beaten in springtime, dried in the sun and put away in trunks with mothballs. In the autumn they were inspected to see if they might last another few months and hung on the line to rid them of the smell of naphthalene.

Kevin liked gardening and cooking. Ratatouille was a favourite, and he loved to make marmalade from fallen fruit on the streets and pavements near his house. Despite ambivalence towards his own children he enjoyed the company of young people provided they were alert to the political ramifications of the new Europe and the tragedy of Cyprus. He cooked simple meals for them, often out-of-doors. However, such company exhausted him and, in unguarded moments, he revealed his epilepsy was making him depressed:

> I am useless, useless.

He wrote to Elizabeth, his stepdaughter,

> every time I do deny fear or, with automatic lightning agility, convince myself that something hellish isn't hell, some kind of epileptic seizure ensues, as if to draw attention to the trick I have just been playing with myself.

Contemporary descriptions have him: raw, on the surface, open, no airs and graces, *morfomenos* (cultured), Tolstoyan, utopian, a big man. Newcomers to the shifting population of expatriates in Athens were less forgiving of his tantrums, regarding him as prickly, selfish, aggressive, exacting, not an easy man. Some said he had abandoned his children. Perhaps the most piercing description, by a sympathetic but critical friend has him as

> A charismatic hero who turned sour, desperately masquerading as a facsimile of his former self. A hollowed out man endlessly performing for the public.

A photograph, probably taken by Liza Mayer early in 1989, shows him with a grained interesting face. Slightly distracted, he is not looking at the camera. His full grey moustache is turned down at the ends, and his ears are low on his head. He wears what looks like an Irish tweed jacket and a heavy red and black sweater. On the wall are old cups, pots and copper pans. His arm rests on a metalworker's vice and he has small delicate hands. He appears tired and old, a man who wants to be alone with his memories and his scars. Comparing this image with the sketch I made of the photograph of Perceval Landon, I see the same shape of head, the low ears, the same moustache, and recall Yvette being impressed by Landon's small hands.

Kevin had retained several Dolmetsch recorders from his schooldays. Visitors to his house often heard music from the street outside as he played along with his Rossini, Monteverdi and Dowland records. Sometimes the wistful voice of his shepherd's pipe suggested the sounds of the mountains and tunes from another age.

When Donald Pitkin, an old army friend, visited Kevin he was struck by:

> the impoverished condition in which he lived in Athens.

He remembered,

> generously allowing me to use his plate, cup, knife, fork to eat the meager lunch he served me in his smallest of quarters - I wondered if romanticism played a part in his impecunious situation - the conversation was not nostalgic, but laced with anger at the USA and the Colonels

Life in Greece is complicated. It can take weeks, even months, to complete a task. An office is closed or it is the wrong office. Or it is the right office and open, but the right person is on holiday. Kevin pottered. It once took him two weeks to find a new hose for his gas bottle. He spent hours in public service offices. He visited the flea market in Monastiraki to look for metal objects like bronze jewellery and old cauldrons. He scavenged for scrap metal from empty lots, and neighbours heard him hammering on his anvil, fashioning things. Apart from his writing he tried to earn a living making jewellery. He was a skilled craftsman and produced simple but elegant jewellery often based on centuries-old designs. These he would sell, mostly to women, and several visitors a week called to order or pick up a necklace, ring or bracelet.

He had absorbed these skills years before from a friend Anita Coudenhove-Kallergis. He used iron, bronze, brass, copper and silver, never gold. Banging away was an outlet for channelling his pent-up frustrations as well as a source of cash. His daughter Ioanna talks of

> his talent for bending the unbendable.

Kevin ate sparingly, often existing on dry bread and beans, augmented by food from his daughters and various women friends. The house was heated by burning dried grape seeds and skins in a *mangali,* an old copper Turkish-style device which gave him and his visitors terrible headaches. He was proud of his ability to scrape by, but would suddenly treat himself to extravagant presents, spending hundreds of dollars on an attaché case or an expensive pen.

He regularly carried his washing in an old rucksack all the way to a public launderette at Pangrati. Long arguments ensued with the woman who washed his clothes because a sock had been lost or some other item had been dyed pink. For a while he would leave his washing with Ioanna until, after yet another row, he set off for Pangrati again.

His day started between 4 and 7 am. He wrote until noon, did his shopping, made his lunch, tried to sleep until six, then wrote some more. He went to bed early because of the pills he took. Frequent insomnia left him leaden and awful the following day. Perfectionism meant his writing output was painfully small. A self-description:

> For one who lets the ink go solid in his pen for fear of using it, pen pushing requires a minimum of 12 hours daily, in the same chair, seven days a week without stopping...

A *prima donna* as both a writer and a man, he flew into rages at rejection, a comma misplaced by an editor, or a line too difficult for the commissioning editorial board to understand.

He spent hours writing to friends and family, tapping away on his old typewriter or meticulously writing out letters by hand with one of his favorite Parker pens. Letters to friends passing through Athens ask politely for Dunhill tobacco (Early Morning Pipe or Standard Mixture Medium) or a Parker 21, once a single volume of Alexander Pope (hardback). The tone is generally considerate although much remains hidden. Sometimes he reveals another side of his character when he describes Nancy as sulphurous, hints at problems with his children, or casually reveals an attempt at suicide.

Various women - Yvette, Nancy, Marion Morehouse among others - sent him money throughout his life. Despite the success of the new edition of *The Flight of Ikaros*, he was keenly aware of his lack of commercial success. He compared himself unfavourably to Paddy Leigh Fermor who, though not a better writer, had better contacts and achieved better publishing deals. It would be too easy to say Kevin was jealous of Leigh Fermor but he was certainly envious and resentful of his sales figures. They corresponded for years and met occasionally in Athens but, whenever Kevin's rage and sense of injustice at an unfair world took over, he used Leigh Fermor as a whipping boy. Matters were not helped by Leigh Fermor's response to Kevin's obsession with Smallwood:

> Ring up my club and talk to Lord Jellico. He will know all about Smallwood.

triggering Kevin's threatening note:

> Watch out when you go to that stupid club of yours (in London) because I will be waiting outside with a big stick that I will clobber you over the head with.

Invited to a literary gathering on March 29 1988 to celebrate Leigh Fermor's achievements. Kevin was able to overcome his feelings and thank the older man for the review of *Athens Alive* in *The Times Literary Supplement,* which led indirectly to the new edition of *The Flight of Ikaros*. At the same party he also met Elizabeth Boleman Herring, an American who worked for *The Athenian*, a news and art magazine published in Greece for expatriates and anglophones. Described then as delightful, charming and witty she showed an interest in publishing his essays and he promised to send her a copy of *Expatriation.* This was to seal his fate.

Ten weeks were spent in Cyprus writing and researching in summer 1988. On return he once again went hiking in the Northern Pindos, this time for eight weeks. After returning to Athens in October, on a whim, he made a lightning tour of Albania. Three days was the maximum permitted stay and tourists were limited to package holidays with approved guides. Kevin expected a diet of state farms and factories, instead he saw a lot of the countryside. He wrote to Marc Dubin,

> Mount Nemetska made my mouth water, but there was no climbing that.

To his surprise he was allowed to walk about in Saranda, Korce and Tirane. He found the landscape terrific but there was little contact with ordinary people other than waiters, tour guides and customs officials, who were

> friendly and informative, if cloudy on historic issues.

He took copious notes of this trip but they never saw the light of day.

THIRTY-NINE

Kythira

In the new year of 1989 Adolf Hakkert appeared unexpectedly at Kevin's front door in Trivonianou with the news that *Greece in the Dark* had sold more than half the 500 copies printed, and that he wanted to publish the collection of Kevin's political essays on Cyprus and Greece. This would have amounted to 135,000 words and was provisionally titled *A Time-Bomb in the Labyrinth*. Kevin immediately embarked on a frenzy of rereading, rewriting and correcting his last major work, but it was not to be. Perhaps the manuscript exists but it was never published.

Two days after his 65th birthday Letta, referred to coyly by Kevin as

> my lady friend,

drove him round Hymettos not far from Athens. Nearby, in 1948, he had camped out in a cave above Liopési where shepherds had their goatpen. He had always wanted to return to this fondly remembered spot. To his shock he found:

> a vast concrete establishment with tables laid out for the lazier excursionists, and built for their convenience over the cave mouth, with a fine view across Southern Attica.

The destruction of the Greek wilderness was a general malaise which Kevin felt deeply. Another ruined location was the spring of Goura on Yeránia, which was

> now accessible by motor road and graced with a rustic Swiss style signpost stating its name in Greek and English.

Even the sacred place where he had befriended the shepherd clan of his *koumbaros* so many year ago had been cheapened. Kevin's felt that description of the Greek landscape in *The Flight of Ikaros* had led to the chapter headings in Marc Dubin's *Greece on Foot.* The Greece Kevin loved was disappearing and he wondered if he shared responsibility for the desecration.

Elizabeth Herring was now phoning regularly and said she wanted to profile him. Kevin was usually susceptible to flattery by younger women (she was some thirty years his junior) but for the moment was unimpressed. He had hoped she'd review *Greece in the Dark* and sent her a copy. But no review appeared nor was he reimbursed for the cost of the book. After paying for the book's publication and spending many hours treking round Athens bookshops trying to sell copies he felt he needed the cash.

Early in February the journalist and commentator, Robert Kaplan, rang on the advice of Elizabeth Herring, asking to interview Kevin about the effects of tourism on Greece. Elizabeth confirmed Kaplan was honest but Kevin should stipulate that his ideas must not be taken without acknowledgement and that the agreement should be written down. Kevin tried to put off Kaplan but they met the next day. Neither was impressed. Kevin thought Kaplan was right-wing, Kaplan thought Kevin was living in the past:

> I was afraid of ending up like him. Mystra's beauty - and that of a handful of other places - had obsessed him for so long that he seemed to have done little more the rest of his life than look back on it.

The interview reveals little about Kevin except his willingness to talk about the intimate details of his origins to total strangers, even when he knew they were journalists. Kaplan duly repeated Kevin's version of his life: Chips Smallwood, Roy Chapman Andrews, *et al.*

> My father was English, my mother American, and I was born in China, so I never had any roots

Kaplan records this in *Mediterranean Winter - A Journey through History,* a lightweight book, nowhere near as interesting as his earlier *Balkan Ghosts*. Unwittingly Kaplan appears to have helped Kevin discard his wife and children, *viz*,

> married at one time to Nancy Cummings the daughter of the poet E E Cummings, Kevin Andrews, at the time I met him, had no family.

Soon after the interview Herring rang again inviting Kevin to a book signing at *The Athenian.* She had read *Expatriation* but offered no opinion. Again the possibility of a profile was raised. Kevin was flattered but still suspicious. By now he was convinced she would not review *Greece in the Dark* but did not know how to ask for it back.

On February 10 Elizabeth Herring phoned again, ostensibly to discuss work she was doing for the Insight Guides to Athens. Kevin did not want to write tourist guides. He was sometimes brought low by what was happening to the Greece that he loved - forest fires, the swing to the right, the consumer society, pollution - and he despaired at the young with their videos and their sub-cultures:

> Greece is such a desert all around me, leaving such a blank within, that nothing stirs, not one creative idea to fill the vacuum… there's nothing to fight for, aim for, interpret.

Then he would turn around and say,

> But there are still honourable people here.

On March 1 Elizabeth Herring finally paid for the copy of *Greece in the Dark* and he took her to lunch Together they went to the Jewish museum in the Plaka. Their next contact was on June 8 when she said *The Times Literary Supplement* had asked her to review a book and wondered whether he or Patrick Leigh Fermor had forwarded her name. She read him the review but he was not impressed. She pressed him for contributions to *The Southeastern Review,* a new literary magazine in English she was to edit. He was a writer; he wanted to see his words in print. He took her some articles.

The following week she phoned twice, asking him to review a book for *The Athenian*. He phoned back to ask about the articles he had left with her. More weeks passed and he again asked about the articles. She talked of offering him work at $50 an hour, an extraordinary amount for the time. Kevin was sceptical about the offer and her response to his writing. In her next phone call she referred to *Expatriation,* then moved to more intimate matters. Unerringly touching his vanity, she asked,

> Have you ever felt suicidal?

He admitted he had, and she made a similar admission. They discussed the novel he had abandoned nearly three decades before. She urged him to try fiction again. Kevin was wary but temptation gnawed away. Several weeks later he opened an old trunk and dug out *The Old Rising Sun*. A tragedy was unfolding.

On August 14 Kevin left a revised copy of *Expatriation* at *The Athenian* offices and, two days later, Elizabeth came to supper at Trivonianou. They sat in the garden and talked. She asked Kevin to read his poems. He had not touched them for fifteen years but few writers can resist attention. She liked his poems.

Letta rang after Elizabeth left, saying she would be back in Athens in three days and suggested they take a trip to Nemea.

The next day, Kevin visited the Southeastern College offices and made three copies of *The Old Rising Sun*, leaving one at Elizabeth's flat in Athens. She asked him to join her and friends that night but he preferred to go home alone.

On August 18 Letta cancelled the planned excursion. She visited Kevin briefly at noon, saying she had sold her flat in Paris. Her fate was decided. His was about to be.

Elizabeth rang to say she had read a third of his novel and suggested improvements. She urged him to find an agent. Kevin was tempted by the idea of a monastic hideaway, without telephones or a postal service, where he might rewrite the novel yet again. Elizabeth suggested they go off somewhere for a few days.

On August 20 she came to Trivonianou and they sat in his garden reading *The Old Rising Sun* together. She talked about her life. At 37 she had been married four times, twice to Greeks. Now 38 and childless, she was separated from her fourth husband, a Greek photographer, who, she said, was planning to withdraw to Mt Athos; both women and female animals are excluded from this holy peninsula but Elizabeth seemed unaware of the irony. She now had a 28-year-old boyfriend from the Mani. She and Kevin planned to eat in the garden but mosquitoes drove them indoors to his study where she said,

> If we went somewhere I would probably seduce you.

What were his feelings? Fear, panic, lust, expectation? He was a complicated man but he knew what he was doing.

He explained that for twenty-one years he had had no love, blaming the wreckage of his marriage and the effect of his medication. Soon they were holding hands across his desk. Then she was massaging his neck.

> You are the sexiest man I have ever seen. You have a the most marvellous face.

Later she told him he had a beautiful voice. Kevin did not know if she meant these words but they suited his self-regard.

During the next three days Kevin amended his novel, using red ink and Snopake. Throughout, Elizabeth phoned to advise, to support, to suggest alterations. Perhaps sensing something was afoot Letta kept in the background.

Kevin and Elizabeth agreed to take the hydrofoil to Kythira. On Thursday August 24 1989 they spent the night together for the first time. The following day he had four *petits mals*, the most in one day for some time. He was clearly under stress and was perhaps reducing, or even ceasing to take, his medication. They bought tickets for the hydrofoil on August 28 and travelled the day after. The hydrofoil is not the best way to travel the islands. It is noisy, smelly and claustrophobic, and the views are limited by salt spray and water running down the narrow windows. Kythira is a small island at the southern tip of the Peloponnese, a quiet refuge between the Ionian and the Aegean seas. A lovers' island. The journey took four hours.

FORTY

Death of an author

Kythira has a wealth of history and its white vernacular buildings fit cosily into a gentle landscape. The people, unusually for Greeks, are mild mannered and quiet. Elizabeth Herring and Kevin Andrews spent their first night on the island in a cheap hotel in Kapsali, a small coastal resort to the south. Kevin could not sleep and got up early, walked to the shore, and swam across the sheltered and shallow bay

The room they shared did not even have a washbasin and Kevin's siesta was disturbed by young men on motorbikes, so they moved to the Hotel Margarita in the old town of Chora just up the hill. Quiet and comfortable the Margarita overlooks a valley and has a rural, even wild, aspect. Its clientele consists of the upper-middle-classes from France, Britain and Germany looking for out-of-the way places. Writers stay there too. Elizabeth and Kevin had a further two days and nights together - talking, fooling, playing games, discussing the future. But things were not well with Kevin. For more than fifty years he kept a diary, daily confiding his thoughts and analysing his personal turmoil. Now, except for a few pencilled notes, he wrote very little. Perhaps he was inhibited because he thought Elizabeth was reading the diary or confused by the direction his life was suddenly taking, On the morning of Thursday August 31 he wrote the following – not entirely coherent - passage which could well stand for his epitaph:

> Woke every two hours through the night for one vigil blacker than the last: every stage achieved reversed, every validity turned upside down. One danger's real in any case: I could give up all work for the sake of playing and making love and talking till Doomsday to make up for all the ridiculous waste sad time stretching before and after and seeing things and travelling together.

Kevin could have been either scared of making a decision or breaking a promise. He may have been guilty about Letta. The black hole of depression engulfed him.

Elizabeth Herring had always sought out literary figures and had admired *The Flight of Ikaros*. Now she had the author to herself but her happiness was short-lived. Eighteen years later she wrote a brief memoir, *Farewell to Ikaros.* The reader is left with the impression that the affair with Kevin lasted much longer than the eleven days they were together and her account differs somewhat from others. Nevertheless she faithfully repeats Kevin's version of his own life, reminding us of his continuing bitterness and of his hatred for his wife and Smallwood.

Westerners tend to believe the summer seas off Greece are always calm but this is not the case. They are treacherous, subject to strong currents, surprise winds and rapidly changing weather. On a day that nearly cost me my life, the dead calm which allowed me to stand on the prow of my boat pulling in my nets, became a raging cauldron in fifteen minutes. Kevin Andrews regularly swam for three, four or even five hours out to sea, leaving his family or friends waiting for him on the rocks. He never had a seizure while swimming. Perhaps he was so absorbed that epilepsy was held at bay. He was fearless in the sea, even reckless. A few weeks before his death, he swam with a six-year-old boy who was told to cling on to one of Kevin's ankles as they went a kilometre offshore. Either Kevin did not care about the danger or did not notice it.

On the morning of September 1 1989 Kevin had two *petits mals*. In the afternoon he and Elizabeth set off for an inlet called Trachylos at the extreme southern tip of Kythira. The path is narrow and rocky and it was a hot day. They lay on the beach for a while and then Kevin set out for the islet of Avgo, thought to be the birthplace of Aphrodite, and supposedly created when Cronus, son of Uranus, cut off his father's testicles and threw them into the sea. The round trip is an eight-kilometre swim. Kevin started off in late afternoon, possibly 5 pm. At that time of year, and at that time of day, the *meltemi* would have been blowing strongly from the north; locally it could easily have reached force seven. Conditions in the inlet would have been calm, but the wind builds up behind the mountains and accelerates down the valley and out to sea, causing waves and a strong current. Waves from a force seven wind are probably less than a metre high but, from the beach, white tops would be visible and swimming would be a battle. So, sixty-five-year-old Kevin, confused about his mother and his father, sexually dysfunctional for much of his life, found himself swimming towards the birthplace of erotic love. Perhaps he reached the island but he did not make it back.

In her account Elizabeth says she saw Kevin wave at about the halfway point. She may well have been mistaken. In my experience, using binoculars from the top of a hill, and knowing exactly where to point them, you might just see a man's white arm in that spray, but from sea level, even standing on rocks, it would be very difficult, if not impossible. Elizabeth says she waited for two hours then, realising something terrible had happened, left his medicine and clothes on the rocks and made her way back to the Hotel Margarita, and then to Kapsali, to seek help. It was dark by then. In her words,

> The fishermen first refused to go out in their caiquia because the sea was too rough.

The sea must have been very rough. Force seven is nothing for a well-equipped *caique* and Greek fishermen are resolute in helping those in difficulties at sea. In any case, when they eventually went out they found nothing. The emergency services were summoned but could do nothing either; on the next day, September 2, the distraught Elizabeth returned alone to Athens by plane. She had done everything possible to have Kevin rescued but the original decision to swim to the island had been his. At Athens airport she was told the body had been found and later she went down to Piraeus, with Corinna, to identify it.

The next few days were a confusion. Elizabeth rang family members and a number of Kevin's colleagues, most of whom did not know her, or were unaware she was involved with Kevin. She told them of his death and how much in love they were. She told Ioanna that Kevin had money in an account in the USA and that she and Kevin were going to live off this and travel the world. She told others that he was so healthy he had stopped taking his epilepsy pills. Using his keys, she unlocked the house at Mets, climbed into the attic where he stored his papers, notebooks and diaries, and carried away more than twenty kilograms of material in a suitcase. In justification, she claims in her memoir Kevin had said,

> Elizabeth, do not let the diaries fall into the hands of my wife, my children. See that they are preserved, published, made available, along with *The Old Rising Sun*, to readers.

No attempt is made to explain why he should request this of a relatively new acquaintance. What is known is that in *Farewell to Ikaros* Elizabeth excoriates Kevin's wife and children for failing to publish the novel and his diaries. She also claims the right to be Ikara to his Ikaros… his beloved, his twin. She even made her own entry on the last page of his diary.

On September 5 she wrote to Patrick Leigh Fermor:

> He was in no way suicidal. He was euphoric, in excellent spirits and form.

That she and Kevin had talked of :

> An escape from their old selves.
> London, a child, marriage, mountains, writing.

Although estranged from Kevin for some time, Leigh Fermor dutifully followed Herring's guidance, writing an obituary which included all the main points:

> death by drowning, untimely seizure... everything had begun to change. He had fallen in love with a fellow writer and poet, remarriage was planned and he was preparing for publication his first novel. He was intensely happy. The fact that these prospects glowed removes all suspicion of suicide from his death..

Interesting that Leigh Fermor should even raise the subject of suicide.

By the time she came to write *Farewell to Ikaros,* Elizabeth tells a different story, claiming that their brief and happy time together released him from the cares of his life. That he chose

> to go out on a great wave, in one of his best loved elements.

Several explanations for the death have been put forward. Some say he had stopped taking his medication to overcome his impotency, some say it was an accident. Elizabeth Herring, in the 2005 version, says it was suicide. At sixty-five, Kevin Andrews went for a swim in rough seas. He had never experienced a seizure in such conditions and throughout his life he had shown little respect for the sea. It was his decision to swim to Avgo and he died.

The Funeral

Having done some errands for Kevin, Marc Dubin returned from England in early September 1989, looking forward to seeing him and handing over Kevin's favourite pipe tobacco, bought at a specialist tobacco shop in the Charing Cross Road, London. Marc phoned Kevin's house in Mets but got no reply. Later he received a call from the deeply upset Elizabeth Boleman Herring:

> I have lost Kevin

It took time for Marc to realise Kevin Andrews had died. Letta was so concerned about Elizabeth's welfare she took her away to the peace of Hydra, staying in a house she partly owned.

The funeral was held on Friday September 8 at Athens First Cemetery where Kevin was buried in the upper tier for writers. His great hero, Panagoulis, was interred nearby.

More than 200 people attended. Nancy, his widow, Corinna and her mother Ioanna, Kevin's great love. By coincidence Kevin's brother George flew on the same plane from London as Nancy, although they did not meet until Athens airport. Kevin's son Alexis was there, together with friends from all parts of Kevin's history. The eulogy was given by Paulos Zannas of the Society of Authors:

> He was not, like so many others, merely a Philhellene: he was a Greek even before he tried to secure his Greek citizenship after the fall of the dictatorship. He was a Greek author...

> You loved and suffered with our country and our people, whom you made your own. Those who knew you, be they known or unknown, simple country people, will not forget you.... farewell our fellow-countryman....

As is often the case with modern funerals, the presence of ex-wives, ex-husbands, current and past lovers means decorum is confused. So it was with Kevin's burial. There was some jockeying for position, some pushing and shoving. In Greece there is a special part of the cemetery where the family greet mourners as they arrive. Nancy was there but so was Elizabeth Herring, introducing herself as Kevin's fiancée. Mourners were understandably confused. One woman records being greeted by the pale, tense figure of Elizabeth Herring, whom she did not know. Then she heard a quiet voice ask,

> You do remember me don't you?

It was her old friend Nancy, Kevin's wife. Still strikingly good looking, plainly dressed and wearing no make-up.

Greeks are not ashamed of openly showing their grief. The depth of feeling is infectious: hands are held, arms extended, kisses made and tears shed. On all social occasions there is movement and physical contact. There was a crowd around Kevin's coffin when it arrived at the grave where Elizabeth Herring struggled to reach the front. She held one of Kevin's *flogera* and asked the gravediggers to open the coffin so it could be placed next to the dead man. The three gravediggers were experienced and knew about decay and putrefaction. They refused to open the coffin and instead the *flogera* was placed on top. Their shovels did the rest and Kevin Andrews - writer, poet, scholar, son, husband, father, lover of Greece and its people - was finally at peace, a state he'd rarely achieved while alive.

FORTY-ONE

Epilogue

Kevin Andrews was much exercised by his own heritage. There is conflicting evidence as to when Kevin was told that Roy Chapman Andrews was not his father, and lingering doubts about his true identity

Kevin's view of all this is easily acquired; he shared it with anybody who would listen. Over and over he says it was close to his thirtieth birthday, over a cup of tea, that his mother told him about Smallwood. Supposedly the revelation shocked him.

Liza Mayer has another story. Very early on Kevin told her he knew something wasn't right. Smallwood, his godfather, was kind to him whereas Andrews, supposedly his father, was always very cold. One day in his twenties while shaving Kevin looked at his reflection and said to himself:

> This is Smallwood's face

Then there is Magouche Fielding who said that Peter Norton, one of Kevin's godmothers, told Kevin the truth about Roy when Kevin was a young man in America. Kevin's response was to dance along beside her, saying how marvellous it was to be a bastard.

Yet another version comes from his brother George. When Kevin was in Greece, between 1947 and 1951, Yvette made a special visit to tell him about Smallwood. This was news to Kevin and shook him. For the rest of his life he was bitter towards Roy, and his relationship with Yvette changed. Yvette regretted the revelation.

These are powerful witnesses, serious people, but each could be mistaken. In any case Kevin's story was different yet again - in a way that insidiously fed his sense of betrayal.

More intriguing than when he was told is the true identity of Kevin's father. George, son of Roy and Yvette, believed Kevin was his full brother. Roy shared this view for much of his life and, as far as I know, never publicly conceded Kevin was not his son. Yet for many years Smallwood accepted the paternal role, and could have been right. But, unless he was very deceitful, his letter to Andrews, late November 1923, shows he was unaware of his imminent fatherhood just a few weeks before Kevin was born. Possibly he did not suspect anything until Yvette's alleged phone call on the morning of Kevin's birth. Or maybe Yvette invented that phone call to please her son and the conscientious Smallwood assumed the obligation imposed by Yvette much later. This makes it easier to explain how Yvette, George and Kevin found themselves staying with the Smallwoods after their epic Trans-Siberian adventure.

But this still leaves Perceval Landon and the echo of Yvette's voice down the years as she tells Pat Glenn,

> It's perfectly possible to be in love with two people at the same time you know.

Adding, she considered herself engaged to Landon. Despite his fame as a journalist and his political influence, little was published about Perceval Landon and I found it difficult to trace his movements. Since he was a close friend of Rudyard Kipling I felt certain – if letters between them existed - he would have mentioned Yvette. I suggested to the Rudyard Kipling Society that Landon may have been Kevin's father. Several members responded. One reply said the relationship between Landon and Kipling was,

> Condoned, if not encouraged, by Kipling's wife.

Another informed me that, after his death, all Kipling's private letters were burnt on instruction from his wife, adding,

> it is a pity that biographers don't tell us the whole truth about people.

The writer of a third said, rather brusquely, he

> would be surprised if Landon were anybody's father.

It was fully two days before the true import of these replies hit home. Kipling was gay and, by inference, so was Landon. But then gay men are not precluded from having children. Kipling had three, and Kipling and Landon could equally be described as bisexual.

Pat Glenn gave me a coloured portrait – possibly a self-portrait - of Landon to take to Ioanna. It was among Yvette's belongings, stored away by Pat after her death. There is a similar picture in Ioanna's files, probably an initial sketch for the full portrait. She showed it to me:

> That's my grandfather, Smallwood. Kevin looked just like him.

But that's not Smallwood, I said, that's Landon. It's the same as the one I have in London. But, says Ioanna,

> I always thought that was Smallwood. It looks so like Kevin.

Medical advice dates Kevin's conception to some time between April 1 and May 7 1923. Where was Landon then? I have been told he was at the Lausanne Peace conference, which opened on April 23 1923, but cannot yet confirm this. In any case Lausanne to Peking is only a week by train and Landon must have taken the train many times from Europe to China. So he could have arrived in Peking by May 1 or could have been there up to April 16. The possibility exists.

I have enlarged Liza Mayer's photograph of Kevin in his sixties on my computer and laid it alongside the portrait of Landon. I looked at the two pictures as scientifically as I could, feature by feature.

The nose was much the same. And the lips and the eyebrows. The chin was an exact match. The low ears and the cheekbones were the same. Landon was wearing a fur hat so it was not possible to see his forehead. However, looking more closely, I saw three vertical wrinkles just above Landon's nose. The photograph of Kevin has the same three wrinkles.

My daughter asked me what I was doing. I replied,

> comparing pictures.

She looked carefully. And said,

> They are not the same person. But he (Landon) could be his (Kevin's) father.

And maybe he was.

If that was the case, Kevin would have had a father he never knew and could not blame. Someone who was sensitive and romantic, a writer, a photographer. Somebody famous, who could match and even surpass RCA, rather than the quiet, worthy, essentially bourgeois Smallwood who refused to recognise him publicly, who did not marry his mother and, perhaps worst of all, insisted on calling him old boy.

I set out to tell something of Kevin Andrews' story, to describe him and maybe explain him. In the main I have used his own words and those of people who knew him. There are many viewpoints. Significantly, none of the many Greek people I interviewed criticised him. Perhaps he was more circumspect when speaking Greek; perhaps he was disinclined to translate his insecurities into another language. He had many friends and they mostly speak highly of him. A typical view arrived unsolicited by email:

> Kevin was a very special man and I cherish the time I spent with him. He was a fascinating story teller and he would share his experiences very readily with an interested audience

And yet and yet… he hated his mother, his wife, Andrews and Smallwood, and was sometimes cruel to his own children. Yvette was a neurotic woman living on the edge of mental illness. Even as a child Kevin was her only support and she adored him. It is difficult to live with a mother who is mentally ill. My mother suffered from agoraphobia, drawn out by God knows what; her sisters all had phobias and her brother took to drink. The family was and is dysfunctional. My mother fretted about her social origins and endured a deep sense of inferiority. I fled from home as soon as I could Kevin never managed to break away. He was a sick man with neurological and psychological problems. Impotent for most of his life, dissatisfied with himself, he seemed happy only in wild and remote places such as the Megara and on Karpathos. I have swum in the same seas, walked the same paths and loved the same people. In different ways we both sought sanctuary in the same places. I am the same age as he was when he died. I do not have his talent nor would I want it. But I think I understand some of his pain. I never met the man but sometimes on Karpathos, on a misty day in spring or autumn, I find myself following an old path up through the wet forest. I see an erect figure moving freely. Then the mist descends and in the shimmering light I am alone again among the dripping pines. There are events in Kevin Andrews' life which are unambiguous, where the details are exact and where the motives are known and understandable. At other times there is far less clarity. Biography is not an exact process; it demands judgement, guesswork and even obfuscation. An indistinct figure on a wooded slope is a legitimate image with which to end this book. It's as close as we will get to the man who was Kevin Andrews.

Index

Lightning Source UK Ltd.
Milton Keynes UK
01 April 2010

152194UK00001B/96/P